THIS ODD AND WONDROUS CALLING

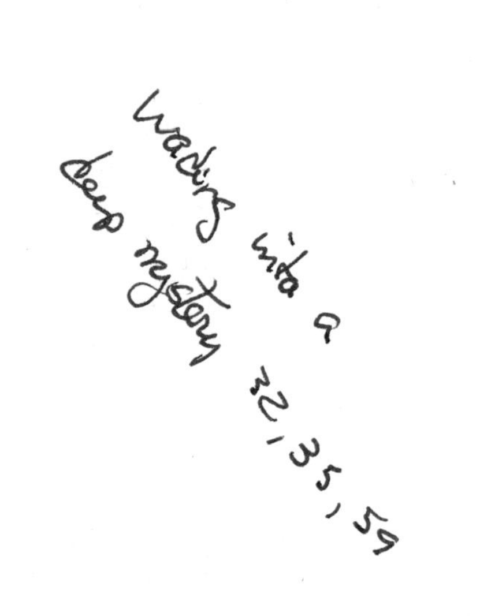

This Odd and Wondrous Calling

The Public and Private Lives of Two Ministers

Lillian Daniel & Martin B. Copenhaver

William B. Eerdmans Publishing Company
Grand Rapids, Michigan / Cambridge, U.K.

Published 2009 by
Wm. B. Eerdmans Publishing Co.
2140 Oak Industrial Drive N.E., Grand Rapids, Michigan 49505 /
P.O. Box 163, Cambridge CB3 9PU U.K.

Printed in the United States of America

15 14 13 12 11 10 7 6 5 4 3

Library of Congress Cataloging-in-Publication Data

Daniel, Lillian.
This odd and wondrous calling: the public and private lives of two ministers /
Lillian Daniel & Martin B. Copenhaver.
p. cm.
ISBN 978-0-8028-6475-8 (pbk.: alk. paper)
1. Pastoral theology. 2. Daniel, Lillian. 3. Copenhaver, Martin B., 1954-
I. Copenhaver, Martin B., 1954- II. Title.

BV4011.3.D36 2009
253 — dc22

2009029273

www.eerdmans.com

This book is dedicated to
Craig Dykstra

Contents

Foreword ix

Preface xiv

Acknowledgments xvii

1. Minute 54 1
2. Shaking Hands 8
3. Entertaining Angels Unawares 18
4. Learning to Pray 29
5. Can We Be Friends? 37
6. So You're a Minister 43
7. I'm with the Band 51
8. Made Better Than I Am 58
9. Crumbs from the Table 67
10. What Shall I Call You? 78
11. "I Was Looking for the Pastor, But You'll Do" 83

12. What Kind of Strange Place Is This? 94
13. Casting Out Demons 99
14. Expertise and Wisdom 106
15. A Cast of Thousands 115
16. A PK in the Ministry 119
17. Recall Notice 128
18. Laying On of Hands 136
19. The Calling Church 142
20. The Twin Impostors 148
21. Married to the Minister 158
22. Married to a Pagan 170
23. Money Off the Shelf 183
24. The Ministry of Angels 194
25. Palm Sunday 204
26. Hospital Visitation 211
27. The Preacher 220
28. Staying in Church 228

Foreword

When in 1968 my class was preparing to graduate from Harvard Divinity School, we invited one of our most revered professors, Dr. James Luther Adams, to address us at our baccalaureate service. Dr. Adams was a man who knew everybody and everything. He had introduced Paul Tillich to the world, and he had been a pastor, a professor, and a prophet of social justice in the Unitarian Universalist tradition. He never said a foolish thing, he was to many of us a model of mind and heart in thoughtful, useful service, and in a time and place where not many of us felt much sympathy for the ordained ministry, "JLA," as we called him, seemed more sympathetic than most to the ministerial ambitions of some. Thus, those few of us who were contemplating ordination were thrilled that so grand a figure as James Luther Adams would preach to us at our last service at Harvard.

The sense of shock and disappointment when Dr. Adams told us that we were entering a profession that was vocationally uncertain and whose eclipse would be a fact for which we ought to prepare is still with me, and although it was perhaps the conventional wisdom of the day, many of us did not want to hear it. God may be dead, as a number of theologians had declared and *Time* magazine had announced on a recent Good Friday cover, but we who wanted to be ministers did not wish to be distracted from our heroic rendezvous with destiny. We listened therefore in sullen silence to the words of our prophet/preacher/professor.

I wish now that we had had this book to read, *This Odd and Wondrous Calling: The Public and Private Lives of Two Ministers,* by Lillian Daniel and Martin B. Copenhaver. We had read all the classic material on ministry, we were more than familiar with the current sociology, and I personally had taken great encouragement from Reinhold Niebuhr's slender volume, *Leaves from the Notebook of a Tamed Cynic.* What was missing, however, was anything by anyone from within the profession who spoke with appreciation, not simply with apprehension, about the ordinary things of the ministry. *This Odd and Wondrous Calling* is full of good things from the collective wisdom of two seasoned pastors, readable for both clergy and laity, and, while anecdotal, it does not descend into clerical anecdote. It is the kind of book that seasoned ministers and seminarians alike should read, the sort of book that would enliven many church groups and probably do more good than much of what passes for devotional and professional reading in church circles.

Why is it good? It clearly comes from the genuine life experiences of its clergy authors, real people writing out of real concern in real situations. One of the chapters tells how the minister learned to pray, something that most people, even most clergy, assume a minister knows or ought to know. One of my favorite chapters has to do with unpacking the Protestant ritual of shaking hands at the church door at the end of a service. Why do we do it? Are there risks? Are there benefits?

Lillian Daniel writes with candor of her early vocational struggles with the Episcopal church and of how her parish found her unsuited to ministry in that denomination. She had problems with obedience and episcopacy, and lucky for her, as she notes, was her discovery of the United Church of Christ. She writes of her troubles with the concept of tithing and the lack of feminine role models for those who want to serve in the pastoral ministry. The familiar problems of clerical identity and authority, especially acute for a young female in the ministry, are well discussed, and she takes up the problem of what to wear and what to be called. Should she, for example, as a young intern in a mental hospital, wear a clerical collar? Would that bring her more respect and professional recognition in a place where she felt a need for clear distinction between the medical staff and the patients?

Martin Copenhaver is the successful pastor of a "tall steeple" church, but he writes from the perspective of a "preacher's kid." How do preacher's kids cope with the burdens of the ministry that they both inherit and experience? He writes with respect and affection of his father, a distinguished clergyman from whom he took inspiration, and also from whom he needed space. Is there any hope for preacher's kids? Few have written better on the subject.

Martin Copenhaver writes with equal conviction and delight on the ordination ritual of the laying-on of hands, a topic rarely taken up in most Protestant circles until it is almost too late. This essay should be required reading for all candidates for ordination, particularly in those Protestant traditions that believe that "something" happens at ordination but are not quite sure what it is.

Both authors take seriously the notion of calling or vocation, and there is a refreshing discussion of the role of churches and congregations in the calling of suitable candidates for the ministry. The vexed question of whether the ministry is a calling or a profession finds careful discussion in this discourse, and especially telling is the distinction between expertise, which most secular professions both require and offer, and wisdom, which appears to be one of the singular requirements of the ministry.

This book is written out of a professed love for the church and its ministry, and it does not claim to have all the answers to the problems of life and ministry. It follows, however, with a clarifying affection, the questions that stimulate and provoke those who choose as their own this amazing vocation.

Speaking of myself, I had had more doubts about the ministry as a suitable calling before I heard Professor Adams's rather dismal assessment. My local church, however, was determined to ordain me, and when I offered what I thought was conscientious resistance to the notion, my old pastor roared at me: "How dare you resist God and the call of God's people? Who do you think you are?" It was reassuring to later hear him say that I was called to the ministry not because I was good but because God was gracious.

A book such as this would have been of enormous help, although it comes not too late for any of us, and I am pleased to commend it to young and old, clergy and laity, believer and nonbeliever as a credible testimony of why women and men still respond to a calling that by most of the world's professional standards makes no sense. This is a book that gets better the more it is read; it does honor to the church and the ministry, certainly to the two worthy souls who wrote it, and we have in it both a classic and a class act. Generations will rise up and call Daniel and Copenhaver blessed, for out of the treasure-house of their distinct yet complementary ministries they share the most fundamental and basic questions pertaining to the peculiar office of the ministry. They do so not in a "how-to" fashion or as a prescription for a course of action, but rather they address the questions that linger in the back of the mind of any serious minister, and particularly in the minds of those who prepare for the serious contemplation of the ministry.

The wisdom contained herein is invaluable, and not readily available in seminary. One chapter, for example, discusses what it calls "The Twin Imposters," praise and criticism, which so often bedevil the pastor. How healthy is the inevitable criticism that comes to the minister, and what should be done with it? How seriously should the pastor take such praise as may come his or her way? Both praise and criticism can intimidate and inhibit a ministry, as we know, but rarely do we talk about it. How refreshing it is, therefore, to have an honest discussion by well-regarded colleagues who in their considerable experience have received a fair share of each.

What of the clerical spouse? Many of us grew up in situations where it was the expectation that in married clergy a church got "two for one," meaning not two clergypersons but a cleric with a spouse who would serve as an unpaid clerical associate. Is it preferable to have as one's spouse someone who is not interested in one's clerical work and may be a secular professional? Is the old model broken, of helpmates in the ministry? How does one deal with the two-clergy household? Are these not issues worthy of our most serious thought? They are given that thought in this book, not in a heavy prescriptive or ideological way, but out of the life experience of two articulate professionals on the case and in the situation.

This Odd and Wondrous Calling is an encouraging book in the sense that it gives strength and courage. For many, especially those in serious contemplation, the ministry is a scary proposition. Suppose I know more of doubt than of faith? Suppose I conform to all of the stereotypes and none of the truths of the ministry? Suppose I worry that I could better provide for my family and myself in another profession, perhaps even in another "helping" profession?

No one really likes to take up these questions, especially in the midst of existential doubt and in a profession in eclipse; and seminary, for better or for worse, appears to be ill equipped to address these matters. At best, such questions are asked in a furtive fashion among close and trusted friends in the earliest, scariest days of ministry, where collegial despair appears to be contagious and epidemic. In such a context, and well beyond it, this book is encouraging, for it speaks with an understanding mind and sensitive heart to real issues from real experience.

I know of no other book like *This Odd and Wondrous Calling*, and I am convinced that it will come to play a useful and significant part in the formation of the clergy of the next generation. If it has many imitators, so much the better, for despite their best efforts, Copenhaver and Daniel have not exhausted the subjects and have provided a splendid model for the interested to think about the ministry. They themselves represent an unusual model of collaboration and colleagueship, writing as they do together yet from quite distinct experiences, and they have provided the basis for many profitable conversations and discussions. For that we thank them, and we thank God.

Peter J. Gomes
Plummer Professor of Christian Morals and
Pusey Minister in The Memorial Church
Harvard University
Cambridge, Massachusetts

Preface

When it comes to ministry, there are plenty of books about how to do aspects of it better, from church growth to fundraising to managing conflict to the latest small group technique. There are books about what is hard in the ministry, and those about the toll it can take. There are books from pastors who have grown large churches and who write so that others might do the same. There are memoirs about the ministry written by those who have left it. But in all this literature for the church and those who lead it, we have found that there was a book missing on our bookshelves and we came to wonder whether God might be calling us to write it.

In our work as ministers, we have both had occasion to reach for a current book that is honest about the challenges of this vocation but still reflects the joy that can be found in it. We have wanted such a book for those considering a call to ministry, for laypeople who want to understand what ministry is like from the inside, and for those who, after decades of ministry, long to fall in love with this odd and wondrous calling once again. We have wanted an encouraging yet realistic book about the ministry written by someone who is still doing it. Some pastors write about how they grew their churches; perhaps we are writing about how our churches have grown us, and continue to do so.

We also realized that we had both done a lot of writing and

speaking on this subject already. Some of that material has found its way into this book. Over the years, both of us have endeavored to write about the ministry appreciatively, yet honestly. In that kind of writing we have found something like another form of ministry to the wider church. And yet our real ministry is what we do with our congregations, week after week. It is to that ordinary work that we wish to draw the reader's attention, to see parish ministry afresh and with the eyes of the heart enlightened. Indeed, writing this book has drawn our own attention to aspects of the ministry in ways that have helped us appreciate it anew.

This book is written by two working pastors who serve churches that are not very unusual — that is, churches that, in key respects, resemble countless other congregations in the country. One of us writes from New England, the other from the Midwest. Between us, we have been in pastoral ministry for a total of forty years, in seven different congregations, large and small, urban and suburban, in the Northeast, Midwest, and West, and we have experienced these realities through two different lenses, because one of us is female and the other male.

The two of us are friends. In our ministries, we are collaborators by conviction and practice. Friendship is an important practice in both our lives and vocations. So the idea of writing a book together seemed quite natural.

After this jointly written preface, each of the chapters that follow is written in the voice of its author, the better to reflect that our experiences are different as well as to preserve our friendship. We hope that the reader is reminded in the switching of voices of the many types of people God calls to this work.

In the process of writing this book, we have critiqued and encouraged one another. Editing a friend's writing can be a risky endeavor, but we found to our relief that we could mark up each other's manuscripts freely and that the book seemed to benefit in the process. Each of us also pushed the other to write chapters that we were not yet ready to write because the subject matter seemed too personal or the feelings around them were still raw. Looking back, those may be some of the most important chapters in the book.

This book also benefited from the input of a wider circle of friends, old and new, who read portions of the manuscript at various stages. This ecumenical circle included colleagues, friends and parishioners, from a variety of traditions, Methodist, Episcopalian, Lutheran, African Methodist Episcopal, Disciples of Christ, and Evangelical, to name a few. We shared this material with lay people, seminarians, teachers of ministers, new ministers, seasoned ministers, and those who simply care about the ministry. Coming from our own United Church of Christ tradition, we have not tried to speak for all ministers or to universalize our experience of the ministry; instead, we simply tell you how it looks from where we sit. Our collaboration with one another and with the wider church has itself been a reminder that ministry is never a solitary endeavor.

We liken our chapters to views of a room through a number of different keyholes. Each one reflects on a different aspect of pastoral ministry. In many instances, the chapters do not address "topics" in the usual sense. Rather, the chapters provide different angles of vision on the ministry. In the diversity of subjects, we have sought to reflect the incredible variety of a pastor's day. We move from comedy to pathos quickly, from story to theology, from scripture to contemporary culture. Much like a pastor's schedule, the chapters deliberately do not all flow from one to another in an orderly fashion. We think this form is fitting, given the subject matter, because ministry is anything but orderly.

We love this disorderly calling. So from the beginning we have wanted this book to be appreciative of the ministry, but also honest about its challenges. Our intent is serious, but we also intend for the book to be fun, because we always take ministry seriously and because we often experience it as fun. We also hope it is clear that we take the gospel more seriously than we take ourselves, because much of the time that is true.

Lillian Daniel and Martin B. Copenhaver

Acknowledgments

For over a decade we have both been encouraged in our ministry by Craig Dykstra. We have also been blessed by his gift of pulling people into conversation in rich gatherings hosted by the Lilly Endowment. So for all he has done for us, and for all he does for the ministry, we dedicate this book to him.

A Pastoral Leadership grant from the Louisville Institute allowed us to travel the country with our book material, testing it out among ministers, seminarians, seminary professors, and laypeople. Jim Lewis was an early supporter of this project.

Sam Lloyd hosted us at the National Cathedral, where Diana Butler Bass, Quinn Caldwell, Mashod Evans, Greg Jones, Jim Wind, and Lauren Winner offered wisdom and good company in a Gothic setting.

In Chicago, Jason Byassee, Kyle Childress, Verity Jones, Peter Marty, and Michael Mooty reviewed early chapters from a view of Lake Michigan, with time later for conversation over Russian dumplings with Rodney Clapp.

Tom Long's consultations were most valuable at various stages of the work. He was brave enough to give us access to some of his brightest students at Candler Theological School.

In Indianapolis, through the efforts of David Wood, we met with new clergy in the Pastoral Residency Program, who told us how the material read in the first years of ministry. Through the leadership of Chris Braudaway-Bauman, we were able to present the material at a retreat of newly ordained clergy on Cape Cod.

It was the new clergy in these two groups who pushed us to write about marriage and family life, which we had not originally intended to do.

In New York, we sipped tea with Stephen Bauman and Barbara Lundblad in her apartment at Union Seminary, which had special significance because Union is where Martin's parents met.

In our own denomination, we received encouragement from our General Minister and President, John Thomas, whom we thanked by losing his only copy of a rare book.

Our friend and colleague Tony Robinson weighed in on the subject of pastoral leadership as only he can, in Cleveland, the City of Lights.

We are grateful for the support of Dale Rosenberger and David Wood, the other half of our small writing group that meets on occasion in Vermont to do more eating, drinking, and talking than writing. We also thank fellow scribes for the church, Shawnthea Monroe and Amy Laura Hall.

Some of this material appeared in some form in the following magazines: *The Christian Century, Congregations, Disciples World,* and *Leadership.* These publications are real blessings to reading pastors, so we are grateful to David Heim, Richard Bass, Verity Jones, and Marshall Shelley.

At one point, Lillian's husband Lou asked, "When are you going to test this out on church members?" So we took the developing book to our own home turf, where members of our churches read and discussed chapters. There we discovered that what we were writing had a much wider audience than clergy. Our church members confessed that they agreed to read the book in order to be nice to their pastors, and that they fully expected it to be boring, but were shocked to discover that it was actually interesting.

So we are grateful to Laura Abernethy, Diane Anderson, Bentley Beaver, Liza Carens, Brad Harding, Vanessa Rose, Linda Smith, Nancy

Smith, Tom Snyder, Barbara Stock, and Molly Weston from the Wellesley Village church. We also thank readers Jon Berry, Todd Buckton, Gabriel Calderon, Lauren Cannon, Seth Carey, Jenny Fischer, Johnny Gillespie, Russ Graunke, Ruth Graunke, Colie Huppertz, Rick Mattoon, Jane Melvin, Dave Mook, Lizz Mook, Gretchen Navarro, Melissa Riley, Kathy Stodgell, Nate Ulery, Debbie White, and Jesse White from First Congregational Church of Glen Ellyn. And of course we are grateful to the members and staff of our two congregations, who understand and encourage our ministry of writing for the wider church. Without their support this ministry would not be possible.

And to the many people whose stories appear in this book, we hope you recognize yourselves in these pages. In most cases, your names have been changed and small details of your stories have been altered — in order to make us look like better ministers, of course. But seriously, in so many ways your stories are the inspiration for the book.

Finally, we want to acknowledge Karen Copenhaver and Lou Weeks, who support this odd and wondrous calling in the best possible way, by caring for their spouses. We thank them with love and gratitude.

CHAPTER 1

Minute 54

Lillian Daniel

I begin my day at the intensive care unit at the hospital, searching for a room. I have entered the hospital under false pretenses, because nobody ever believes I am a minister.

Put aside the fact that I am neither male nor wearing a collar in this Roman Catholic town. I am not even accepted as a Protestant, because the church recruits fewer and fewer first-career clergy.

The way this fact trickles into my life is that often when I show up at hospitals I am judged to be too young. "You couldn't possibly be a minister," I am told, by people who say this as if they are the first people to honor me with their refreshing candor, but of course being called too young does get, well . . . old.

So I have adopted the custom of entering hospitals without wearing my clergy badge, walking the floors with a certain sleepy confidence that I copy from the doctors, more of whom tend to be my age. Too young to pray at bedsides, apparently I am just the right age to wield a scalpel. Without my clergy badge, I get in everywhere.

It's like *The Wizard of* Oz. Wake up, Lillian. You're not in Christendom anymore.

And now I find myself at the intensive care bedside of one of the saints of our church, who has struggled with cerebral palsy since her childhood. Now, after a rich life, in old age she is slipping away from a world of pain.

Her words are slurred these days but her mind is sharp. Together, in the midst of beeping machines and anxious faces, we try to get the doctor's attention.

We ask him to change the policy of limiting visits to family members. She has no living family. But there are church members who have visited over the years, and now they want to visit one last time. Finally, the doctor understands.

"Okay. It's like the church is her family," he mutters, making a note on her chart. Perhaps it is the same note that God made long ago in the book of cherished life.

Our conversation ends in her making a living will with this doctor. As I listen to these words being exchanged, I realize that in the Christian walk we pay holy attention to one another, eavesdropping on moments and words that the world may not understand.

It takes a holy imagination to know that the living will in her medical chart is not the last word; rather, the Word that was in the beginning has given and will give her life.

Wondering if it is ever a good time to leave her bedside, I eavesdrop back through the centuries to Jesus' promise to his disciples in John 14:18, "I will not leave you orphaned."

I love being a minister. Even when the ministry is hard, it's more fun than any other job I can imagine. Where else can you preach, teach, meet with a lead abatement specialist, and get arrested for civil disobedience all in the same week?

Where else can you be invited into the living rooms of new mothers and into the hospice rooms of the dying, and find hope in both places? I do love being a minister. I love the agility it calls forth, and the chaos that only Jesus could organize into a calling.

But mostly I love observing God's presence in the lives of people of faith. Mostly I love those moments when, from the position of paying holy attention to my own community of faith, I notice the power and presence of God. There are moments when we are practicing our faith together in ways that have become ordinary, but God's grace breaks in and we realize we are part of something extraordinary.

Somehow God calls us into practicing our faith together, not so that we will all march in lockstep but so that we will move like a dance troupe, in which each one of us contributes a somewhat different step to the unfolding work and beauty. Practicing our faith is like dance. Each event is unique and unrepeatable, but we are moving in patterns and steps of a tradition and a people. We are called to dance together, not just with those we meet in this life but with a cloud of witnesses and a slew of saints from our past and future. We work at it, and practice for the gift, every now and then, of a loss of consciousness of our own clumsiness and the sense that we are soaring, doing what we are called to do.

When I think of how all of our callings come together, I think of this.

There is a woman in my church who suffered a stroke, from which she is gradually recovering her ability to speak. But the last thing to come is our names.

Church people visit her, and she can speak to us in ways that indicate she knows exactly who we are, and has known us for years, but she cannot speak anybody's name. Instead she pulls out the church photo directory, that lightweight book full of carefully posed photographs of church members.

People outside the community might make fun of those church directories, where we all take turns sitting in front of the same strange backdrop of dark swirling clouds, family members trying to smile at the same time. But to those who know one another, these photos are full of meaning. A cheerful Christmas sweater does not distract us from the pained smile of the recently divorced. The missing family member points to grief that the whole community endured. A newlywed's swelling tummy pulls us toward promise, while the childlessness of another family photograph in yet another year reminds us to keep praying.

When one of us from the church walks in to see the woman whose speech is failing her, she waves that sacred church photo directory at us, as if to say that she does not know our names, but she knows the way in which we are all related. She may have forgotten our names but she knows us as we truly are.

When I look back to the education of my generation, college in the 1980s and seminary in the early 1990s, I realize that we spent a great deal of time on names. We wrestled with questions of language as if our lives depended upon it, drawing lines between ourselves based on our words and our names.

But in the life of my local church, where we grow and change our membership as the Holy Spirit is with us, we are forgiven if we forget one another's names. We're allowed to remember, instead, the ways in which we are related.

It's that sense of being related that takes me in my walk of faith to the places I do not want to go. Many of us are drawn to religion thinking that we are entering a world of ideas, when really it is such an earthy calling. Nothing in my training could have prepared me, a person who once had the luxury of fainting at the sight of blood, for the time I would be required to spend in hospitals.

Nothing could have taught me how to pray through the beeps of machines and to hold hands around working nurses' aides with wet washcloths. Nothing could have taught me how to sit by a bedside and pretend not to notice the strong smell of urine.

Nothing could have prepared me for how tiny and small the CEO looks in his hospital gown, of how people's faces seem to fold into blandness when they lie in a coma. Nothing could have prepared me for how terribly earthy the life of the church community is, how incarnational.

Nothing, I should say, except Jesus, and the trust that for some reason God chose to come to this world of pain in bodily form. Sometimes, my calling as a Christian is to count the broken bodies in the world and call them God's.

It seems to me that the church I was trained to expect was some sort of cocky, country-club fortress that needed to be taken down a peg or two. We, the new ministers, would come flying in like Underdog, armed with new hymnals, new language, and new ideas, inspired by professors who were still passionately processing their two years in the ministry fifteen years ago. The church I was trained to expect was a church that needed fixing, not in its weakness, but in its hubris.

But the church I was called to serve as a minister turned out to be a body broken in different ways. It's true that some of our congregations dress up in statistics that seem sleek. Yet today the average seminarian who is called to parish ministry will probably go out to serve a struggling church, perhaps even a couple of struggling churches.

Having read about megachurches, we may instead find ourselves worshiping in the shadow of the nearby megachurch, wondering what our congregation is doing wrong. Meanwhile, at the megachurch, they are wondering what they are doing wrong, as more members slip out than skip in. Most churches do not need taking down a peg or two at all.

Some of our churches have been taken down so many pegs they feel the next step will be the ground, and so they snarl and hiss at change as if they are about to die. Because some of them are. But some of them are about to live.

In school, I was taught the tools of critique, and how to search out the weakness in the argument, even the signs of death and decay. But what about life?

Are we schooled in searching out the life? Can you be taught how to look for signs of grace? If there is a pastoral imagination, this must be at the heart of it.

I think back to the visit to the intensive care unit that morning and how unprepared I was for the scene God was unfolding. As carefully as I try to plan, as much attention as I give to the details, I never know what will happen in the life of our church. I realize that when you are following God's plan in community you'll never be an expert, just a person who can notice grace in earthy places.

Back at the church, the trustees are meeting. The trustees are indeed the trusted ones, the lay leaders entrusted with managing the financial and physical resources of our church. We Protestants are fairly earthy ourselves. We like to say that the members run the church, not some faraway hierarchy. Of course, when the members run the church, that probably doesn't leave quite enough room for Jesus.

At this meeting, I am thinking about the woman I visited in the intensive care unit at the beginning of the day, imagining the great hand of God cradling her tiny body as she wafts in and out of this world. I am tuning in and out as the trustees discuss another of their duties: they must take their twice-yearly turn preparing and serving the meal at the homeless shelter.

Is the discussion about hospitality as a practice of the faith and the theology behind it? Is the conversation about how we could do more to solve the problems of homelessness as a systemic evil, instead of simply serving food? Alas, no. The heated discussion is about the correct recipe for chili mac, that strange American casserole that dares to cross macaroni and cheese with canned chili and call it food.

As I consider the nature of the holy imagination, I sit through a forty-five-minute discussion about chili mac. Do you get the large cans of chili or the small ones? Does anyone have a membership to a discount warehouse? And then there is the particularly contentious issue: should we buy grated cheese or grate it ourselves?

Someone remembers that they do not have a cheese grater at the shelter. Should we buy one or just spend extra on the grated cheese? Let's do a cost comparison, someone suggests, whipping out the calculator. This is the board of trustees, after all.

Just as we are nearing a decision, a new board member asks, "Why do we always make chili mac? The last time, the people said they were tired of it. Besides, some of the homeless are vegetarians."

I know what's coming next and I cringe . . .

"How can you be homeless and be vegetarian?" a veteran of the board inevitably asks.

The younger members of the board glare at him.

Now it's been fifty minutes. On chili mac. This moment is eternity. I am losing my religion. I have lost my eschatology. Fifty-one minutes.

I find myself dreaming of the past. I remember feeling a call to preach having never even once laid eyes on a woman minister until I set off for divinity school, basically on a hunch that they did indeed exist.

I think back to the papers I wrote, staying up all night on fire for God and the theology of one person or another. Was my first inkling of the pastoral imagination my own call to the ministry?

I think of the prayers I said earlier that day at the hospital bedside, and wonder if the woman I prayed with is even still in this world.

"Can I go back to an earlier point?" the clerk of the trustees asks. "Did you decide on the grated cheddar cheese or to purchase a cheese grater? I need to get this right for the minutes."

For this I spent three years in graduate school.

Sometimes it takes holy imagination just to remember a call, to imagine one, not in the sense that the call is an illusion created by us, but when we imagine, we see what we do not know; we see the possibilities God has for us.

We see God's possibilities even in the midst of grated cheese or broken bodies, because in the end they are not so different. They both point to the fragility of life, the desperate delicacy with which we try to live with order, balance, and meaning in a chaotic world.

When I think of the holy imagination, I consider that we can be prepared by one another for what is really out there, but it is God who prepares us for what might be out there. God will not leave us orphaned.

Christ crucified and resurrected prepares us to find majesty in the ordinary, mystery in the concrete, love in the midst of feuding, a ministry of tending to the details in the midst of grated cheese.

"I'd hate to be homeless, on a cold night like this," one of the trustees says. And for a moment the clerk puts down his pen, the calculator is pushed aside, and everyone is silent, and I feel as if I hear God's pen making a scratchy note in the book of our cherished lives.

And then the meeting goes on, to the church space requests and the broken window panes, but there was that moment when we were all quiet, and we could hear each other breathe, and we could hear who had a cold, and who was a runner, and who was choked up.

That was the moment that was really eternity. Grace had broken in. It carried us soaring into minute 54.

CHAPTER 2

Shaking Hands

MARTIN B. COPENHAVER

Worship is over and I am standing in the doorway shaking hands. In front of me is a couple I do not recall seeing before. I say, "Good morning! I'm Martin Copenhaver." By my manner and my tone of voice you might think that I am greeting long-lost friends, rather than introducing myself to these people for the first time. The woman of the couple responds, "Good to meet you. We are Jill and Bob Townsend."

"Welcome. So good to have you here." I think, *Focus on their names. Catch the names before they simply drop to the floor.* But while I am chatting with the new couple I see out of the corner of my eye, next in line, someone whose grandmother just died. I give a nod in her direction to let her know that I want to speak with her, but not yet. I need to be attentive to the new couple for at least a few more moments: "Are you new to the area or just new to us?" *What is their name? Townsend! Whew. Still got it.* My thoughts spin back toward the one who is next in line and I begin to second-guess myself. *Wait, was it her grandmother who died or her grandfather? Actually, I think it was her grandfather.* And then my mind lights ever so briefly on the person she is talking to, a parishioner I have not seen in worship in some time. I think, *It's been, what . . . almost a year? I wonder why she is back today?* But I need to stay focused on the new couple. *Quick, file away their names before you lose them. Townsend. I can re-*

member that because they are "new in town." Jill Townsend says, "We've lived here for years, but we're looking at other churches." *Okay, Townsend, as in "not new in town."* I say, "Well, I hope you can stay for some coffee." She smiles and says, "Not today, but I'm sure we will be back." I look for someone to introduce them to, but they are out the door before I have a chance.

Next is the woman who lost her grandfather. Or was it her grandmother? I say, "I'm so sorry to hear about your loss." She says, "Thanks. I so appreciate that. But it was a blessing." I ask, "Was your whole family able to gather for the service?" It's a rather lame question, but I am stalling for time, hoping that she will drop a personal pronoun in reference to her grandmother. Or grandfather. Before she can respond my teenage son comes up behind me and drapes his arms over my shoulders: "Dad, you know you want to give me money so I can get something at the bake sale." Normally I would remind him that this is no way to ask me for something, but I don't have time for a lesson in manners. "Sure, Todd, here." I give him a ten dollar bill. It's all I have. "Thanks, Dad."

I turn back to the grieving grandchild. She says, "Yes, the whole clan gathered. He would have been very pleased." *Bingo. "He." I should have remembered that it was her grandfather.* I say, "Well, I know you were very close to him. We will continue to hold you in our prayers." She responds, "Thank you. And you know Mary, don't you?" indicating the member of the flock who has been missing in action. And I do remember her very well. I say, "Of course, it's great to see you, Mary." Mary says, "Yeah, well, I haven't been around for a while. There's just been a whole lot going in my life." I think, *Okay, there's something to follow up on.* I say, "Well, it would be good to catch up when you have a chance." She says, "Sure. Any time." Using a common pastoral way of closing a conversation, I say, "I'll call you." And then I hope I remember to call.

A teenager approaches with a cast on his right arm. I search my memory: *Did he have on that cast last week?* I playfully extend my right elbow and he does the same. As our elbows touch we share a little laugh. I say, "How are you hanging in there?" He responds, "Okay. I broke it playing soccer." *So the cast is something new.* I ask him how it happened and he tells me the story. When he is finished I put my hand on his shoulder and say, "I'm so sorry. But you should see the other guy, right? I'm just glad you play soccer instead of tennis so that you can keep at it."

A man about ten years younger than I, who has been waiting in the wings, suddenly steps forward for his moment: "You don't remember me, do you?" He does look rather familiar, but more like the way a person can remind you of someone else you know. Fortunately, he bails me out: "I was in the first confirmation class you taught, twenty-five years ago." I say, "Of course I remember you. Absolutely. But I have become very bad with names in my old age. Help me with yours." He replies, "I'm Scott Harrison." Shaking my head in contrition, I say, "Of course you're Scott Harrison. Absolutely, I remember you. That was a great confirmation class. How have you been?" Then, after a few more snippets of conversation, I offer him my hand again as a way to draw this conversation to a close.

Someone else approaches who says, "I really have to take issue with your sermon today." I say, "The sermon is just the beginning. Then comes the conversation, which often is the best part." He says, "Well, maybe that's a conversation we'll have." I say, "Great. I welcome that. Will you call me?" In this instance I want to put the onus on him to call.

This entire sequence lasts only about ninety seconds, but it contains worlds within worlds. And that represents only a small portion of the line of people who wait to shake my hand. No wonder I always come home from worship ready for a nap.

And the thing is, I do think that the sermon is just the beginning, that one sign a sermon has done its work is that it prompts continued conversation. And I do remember that confirmation class from twenty-five years ago. Sort of. And I really do want to offer a word of genuine comfort to the person who has just lost a loved one. In the moment I may not remember whether it was that person's grandmother or grandfather, but it is a loss that needs to be acknowledged. I want to make the newcomers feel welcome, as well as the person I have not seen in twenty-five years. I really do want to remember everyone's name. It's not merely that I want people to know I care, although that is part of it. I want each person who comes through the line to experience something of the embracing love of God. After all, not a sparrow falls without God's knowing and caring. Then again, sparrows do not have names and I am not God.

Through the years I have learned the historical and theological foundations of practically every word and gesture in the liturgy, but no one has ever explained to me why pastors stand in doorways and shake hands with worshipers following worship. I just know that you better do it. It is an essential part of Sunday morning. If after worship one Sunday, rather than stopping at the door to shake hands, I went directly to my study instead, I imagine that there would be a bit of confusion and perhaps even some grumbling, as if something were terribly amiss.

One reason the ritual of shaking hands seems indispensable is easy to identify: it is an intensely concentrated time of interaction. As a pastor, you learn a lot about what is going on in your parishioners' lives while shaking hands after worship, much of it mundane, but some of it momentous as well. People often are willing to say the most remarkable things in such a moment. Perhaps that is because, with their hearts fresh from worship, they are more willing to take risks. Perhaps it is because they can say something quickly and then immediately leave without having to face an extended conversation. Perhaps it is simply because they are seizing the moment. Whether for any of these reasons, or other reasons entirely, people will often say extraordinary things at such a time, not just about births, deaths, divorces, job losses, and moves, but other things as well. There was the man who said, as dispassionately as if he were reporting on the certainty of rain that afternoon, "The doctor has given me three months to live." Or, the woman who looked at me with begging eyes and said, "I just learned that my son is a drug addict." Or, the man who was barely able to get out the words, "My wife left me last night," before collapsing in my arms. In each instance I do not remember how I responded, but I recall the words of each with vivid clarity.

Then there was the time when a woman I had never seen before, obviously great with child, stopped at the door and rubbed her belly with what I took to be both wonder and pride, and asked, "Will you bless my baby?" I hesitated, not because I was reluctant to offer a blessing, but because I wasn't exactly sure how to go about it. So I asked, "Do you have a picture of how you would like me to do that?" She responded, as if giving me remedial instructions, "Well, I'm not sure exactly, but I would like you to put your hand over the baby and say a prayer." So I put one hand on her shoulder, the other on her belly, and I offered a prayer. It was a brief prayer, but before I finished the line at the door had turned into an intimate little circle around the bold expectant mother and the suddenly shy pastor.

In much of our worship there can be so many words offered, often at a distance, from talking heads that peer over pulpits, like television newscasters who only seem to exist from the shoulders up, that we can get the impression that worship is about disembodied words. But you don't have to have your hand on the belly of a woman you have never met before to be reminded that the Christian faith is insistently incarnational. The reminder is right there in the ritual of shaking hands. The word is always enfleshed — in Jesus, of course, but also in the preacher, and just as surely in the worshiper as well.

Not all of it is that serious, of course. Every preacher I know has a collection of memorable comments that have been made by parishioners as they shake hands following worship. Perhaps the most prized example in my own collection is the comment I received not long after seminary from a man who said to me, "You know, Martin, every sermon seems better than the next one." He was in his car and driving away before I realized what he had said.

There are the comments that, in one form or another, every preacher has heard, that communicate in a kind of code.

Someone says, "I wish my sister were here to hear that sermon. I've been saying something like that for years." Translation: "She has stopped listening to me. Maybe you can get through to her."

Someone else says, "Well, you certainly gave us a lot to think about." Translation: "I don't agree with what you said this morning." Alternative translation: "I didn't understand what on earth you were talking about."

Or someone speaks about what a sermon meant to her. In the process, she paraphrases what I said that she found so helpful — and it is as if she is talking about someone else's sermon, because I do not recognize a word of it. The thought she is so joyfully carrying away is not the thought I meant to convey. When that happens, I usually conclude that I have not done my job as a preacher or the other person has not done her job as a listener. So I have to remind myself that there may be another explanation. Perhaps the Holy Spirit has taken my words and spoken through them in ways I did not intend.

When preachers stand in doorways and shake hands it is a reminder that the clergy are not performers and the congregation an audience. Rather, in worship we are all performers before the true audience of worship — that is, God. But both clergy and laity sometimes get confused about this. The practice of shaking hands after worship is one way to reach across a divide, either real or imagined, that may have developed between chancel and pew, between worship leader and worshiper. After all, in worship an illusion can emerge that the worship leader is somehow set apart, someone who is not to be confused with God, but sometimes is. When the worship leader comes down from the rarified heights of the pulpit or the chancel and shakes hands with worshipers, it is a palpable way of reminding everyone involved that he or she is just a fleshly creature. It is a way of saying, "We may have played different roles this morning, but we are part of the same company of players in this drama."

Some preachers — mostly the celebrity preachers, the leaders of megachurches — do not shake hands. I can see why. Celebrity requires some distance and at least a dash of illusion.

In the theater there is a tradition that actors are not to be seen by the audience before or after a performance, and particularly not in costume. There is a certain illusion that is to be maintained that requires some kind of divide between player and audience. If, for instance, you see the actor who is playing King Lear munching on a bagel backstage before the curtain goes up, it will be more difficult to fully accept the actor as Lear once the play begins. Also, it would be odd, and more than a bit disconcerting, to have Lear and his daughters greeting theatergoers at the door following the performance. Actors collaborate with members of the audience to create, for a time at least, a kind of illusion that they are the characters they play. Anything that exposes that illusion is usually unwelcome. As a preacher who shakes hands, I believe worship leaders have a quite different job: to expose illusions at every turn, including the illusion that they are something more than fellow-players in the drama of worship. Shaking hands after worship is one way of putting the worship leaders in their place.

I have learned that this is a time in which the worshipers rightfully take charge. The preacher has had a chance to speak, sometimes at great length and perhaps from a high pulpit that is "six feet above contradiction," as one parishioner of mine wryly put it. During worship the members of the congregation have sat in silence or they have read words that someone else has written for them. This moment of greeting the worship leader is an opportunity for them to offer their own words. It is a chance to say a word about their lives as a kind of testimony in miniature or to add a coda to the sermon by pointing out something that, in their opinion, the preacher left out or got wrong.

On the eve of the first Gulf War I preached a sermon in which I expressed my opposition to the imminent invasion. I did not want to use the pulpit merely as a soap box from which to expound my political views. I wanted the folks in my congregation to hear reflection on the war that they would not find in the editorial pages, to help them think about the issues as Christians, and not merely as citizens. So I was careful to interpret my opposition to the war through my understanding of both scripture and Christian tradition. I spent a good deal of time preparing that sermon and I delivered it with confidence, even though I knew that there would be many in the congregation who would take issue with it, because I believed that what I was saying had integrity.

After worship I shook hands at the door. Some people found various ways to tell me that they agreed with me. Others wanted to let me know that they did not. Many did not comment at all on the sermon, which left me free to interpret their reactions. Then one older member of my congregation approached me, a retired general who was normally quite soft-spoken. As I have indicated, usually I remember what people say to me as we shake hands but I don't remember my response. But this encounter is different. I don't remember what he said. I just remember how angry he was. I do remember what I said in response: "Reg, you are a military man. You of all people understand the chain of command. Well, in the chain of command I am obliged to follow the orders of Jesus. And that's all I was trying to do this morning in saying what I did — obey orders." I do not even remember what he said after that. I just know that I immediately regretted saying anything. I had already had my turn to speak. This was my turn to listen.

When Paul finished preaching in Antioch, the worshipers who shook his hand at the conclusion of the service said, "Please preach that sermon again next week" (Acts 13:42). What a startling request. To be sure, no one has ever said that to me. After all, we want to be up on the latest. We read today's newspaper with interest; tomorrow that same paper will seem good for nothing but starting a fire in the fireplace. The people of Paul's day were no different; it was a new day and ordinarily they would want to hear a new message.

So what could Paul have said in that sermon to elicit such an unlikely response? Quite simply, he told the story of God's fierce love affair with the world, first through the people of Israel and then through Jesus of Nazareth. Paul spoke of God's faithfulness throughout history, about the covenant God established with Israel, and about how God rescued the people from slavery in Egypt and led them into the Promised Land. He told them that all of history had been preparation for Jesus' birth and that, when the right time came, God sent Jesus out of God's own being. Paul told the people that, though Jesus was blameless, he was crucified, but the promise of his coming was fulfilled when he was raised from the dead. And in his life is the source and meaning of our own lives. To that sermon, the people said, as they were shaking hands with Paul, "Please preach that sermon again next week."

When Michael Greene, a British historian of evangelism, addressed a gathering of United Church of Christ ministers a number of years ago, he sparked lively debate by defining evangelism as "chatting about Jesus" and by asking us, "When was the last time you told your congregation what Jesus means to you?" At the hotel bar afterwards Greene's remarks sparked a lively exchange. Many felt that Greene's question was dangerously simplistic, smacked of fundamentalism, and represented the kind of piety they had hoped to escape by joining a liberal denomination like the United Church of Christ.

I was among those who felt that Greene's question was a challenging and appropriate one. In fact, I was haunted by it. I could not answer it with certainty. As a Christian preacher I talk about Jesus a good deal, but talk about is quite different from expressing devotion. It is the difference between talking about a loved one and sending a love letter.

Greene's question was still in my mind when I preached for the last time to my congregation of nine years, First Congregational Church (UCC) in Burlington, Vermont. I spent almost the entire sermon speaking devotionally about Jesus, which would be about as unremarkable in some traditions as it was startling in my own. Here is how I concluded that sermon, which I entitled, "What It's All About":

> As I am about to leave, there is something I want to tell you. I want to tell you what Jesus means to me. I want to share my belief that everything depends on him. I want to urge you to learn from him. I want to assure you that you can lean on him in times of trouble. I want to ask you to listen to his words of challenge. I want to tell you that I believe that you can entrust your life to him. I want to affirm that he is Lord of this church, and that in his name you are freed to love one another and empowered to share that love with a hurting world. I want to profess that, though once people could not look at the face of God and live, now we are invited to look at the face of God in him, in Jesus, and live as we have never lived before. He is Emmanuel, God with us, God with us all, whether we are together or apart. That's what it's all about. That's all I know. Amen.

At the conclusion of that sermon I stood at the door and shook hands with the members of the congregation for the last time as their pastor. One woman, a beloved saint of the church, came to the head of the line but was so overcome with emotion that she could not speak and went to the back of the line. I assumed that she simply did not know how to say good-bye. When she finally reached me again she extended her hand to shake mine, her shockingly blue eyes magnified by tears. Her voice cracked as she asked, "Why didn't you tell us this before?" It is almost as if — if she could have — she would have said, "Please preach that sermon again next week."

I did not know how to respond. And now it is her question that haunts me.

CHAPTER 3

Entertaining Angels Unawares

LILLIAN DANIEL

At the beginning of my ministry at Church of the Redeemer in New Haven, in 1996, I worried each Sunday that the choir would outnumber the congregation. Everybody knew we had to grow.

"We have to grow, you know," they'd say, like members of small churches everywhere do, with all the enthusiasm of a person scheduling a dental appointment.

"We need to attract new members and change," they would say. There was desperation to the announcement, but a stoic resolve at the end. Like a surgeon who announces, "We'll have to take that thing out."

Our beautiful New England sanctuary was built for greatness, the third building of a congregation gathered nearly two centuries ago. It was an elegant red-brick structure, with white pillars, three great white doors, and a steeple, set back from the main road on which it stands. The interior, with its cream-colored walls, lofty ceilings, tall windows behind still more white pillars, and spread-out pews, was meant to project space for God, and clearly space for congregational growth. But after a couple of decades of membership decline, that cavernous interior simply projected emptiness. How could we ever fill this grand church?

It was built in and for the days when people drove in from the suburbs surrounding New Haven to attend church in the city, back in the days when cities were a destination for wealthy shoppers, not struggling panhandlers.

For years, families had been leaving the city in order to live and attend church in the suburbs, where strip malls were becoming one-stop destinations for commerce as well as conversion. What hope did our churches in the city have, where there were way too many of us with expensive buildings, dwindling resources, and wistful remembrances of a better time? We were like beautiful girls lining the wall at a dance where the boys had failed to show up.

At least that's what I had been told by the books I'd read and in the conversations I'd had before I arrived at Church of the Redeemer. One local pastor told me that he had commissioned a sociological study of our urban neighborhood, in order to gather information about the possibilities for church growth. The survey told him what we all knew. There were way too many churches in our East Rock neighborhood, home to Yale graduate students, professors, and Irish and Italian immigrants, most of whom were categorized as "happily unchurched." Long gone were the days when business and social connections came through the church. Now, the decision not to attend one of the many sanctuaries our neighborhood had to offer was a well-thought-out choice.

Like so many other churches in the city, we had a handful of children in the Sunday school — two of whom were mine — and a long list of what I began to call "ghost families." These were families who had once built the Sunday school, who had once worked so hard to build the committees, who had once driven in from the suburbs for years with their children, who had once been gifted and dynamic leaders of the church. The current leaders, wonderful committed people in the church who had these qualities themselves, would speak of the ghost families with a holy reverence, as though they were different. "If only you could have known them. They were such workers. How they struggled to turn things around." Until they had quit. They hadn't died; they had just left.

The ghost families haunted me in those early years.

A few of them quit just weeks before I was to begin my ministry.

Some of them were nice enough to call me at home before I came on board. "We're tired, we're exhausted, and we can't keep going," they'd say, as they explained a transfer to some thriving suburban church. "And we wanted to quit now, before you started, so that no one would blame you for our leaving."

"Can't you give me and this new ministry a chance?" I would ask over cookies and tea at their homes, where they tried to be kind but still eyed me like the alcoholic cousin who has come asking for money.

"No," they would say, after telling me everything that was wrong with the church, and why they had given up on it.

And then, just when it couldn't get worse, it did. After a few of these ghost family visits, I learned the drill. Having heard what was wrong with the church they were leaving, I'd then have to listen politely as they told me about their new church — how *beautifully* the large Sunday school functioned, how *many* youth attended the youth group, how *inspiring* the preaching was, the *thrilling* capital campaign around the corner that instead of feeling like a burden had strengthened the whole community.

"It sounds *wonderful,*" I said, determined to make one last cross-court eschatological shot. "But one day in the future, we could be like that too."

They smiled indulgently, like hardened ranchers in the company of a vegan. "Better for us to resign now, so that your feelings won't be hurt when we resign later," they said. "But good luck," they would add, seeing me to the door and collecting my mug of cold tea. "It is a wonderful church. They deserve a wonderful minister."

But I wasn't that minister, apparently. I was losing members before I had even preached my first sermon.

So, still mourning the ghost families, our congregation, like others that have become more used to shrinking than growing, had perhaps grown wary of newcomers. Our members dwelled in the stories of those ghosts who had once fought valiantly and left. I began to suspect that in order to truly be appreciated as a church leader in this system, you had to resign, join another church, and then ascend to your previous church's sainthood.

I thought I was ready for all this. I had read all the books about pastoring small churches, mostly written by pastors who had turned them into enormous ones. I had immersed myself in the study of church growth, attending seminars and reading voraciously, particularly drawn to books that featured some kind of "how-to" section. I listened to tapes of pastors who had performed market surveys of growing suburbs before opening the perfect church for that group's demographic and marketing needs. And I learned that my church had all the markings of the type least likely to grow — founded in the 1800s, no parking lot, in a city. But I also soaked up the ten steps to fixing all that, the workbook that would turn us around, the self-study that would break it all open, delighting in the great thoughts of great pastors who had grown their mighty churches — with Jesus' help, of course.

The Protestant church long ago rejected the doctrine of "works righteousness," which claimed that we could earn salvation through our own good works. Rather, Protestants take the view that salvation is not ours to earn, but comes from the generosity of God's grace. I have found, though, that as small churches wanting to grow, we can sometimes lose sight of grace, and put our faith in our own efforts instead.

As I look back, I suppose that the church growth movement had so soaked my consciousness that I had come to believe that my call was to shape the church, and I was far less interested in being shaped by the church. My calling was to fix, not to be fixed. We all knew we needed to grow, that we had great work ahead, but it turns out that grace was waiting for us, waiting to be noticed.

The first Sunday I preached in my church, two men visited for the first time. Tim and Jack came to coffee hour and introduced themselves as "partners" to one older member of the church.

"And what kind of business are you two in, then?" she inquired. They shrugged, and politely explained their two entirely separate careers.

"Two such handsome young men," she told me later, with a wink. "But these young people . . . how can you be partners if you don't work in the same business? Perhaps they're in investments."

The week after my very first Sunday and theirs, I called on the two men in their beautifully appointed Victorian home in the historic Westville section of New Haven. We sat on velvet-covered love seats and sipped tea from translucent English china. My hands shook as I tried to balance a cookie on the side of my saucer. This would be my first effort at evangelism in my new church, if you didn't count my failed attempts to keep those members who left before my arrival. I was ready for a clean start.

I said a little prayer and made three promises to myself as I surveyed the floral wallpaper, the polished antiques, the tasseled silk lampshades, and the porcelain figurines. One, that I would handle myself with appropriate poise in such a beautiful and formal home. And two, that I would not make a big deal about the fact that these men were gay. And three, that I would not convey an air of desperation in my efforts to recruit them. I took a deep breath and another cookie.

Then I noticed that I had tracked dirt onto the exquisite Oriental rug and that my tea was filling my little saucer. The first cookie was starting to decompose in the liquid and float. I wondered how I could possibly get it out of there. As I tried using the second cookie as a pusher, it began to soak up tea as well, and I realized I was creating a little cookie quicksand that was threatening to spill over the edge . . .

"So tell us about your church," they said.

Ah yes, I thought to myself — the perfect opportunity for me to reflect on my seven days of ministry and all the knowledge I've gleaned about our community from the members I drove away before I even started.

"Well, I should tell you up front that we don't have any other gay couples in our church," I announced. I put down my saucer with a bang and a splash of cookie mush hit the antique table.

They looked at me strangely.

"But you're welcome to come." I continued, "In fact, we desperately need new members or people say we'll close down. We've been losing members for decades, and I just got here . . . but I've been reading a lot of great books about how to grow the church."

So, with all three promises to myself broken, I took a deep breath, wiped the spot of cookie mush off the antique table and started over.

When I described the church I wanted these two men to join, it was not the church in the present, but the church I dreamed it could be, a place where all people would be welcome and God's grace would abound. I waxed eloquent about a church that probably bore little resemblance to the one they had visited, but they listened politely to all my big plans.

Finally Jack interrupted me to say, "Since receiving your phone call, we've prayed about it and we believe that God sent us to church on your very first Sunday for a reason."

A few weeks later, Tim and Jack were part of our first new members' class, which also included a newly baptized lawyer from Taiwan, a Yale physics student, and a ninety-two-year-old artist.

Years later, we talked about that conversation in Jack and Tim's living room. It turns out that to Tim and Jack my awkward and clumsy statement of welcome, the one I had wanted to shove back into my mouth in sophisticated liberal nonchalance, was meaningful. It turns out that my trip to their beautiful home gave them a chance to show me what their ministry with our church would become — a ministry of hospitality. While I had been thinking about how to welcome them, they had been thinking about how to welcome me. Hebrews 13:2 says, "Do not neglect to show hospitality to strangers, for in doing so, some have entertained angels unawares." It strikes me that on that awkward visit, all of us had been entertaining angels unawares.

Shortly after they had joined our small church, long enough for a little of my grand vision in the living room to have happened and long enough for much of it to have been exposed as nonsense, Jack and Tim invited the entire congregation to their house for an Epiphany party.

Epiphany is that day in the church calendar that comes twelve days after Christmas — the day, it is said, when the Wise Men visited the baby Jesus and immediately recognized him as the Messiah. (When children ask me to explain the word *epiphany,* I describe it as a light bulb, a sudden recognition, or an "a-ha!" moment.) Around New Haven, the Latino community is large enough that this twelfth day after

Christmas is a city and school holiday known as Three Kings Day; in terms of shared meals and worship, it left our Congregational attention to the day looking sadly perfunctory. So the idea of an Epiphany party filled me with delight.

By now the congregation had sampled Tim's gourmet baking at church coffee hour and raved at his skill. Having visited their home, I knew this party would be on a grand and extravagant scale.

Yet while church members had stopped trying to fix the two men up with the single women, still I worried. I knew Jack and Tim had taken a leap of faith in joining our church rather than another, more explicitly welcoming church. I knew that for Jack and Tim, the hospitality they gave so generously could well have been denied to them in the past.

I knew that our church and I were learning hospitality all over again as we moved away from desperation for growth for ourselves as a church, to a warm welcome for the sake of God and the other, and away from a desire for the church of the past, to a vision for the church of the future. Would people at church understand the significance of the Epiphany party invitation? Or would busy schedules and bad weather conspire to keep us isolated from one another?

The night of the party the weather was icy and the roads slick. I arrived late myself, terrified of what I might find. Yet when we pulled up to the house the lights from the window and laughter behind the door pulled us into a stuffed house more crowded with church members than our average Sunday service. Everybody had shown up.

Children ran up and down the stairs, giving their parents a gasp as they brushed by the many fragile things. Some of the little ones marveled at Jack and Tim's Christmas tree, which was the biggest and widest I had ever seen. Every ornament was Victorian, and silver kittens and rose-cheeked ladies smiled down from a softer time.

The older members had set up camp in comfort on those same love seats I had perched on so awkwardly. Later I realized that while I had been wondering who would come, they had been organizing rides for one another and reaching out to the newest members.

Now, they looked right at home, the women still in their bright

Sunday suits and sensible shoes. They balanced tea sandwiches and petit fours on their saucers with ease. One of them gestured to Tim who was standing solemn sentry at the enormous silver punch bowl, ladling pink liquid into tiny cups.

"Now this is a party the way we *used* to do them," she said. All the ladies nodded in recognition, pointing out the doilies under the cookies and the lavishly set table, and the home arts that they worried had passed away in the march of time. Tim and Jack glowed and eased under the endorsement of a great generation who appreciated their details, on a snowy night, in the midst of a cold world that didn't always appreciate their lives. Here around the tea table, generations spoke through the practice of hospitality about what changes in life, and what does not.

"Today women don't have time to do all this," the women said. "You women today, you work and have careers, and children," they said, glancing toward their new pastor as a member of this species. "But this party just takes me back to the old days."

It took us all back, but forward too. For hospitality is not a lost art. It is a practice, and an act of faith. It is one that our church came to practice well, thanks in large part to Jack and Tim and many others, who naturally bring beauty and welcome into everyday encounters.

I would go on to discover that I was wrong that day in Tim and Jack's living room — our church already had gay members. We would go on to receive more, and to write a statement marking ourselves as open and affirming to all people, regardless of sexual orientation. We would go on to grow interracially, and to wrestle with differences of class. But to my mind, our congregation's practice of hospitality was honed by the Holy Spirit at that Epiphany party, when on a cold winter's night people who had been strangers suddenly strangely warmed one another.

That Epiphany, the hospitality went many ways. Our hosts invited us into their lives and their world. The church accepted the invitation, which in turn invited Jack and Tim deeper into the church's life.

But first God makes the invitations, when we take a moment to welcome a newcomer, when we make an awkward visit, when we serve a cup of tea, when we entertain angels unawares.

Built for a time when ladies had time for elegant teas, our church, like many New England Congregational churches, had an old-fashioned ladies' parlor that we seldom used. Grand in proportion and furnished with oriental antiques in need of repair, too big for our average events, the parlor had become dusty, tattered, and seldom-used. It wasn't long before Tim, who had taught himself to upholster, had befriended a longtime member who could hang wallpaper. Between the two of them, they used money raised by a series of elegant dinners to renovate the ladies' parlor. The end result looked a lot like Jack and Tim's living room: handmade silk Roman shades, pink Victorian wallpaper full of exotic birds and flowers, and velvet love seats everywhere.

Some people are shocked to see such an extravagant room in a New England church, and more shocked to see how much we use it. After all the work the men had put in, we couldn't continue to call it the ladies' parlor, especially when we wanted it to be used often and by everybody. So gradually it came to be called the upstairs parlor. Sort of a frilly version of the upper room, without all the betrayal and desertion.

We came to be known for our deacons' extravagant silver teas after church, on special Sundays in the church year, when we pulled out all the good china. The older members taught the newer members how to make those tiny cucumber tea sandwiches from another era.

Sometimes, as a congregation, we wondered whether the frilly fun of silver teas might seem self-indulgent to an outsider, but it felt like ministry to us. We knew, for instance, that the parlor was not just restored for our pleasure but also for the nursing mothers' group, the environmental activists, the labor unions, the teenagers, and the social workers who met there for retreat. When such groups found out they would be meeting in the upstairs parlor, generally they took in their breath. "Surely this room isn't for us?" they asked. But it really was. And the ornate wallpaper continues to take in the shouting of union stewards, the tears of women with postpartum depression, the strategizing of community mediators — and a few antique chairs do get nicked along the way.

I recall the scripture passage in which the disciple who will become the betrayer, Judas, castigates Jesus for allowing Mary to perfume his feet when there were poor people to be fed, and Jesus' angry response. "The poor you will always have with you," he said. But Jesus would only be there for a little while. And Judas, who had lost his sense of extravagant beauty, would soon lose his sense and his life.

We're not Jesus, but like him, we are only here on earth for a little while. And so we long for a life lived richly and deeply. We know there is something wrong with the patterns of the world, of people who starve while others live in absurd wealth. We know there is something wrong when homeless people die of exposure after funding for their day hospital is cut. We know there is something wrong when so many families are too poor to be able to serve their kids breakfast, so it becomes a part of every child's New Haven public school day, leaving even less time to learn. There is so much wrong in the world that Christians must attend to. It can feel overwhelming to turn to the practice of hospitality in a broken and inhospitable world.

Yet we found that the hospitality of a silver tea offers both pleasant comfort and prophetic correction. For at the silver teas, I look around to see people who do not have this elegance at home enjoy it in community. I see people who have no china of their own get to own the china of the church. People whose usual lunch is a yogurt slurped down while standing in front of the refrigerator get to sit down instead in the parlor, with a lovely plate full of treats, and gaze upon floral arrangements that seem too grand for any one house but are fitting for the whole people of God. There, in the church's shared finery, we can dream of a day when the beautiful things in life would all be shared.

Busy parents who think they are too busy during the week to sit down to eat with their children stand around the old sink after silver teas, lovingly washing each piece of china, and they wonder if a sliver of this hospitality might find its way back home. Teenagers, who claim to love nothing more than eating fast food in the car, instead play "mother" and ladle out the sherbet punch to the children, who marvel that they are allowed to use such pretty things. In a world of hoarding, extravagance breeds extravagance. Together, in our old formal church parlor we are practicing hospitality, taking one another in and receiving one another's gifts.

A recent widow who lives alone gets to preside over the pouring of the tea. She sits behind a silver tea service that generations before her have washed, polished, and drunk from. Here she presides over a crowd. As she is pulled out of loneliness, tentatively stepping out for a moment from the shadow of her grief, there at the head table, she pours out for others what has already been poured out for her.

CHAPTER 4

Learning to Pray

MARTIN B. COPENHAVER

One evening during my first week as a student at Yale Divinity School there was a knock on my door. Sitting at my desk, I tossed the words, "Come in!" over my shoulder. The door opened and there stood a student from down the hall. He and I had already had a few glancing conversations, over a meal or two and while brushing our teeth in the communal bathroom. I remember liking him, even though he had a brilliant smile and a mane of windswept hair that, once I learned he was from California, made him a bit suspect. He introduced himself as "Toph," which didn't help much, either. I was from New York, so perhaps I can be forgiven for assuming that the next thing I would learn is that he went to college on a beach volleyball scholarship.

Toph asked, "Am I disturbing you? We could talk later." I replied, "No, this is a fine time." I stayed at my desk and he remained in the doorway. He started with something of a Jimmy Stewart stammer: "I was, you know, just wondering if you might be, well, interested, or could be interested — perhaps — in having a prayer group." I did not respond immediately, so he continued, "That is, if that might be something you would be interested in doing. Or not."

"Uh-oh," I thought. "Here it is." I did not know this fellow and I had my own stereotypes of the sort of person who would issue such an invitation. That reaction was part of a larger concern. I did not yet know any of my fellow students very well and I wondered how I was going to fit in. The day before registration, just a week before, I had dropped some things off at my room and then left campus as quickly as I could, in something of a panic. I drove back home to New York and, over dinner with my parents, I tried to articulate my fears: "I'm just afraid that I will be stuck for three years with a bunch of religious nerds." My father suggested that, if I was going to be a student there, it's a pretty good chance that there would be others like me, probably many of whom had the same kinds of questions I did. But I was not consoled. Up to that point in my life I had not been around people my own age who took their faith seriously and I did not yet know what to expect.

My first few days on campus had been somewhat reassuring. I met a number of people I liked, but I was still a bit wary.

Now here was this fellow I didn't really know, asking me to join a prayer group. He was standing in the doorway because I hadn't invited him in, but now it seemed like he was blocking the door and I felt trapped. When I finally responded to his stammering invitation, I hemmed and hawed a bit myself. I remember expressing some reservations, but I don't remember much of what I said. I just remember feeling uneasy and a bit anxious. One reservation that I probably did not express at the time was that I did not know how to pray.

I am the son and grandson of ministers. I grew up in the church. I had been on the staff of a church during two of my college years. I felt called to the ministry. But I had no real experience in prayer and, if I believed in prayer at all, it was only in a rather vague and meager way. Oh, to be sure, my parents said bedside prayers with me when I was young, and in our family we always began our evening meal with a prayer we said together. But otherwise prayer was not really a part of my life and, if asked to offer a prayer, I would know to start with "Dear God," and end with, "Amen," but as for what might go in between, I was largely clueless.

So I hesitated in response to this invitation because I had visions of being stuck in a small dorm room with a bunch of people who were very comfortable — perhaps all too comfortable — with prayer, when I was still not sure what to believe about prayer or how to go about it.

I asked Toph what we would do exactly. He said, "Well, I'm not sure. We can decide that. But I could tell you what we did in our prayer group at Williams." Hearing that he went to that Massachusetts college forced me to reassess my beach volleyball theory, which may have left me open to reassessing a few of my other assumptions as well. Toph explained, "We would begin by reading a passage from scripture — just whatever anyone wanted to read — and then we would reflect on that a bit. Nothing formal or prepared. Then we would share prayer concerns and use those as the basis of our prayer together. And we would commit to praying on our own during the week and to remember the prayer concerns that were raised during our gathering." It was just as simple, and just as foreign to me, as that.

I told Toph that I would give it a try. We quickly assembled a list of others we would invite to join us. There was David and his roommate, Dale, and Arnold from down the hall. None of us knew each other very well. Everyone agreed that we would meet on Wednesday night at nine.

I don't remember much about that first gathering, probably because it followed the same pattern we used every Wednesday from then on. We always met in my room (whether I offered to have the gatherings in my room because I like the role of host or because I was trying to maintain some measure of control, I cannot say for sure; both are plausible).

We followed the format Toph had outlined when we first talked. We began by reading a passage from scripture, but we didn't read it the same way we read it in our classes. We didn't dissect the passage using the standard tools of scholarship. This was not a time to pick apart a text in all the ways our professors were teaching us how to do. Rather, this was a time to let scripture speak to us. We sought to relate what we were reading to what was going on in our lives — which I realize may not sound too remarkable, but it was quite different from what was going on in our classes or most of our conversations at the divinity school.

A story about one of our professors that was in circulation

among the students helped us to keep the distinction straight. At a gathering of the faculty a professor of New Testament had read a paper about the story of the multiplication of the loaves and fishes. The scholars present entered into a debate about the veracity of the account, its various literary and historical influences, and different theories about how the story had taken its final canonical form. Then someone turned to Paul Holmer, a professor of theology, for his opinion, because he had been uncharacteristically quiet during this exchange. He said, "Well, I don't know about all of that stuff. I was just thinking that if Jesus could feed all of those people, perhaps he can feed me." We kept that story before us. We did not want to be content with carving up the text. We wanted to feast upon it.

Then we would review the prayer concerns that were raised the previous week. "How is your aunt doing after her cancer surgery?" "Is there an update on your brother's search for a job?" "Did you get through that exam okay?" "Obviously, we need to keep the starving people in Ethiopia in our prayers." "And all of those people who are going to have a hard time heating their homes this winter." "And your visit with Patty this weekend? How did that go?"

At first, the practice of going down our prayer list from the previous week seemed an odd exercise. At times it felt almost like we were attempting to keep track of God's batting average. And there were stretches when God seemed to be in a terrible slump. There were items that appeared on our list week after week, for which there was no discernable answer to our prayers, even with the broadest understanding of what it might mean to have one's prayers "answered." Nevertheless, over time, what was most remarkable to me was how often we could sense some kind of movement in the areas of concern that we brought to God in our prayers. To be sure, God did not always seem to respond to our prayers in the ways we might have hoped, but I was surprised to see how often something would happen, whether always through the movement of God's Spirit or not, I cannot say for sure. I was beginning to conclude that there was more to this prayer business than I had previously imagined. I felt as if I was beginning to wade into a deep mystery.

Then, when we had fashioned a list of prayer concerns for the coming week, we would hold hands and each of us would offer a prayer. The prayers were as conversational as anything that preceded them. We simply shared our lives with God in much the way we had shared our lives with one another in the conversation leading up to prayer. Often our prayers were seasoned with laughter, and occasionally punctuated by tears as well. It seemed quite natural that both would be part of our prayers. All of this was quite new to me.

Over time, what was becoming increasingly important to me was not the question of whether God answers our prayers in any conventional sense, but the ways in which those times of prayer seemed to usher me into the palpable sense of God's presence. And the people with whom I entered into God's presence week after week were becoming increasingly important to me as well. Those Wednesday night gatherings became the axis on which the rest of the week seemed to revolve. I developed a great appreciation for the others in the group. Like others I met at divinity school, they were among the most engaging, fun, and interesting people I had ever been around. No longer was I wondering if there would be anyone like me among my fellow students. Now there were ways in which I hoped that I could be more like them.

During Lent of that first year, four of us decided to have a weekend spiritual retreat. In the midst of the rigors of study, we wanted to immerse ourselves in the ways of prayer. And what better place to do that than a monastery? So we made arrangements to visit Mount Saviour, a Benedictine monastery in upstate New York.

When we arrived on Friday night we were greeted by Brother Timothy, who showed us to our rooms. When we unpacked our bags in the sparse rooms, we had to laugh because, without consulting one another, three out of four of us brought brown sweaters to wear. After all, we each must have been thinking, what could be more appropriate to wear in a monastery? You certainly wouldn't pack a paisley shirt.

After we were settled in, we met with Brother Timothy, whose turn it was that week to talk with the guests. I mean that quite literally. The Benedictines observe a discipline of silence. They do not speak to guests and do not speak to one another, except once a week, when the monks have a meeting to talk over concerns in their community. I remember asking Brother Timothy what sorts of things they talk about when they gather at that meeting. He said, "Oh, you know, the usual: we talk about the little grievances and silent arguments that arose during the week." At the time we thought that quite amusing. When the monks finally have a chance to talk, conversation does not concern spiritual insights they have gained in the silence, or anything like that. Instead, it's about things like who forgot to put the cap back on the toothpaste.

The rest of the weekend we joined in the monastic life. We did not speak with one another, except in whispers behind closed doors in the guest quarters. We attended worship, all seven offices (that is, worship services) a day, beginning with matins at four o'clock in the morning. We shared the simple meals with the monks in silence. We joined the monks in manual labor. Cleaning out the stalls in the barn with one monk, I wondered what he was thinking about on his side of the veil of silence.

We found the discipline of silence rather demanding. Our group of four verbose, opinionated seminarians usually had conversations that were more like one of those rambunctious political talk shows on television. But for that weekend, for the most part, we kept the discipline of silence.

On Saturday night, we gathered in one of our rooms. We had a Bible study and then, after we said a few prayers, there was silent prayer. And after the silent prayer there was the very different silence of four young men in desperate need of something else. One of us said, "You know what I could really go for right now? A pepperoni pizza and a beer." It was the quickest consensus we ever reached.

Not wanting to disturb or disappoint the monks, we pushed the car out the gate of the monastery, without turning on the engine or the headlights (our own version of keeping the vow of silence) and then we piled in and drove to a greasy spoon in this little rural town. We had our pepperoni pizza and beer. We talked about what was going on in our lives, about what God might be up to in our lives, about our fears and our joys. We played some of our favorite songs on a jukebox. We told stories and laughed. In fact, we were so raucous that the people in that little dive stared us, this group of young men in brown sweaters, whooping it up.

When the place was about to close, we drove back to the monastery, too tired to push the car anymore, but once again we did turn off the headlights. We slept a little, and then got up for matins at four in the morning, our eyes half closed — in prayer, of course.

All of us were grateful for the experience at the monastery, but that was the only time we went there, or any place like it. We concluded that we didn't have to go anywhere special to deepen our experience of prayer. The little dorm room would do. When we gathered there on Wednesday nights, as we ended up doing each week for four years, it felt like something of a holy place. Over the course of those years a few others joined us. The format was largely the same, but the prayers that we brought continued to widen in scope to include the range of public issues of the day, as well as the joys and burdens of our individual lives. During our four years together, five of us married (including two who met one another in the group), one divorced, one came to the understanding that he was gay, a number of us were ordained, one decided not to pursue ordination. One group member's father was sentenced to prison for embezzling money. Another member's parents divorced. And then there were all the everyday vicissitudes of life that we shared in those years: the academic pressures, the questions about vocation, the challenges of being new to ministry, the tattered or torn relationships, the financial concerns, the shared meals and shared jokes, the times we worshiped together, or studied together, or sought shelter in one another. Among the closest friends I have ever made were people I met in that prayer group I was reluctant to join. And I am convinced that those relationships are particularly strong because they were formed in the crucible of prayer.

It has been a long time since we met together in that little dorm room, but I continue to pray for the members of that group, and I know they do the same for me.

Last fall I called Dale, a particularly close friend who was part of that original prayer group, and I told him about a trip to Israel I had heard about. I said, "I'd love to go, but I want us to go together." He immediately agreed. Neither of us had ever been to Israel before. We were scheduled to leave the day after Easter. Before our departure, the leaders of our group had suggested that we invite the members of our congregations to write prayers on slips of paper that we could then take to the Western Wall in Jerusalem. The Western Wall is the foundation wall of the temple that was destroyed a generation after the death of Jesus, the only part of the temple that remains. The Western Wall is the holiest of Jewish sites, a place of prayer. Pilgrims stand before the wall to pray and many put prayers written on slips of paper in the cracks of the wall.

As Dale and I approached the wall, he had a large pile of prayers on slips of paper that he had collected from his congregation on Easter Sunday. Since I had no written prayers with me, he handed me a stack of his. We stood next to each other before the wall. I put my hand on one of the huge stones of the wall and noticed how shiny it was, worn smooth as a gem by all the hands that had touched it through the years. Then I read each prayer in my stack from Dale's congregation and made them my own prayers, prayers from people I do not know, but with whom I now felt an intimate connection. There were prayers for healing, prayers for those who were grieving, prayers for aging parents, prayers for wayward children, prayers for those who were homeless, prayers for those who fought in wars, prayers for peace. Here in Jerusalem, that great broken heart of the world, people were pouring out the deepest yearnings of their own hearts.

And then I came upon one prayer that stopped me. It was written in Dale's familiar scrawl. It was a prayer for me. Just seeing my name on that slip of paper was something of a jolt. The prayer was simple: "For Martin's health and his vocational discernment at this time." Dale and I had prayed together often through the years and had assured each other of our continued prayers when we were apart. But here in my hand was a prayer for me he did not know I would see, that was intended for God alone, and yet I was allowed to overhear it. And in that moment, that place, soaked in the prayers of pilgrims over centuries, became a most holy place for me, as well.

CHAPTER 5

Can We Be Friends?

LILLIAN DANIEL

I remember the quiet summer night when things changed between my neighbor John and me. We were sitting on his front steps, having a beer, watching our children run up and down the sidewalk, which was our usual routine as we waited for our spouses to come home. We were sitting there, talking about nothing, when he ventured into new territory.

"I'm thinking I want my kids to go to church," he mumbled. "I wondered if you knew anything about that Methodist church up the street from us."

The words came out of my mouth before I had thought them through. "What on earth are you talking about? Here you are living across the street from a Congregationalist minister. Suddenly you wake up one morning, finally feeling religious, and you want to go visit the *Methodists?* Why wouldn't you come to our church?"

"I don't know," he said, staring out at the kids. "I guess I do want to try your church." I wondered if he had just made a nice save. "But I didn't know how you'd feel about that."

But by then I was in work mode, not feeling mode. I saw a potential member for my church and zoomed in like a telemarketer on speed. Before John knew what had happened, he had agreed to come to church the next Sunday and was saved from his near brush with Methodism.

John and his kids stayed in our church. He became a leader in our community-organizing program and later a deacon. He has told me that his life is richer now. We've discussed tithing, salvation, communion rituals, and politics; and now, as his minister, I know something about his nine-to-five work as well as his inner life.

But as for drinking a beer together on the front steps with nothing to do but watch the kids — that passed away. As pastor and parishioner we now had a relationship centered in a community. And we became items on one another's to-do lists.

I wouldn't trade the new relationship, but I do miss having someone to sit on the steps with. Looking back, I think I understand why John wanted to visit a church other than mine. Perhaps he saw what I did not see: that after we became pastor and parishioner, we would no longer just sit on the steps and talk about nothing.

Being in the ministry, where so much of my work is devoted to the building of relationships, I worry about losing the ability to just sit next to someone and talk about nothing. Evangelism has become a part of my personality. Even when I try not to draw people to my church, they must see an invisible sign on my back, a sign like the ones we stuck on unsuspecting victims in grade school: "Kick me!"

Ask me a question about religion, tell me about the nun who rapped your knuckles or the pastor who ran off with the music director, or the fact that you're a very spiritual person but you just don't believe in organized religion, and I'll start telling you about my church. I can't help myself. So as I establish friendships outside the church, my friends join the church.

It is not happenstance that my family had a gym membership at the Jewish Community Center. Proselytizing there would be rather bad form. I found that I could go to the gym there, eat at the snack bar, watch my kids run around, and talk about nothing. Few people there knew that I was a minister, and I liked it that way. But I wonder if, in hiding out at the Jewish Community Center, I was ducking some hard questions.

I remember the debate in divinity school regarding whether a minister could have real friendships within his or her congregation.

Back then it seemed as though it would be simple. But the end of 2 Thessalonians 5:12 reads like a mass of contradictions that comes closer to the reality of Christian leadership: "But we appeal to you, brothers and sisters, to respect those who labor among you, and have charge of you in the Lord and admonish you; esteem them very highly in love because of their work."

The words *respect, have charge of, esteem,* and *work* seem to imply a sense of being set apart. That distance is then unraveled by the intimacy of words like *brothers and sisters, among you,* and *in love.*

I know that I have friends in my church. I am also aware that there are limits to those friendships, ways in which we are set apart from one another. The major focus of my life, my ministry, is a topic that is, for the most part, off limits. I must find other friends with whom to vent about the frustrations of work, from staff conflicts to the occasional vocational vacuums.

So for that reason, I have learned the value of friendships with other ministers: collegial friendships. Two months into my first ministry, at a lobotomizingly dull denominational gathering for new clergy, I caught the rolling eyes of two other women about my age. Since that day I have kept a monthly lunch date with these colleagues in ministry, for eleven straight years.

Together we have been through two ordinations, four births, five job changes, one wedding, and one coming-out story. We have prayed for one another in hospitals and gone shopping together for interview suits. Between us, we disagree politically and theologically. We have radically different understandings of our calls. Yet nothing could have prepared me, eleven years and 132 lunches ago, for the way in which God has used our friendship for both holy encouragement and prophetic correction.

When I served on my denomination's subcommittee dealing with pastoral misconduct, I cynically scrawled on one thick folder the title "Bad Boys." But as we heard case after case of sexual misconduct, a common theme emerged: cases of misconduct regularly involved men who tended to be lone rangers. They generally told stories of loneliness and isolation from their peers.

Later, when I learned that it wasn't just the boys who were straying and that the girls lapsed too, I realized that I had been blessed with a covenantal group of women to hold me accountable. As we had been honest with one another, this had become a place where we shined God's light on our own shadows.

I am haunted by the ending of the Letter of James, where the author tells Christians of their need for one another. "My brothers and sisters, if anyone among you wanders from the truth and is brought back by another . . ." Ministers without collegial friendships have no one to bring them back.

I'm struck by how often the epistles begin with words about friendship. The early church must have valued it greatly, with all those loving blessings and holy kisses between brothers and sisters of the faith. Sometimes it seems to be lifted up as a practice of the faith, even a discipline that Christians are obligated to enter into for their own mutual formation.

Yet at the beginning of Paul's letter to Titus, a friendship is described differently: "To Titus, my loyal child in the faith we share, grace and peace from God the Father and Christ Jesus our Savior" (1:4). The letter goes on to encourage Titus to seek out elders in every town. And so we are reminded that not every friendship is between peers in age or cohort group. We cross boundaries in our friendships, and so we grow in the faith.

Some collegial friendships are teaching friendships. In a male-dominated field, my mentors tend to be men. There have been times when I have found myself invited into a room of men whose experience of the ministry and the world is radically different from mine. Sometimes I sit like a country cousin in the old-boys' club, waiting for the subtitles to appear or the translator to arrive.

But more common are their quick responses to my urgent telephone calls, patiently nurturing me through some crisis in the ministry. It seems there is no crisis that one of them has not seen. These friendships between older men and younger women in the ministry are breaking new ground. Together we have struggled across the differences in age and gender to find a way to make disciples of one another.

But the crossing of boundaries for the sake of Christian friendship is nothing new. Like Titus, I need my elders in every town.

Then again, perhaps such a vision of friendship is too limited. Perhaps there is a place for church members among a minister's friends. I know that I should not gripe to church friends about a member of the church staff, for instance. But I have come to realize that withholding such information does not necessarily create distance. In a secular world that defines people too much in terms of their work, perhaps there is something helpfully countercultural about having friendships in which work, and workplace gossip, cannot be a central focus.

When my mother died, a quartet of church members flew down to sing at her funeral in Washington, D.C. When our senior deacon spoke at her service, he explained that he represented the church. It occurs to me that that is what we do in all Christian friendship: we transcend the needs of the individual to point to something larger than ourselves. I had my little rules about not discussing work with my members, but here they were proclaiming the gospel in song at the saddest moment of my life. What greater intimacy could there be?

After the funeral, I looked around my mother's house, full of people gathered for the reception. A table full of canapés had replaced the hospital bed in the living room, where she had died just days before. The smell of my stepfather's Greek food had mixed with the sick scent of a weeklong coma. My ability to make small talk was wearing thin.

At that point, I needed my collegial friendships — not the neighbors or even the family, but the Christian ministers who had accompanied me in the walk of loss along the way, who understood what it meant to visit the sick of your church while your mother was dying somewhere else. I thought of Paul's greeting in Philemon 1:2 to Archippus, whom he describes as a "fellow soldier."

And there, showing up at my mother's home, was the minister from another church back home, a church that in the language of the world should be my church's "competition." Upon hearing the news of my mother's death, Shep had quietly booked a flight down to Washington and simply appeared at the service.

Shep had been many things to me over the past ten years, first my pastor, then my mentor, and then a colleague down the street. I'm not sure what role he was playing in my life at that moment after the funeral — perhaps all of them at once. Simply seeing him standing among the mourners, amidst the small talk, gave me the witness that I had a life waiting for me at home. This death would not be the last word.

The members of my church who had come to sing at the service approached me to say goodbye. "We're heading back to the airport. We're not going to stay for the reception," they said. "If we do, you will worry about us. You'll feel like you have to introduce us to all these people."

They were right, of course, that I would fuss over them. But how greatly they underestimated the power of their presence. I didn't know how to put it into words, but perhaps they saw it in my silence. They did not leave.

"Okay, we'll stay for the reception," they said, "but only if you promise not to act like the minister. Because right now you should just be the grieving daughter." Their understanding of those boundaries made me realize how permeable they could be.

"Please stay," I said. "And I promise to ignore you." It was the first time I had laughed all day.

I thought back to when I used to sit on the steps with my neighbor John. As I watched the church members mingle into the crowd, I realized that these church members and I had finally come to the point where we could simply be near one another and talk about nothing. We were friends.

CHAPTER 6

So You're a Minister

Martin B. Copenhaver

Most professions, it seems, have their characteristic pet peeves. Doctors can become quite crabby about how a social occasion can turn into a professional consultation when an acquaintance describes his ailments at length during a cocktail party. Teachers I know get annoyed when people comment on how nice it must be to have summers off, probably because teachers often have to take on a second job in the summer just to make ends meet. Attorneys complain that if they never heard another lawyer joke, it would be too soon.

And we ministers are not immune. We, too, have our pet peeves. There is one in particular that I feel compelled to confess.

But before I go any further with this, I need to warn you: I don't think there is any way to describe a pet peeve without sounding . . . well, peevish. At least I have not found a way.

So here goes: Ministers are often annoyed by what people say to them when they find out that they are ministers. In social situations or other settings, when someone finds out you are a minister, often what you hear in response is something so lame that you simply want to extricate yourself from the conversation as quickly as possible. Often that is not possible, however. So, instead, you are treated to another trite generalization about the state of organized religion or some hackneyed explanation about why this person does not attend church.

When this pet peeve is given free rein in a gathering of ministers, we will come up with the same examples of things that are said to us. Over and over again, we all hear the same things. We often fantasize about offering snappy comments in response. And, on occasion, we might find ourselves actually saying those things.

Someone says, "All religions are really alike, aren't they?" Response: "Do you really think that is a respectful thing to say to people of other religions? Usually that just means, 'Your religion says the same thing mine does, only not as well.'"

Or, "I don't belong to a church because I feel closest to God in nature." Response: "Okay, but during a walk in the woods what exactly do you learn about the nature of God and about how to live your life?"

Or, "Every time I go to church, they seem to be talking about money." Response: "Yes. It's called an offering."

Or, "I don't believe in organized religion." Response: "But do you believe in community? If religious faith is a solitary matter, you'll be fine. But if responding to God involves community, before long you'll have some kind of organization."

Or, "I thought it was important to go to church when my children were young, to give them a spiritual foundation. But now they are grown, so I don't go to church much anymore." Response: "So you wanted to give your children a foundation in something you don't really care about much yourself?"

Or, "I think of myself as spiritual, but not religious." Response: "So you like to pick and choose your beliefs, wherever they may be found, which really means that it is all about you."

Or, "Every time I come to church they talk about the same things." Response: "Perhaps that is because you only come at Christmas and Easter."

Or, "I'm into Native American spirituality." Response: "Really? Which tribe?"

Or, "I don't believe in a God who [fill in the blank: created the universe in seven days, would give children cancer, condemns all Muslims to hell]." Response: "Did it occur to you that I might not believe in that God, either?"

Or, "I stopped believing in God when I looked at all of the terrible things that have been done in the name of religion." Response: "So God is to blame for all the things that misguided people have done in God's name? How about all of the things that have been done in the name of the nation-state? Are you going to become an anarchist as well?"

Or, "I don't come to worship anymore because I don't get much out of it." Response: "Well, maybe that's because it's not about you."

See what I mean about how difficult it is to describe a pet peeve without sounding peevish?

What these comments ministers often hear have in common is that they represent a rather shallow understanding of God and the church. They are offered as if they represent a novel insight, when in fact you have heard it all before. And, in most cases, the remarks are so closed-ended and self-justifying that they do not lead to much in the way of conversation.

So most ministers I know avoid even saying any of the snappy responses they might imagine and opt instead for getting out of such conversations as soon as possible.

When I used to travel with Dale — an old friend of mine, and a fellow pastor — we used to go to some lengths to avoid having such conversations at all. We would take on the professions of our wives for the duration of the trip. If we got into a conversation with someone on the beach or in a bar, he was a clinical psychologist and I was a corporate lawyer. We knew enough about our wives' professions to bluff our way through a casual conversation and, in that way, we could avoid getting mired in the kind of conversation you can have with strangers when they find out you are a minister.

When someone finds out you are a minister, sometimes you have to listen to more than their theories about God and the church. You also may have to deal with their assumptions about ministers.

For some time after I moved to the church I now serve, I was in search of a good barber. I wasn't looking for anything fancy, just someone reliable. The sexton of our church suggested I try his barber, who had his own shop in the next town.

When I walked in the door, I was optimistic. It had the look and smell of an old-fashioned barber shop. The barber was friendly and seemed competent. He chatted away to the man in the barber chair, and occasionally directed a word to me.

There was a television on, broadcasting a news program. When the newscaster turned to the story of the Clinton impeachment hearings, which were going on at the time, the barber stopped cutting hair and looked for a moment at the television. Then he turned to the customer in the chair and to me and said, "Ridiculous. Completely ridiculous. I'm from Greece. This would never happen in Greece. He's the President of the United States, for God's sake. He's the leader of the free world. And he's being impeached because he got a . . ." And then he used a crude colloquialism for oral sex. He went on to repeat his point a number of times, without much variation, using many of the same words, sometimes with fervent indignation, while other times muttering the words under his breath. I listened, which is what ministers do, and perhaps nodded my head, which is another thing ministers do a lot, and then I went back to my magazine.

When he finished with the other customer, he ushered me into the chair with something of a grand gesture. He put a tissue paper collar around my neck and, like a magician unfurling a cape, he draped my torso with a large cloth.

As he began to cut my hair, he tried to start a conversation: "Where do you live? Do you have children? Are you a baseball fan?"

Then he asked, "How did you find us?"

"John Willard told me about you."

"Ah, yes, I know John. How do you know him?"

"Uh-oh," I thought. "I don't like where this is headed." I said, "John and I work together."

He came back, "But John works at a church."

"Yeah, he's my colleague." I knew I wasn't going to get away with this.

"And what do you do there?"

Checkmate.

"I'm a minister," I said, bracing myself.

But I wasn't fully prepared for what happened next. He staggered back from the chair as if he'd been punched in the stomach. There was a look of sheer horror on his face. After a moment, he placed his right hand over his chest, which I took to be a gesture of grief and contrition. I was hoping that he would consider the gesture sufficient and simply go back to cutting my hair.

"I am so sorry. I had no idea. If I had only known, I would not have said what I did about the President."

"No, it's okay," I said. "Really, it is."

But he wasn't buying it: "I am so embarrassed. I had no idea. To think that I insulted a priest like that. Will you please forgive me?"

And what was I to say to that? To say that I forgive him might be the shortest route to getting back to my haircut, but I actually didn't think he had done anything to require forgiveness. If I said that, however, that might only prolong the conversation. I saw no way of reconciling his assumptions about me with the reality, at least not in the length of time it takes to get a haircut.

What I wanted more than anything else was to get out of there. He was only partially done, however, and if I left now my hair would look ridiculous. Besides, I couldn't see any way of leaving at this point without increasing his embarrassment and, at the same time, reinforcing his assumptions about me.

So I settled for saying something like, "Really, let's move on. What do you think of the Red Sox' chances this year?"

That did the trick. Almost. We engaged in banter about the hometown team, but it was interspersed with more of his apologies, mostly mumbled or whispered, as if they were said in a confessional. I did not respond. When he finished cutting my hair, I gave him an unusually large tip, through which I was trying to say, in a tangible way, "It's okay. Really." That seemed not to work, however. As I stood up to leave, he stuck out his hand to shake mine and said, yet again, "I'm so sorry." I replied, "Have a great day."

It was a good haircut. I never went back. If only I had told him that I was a corporate lawyer.

Not long ago my wife Karen and I went to a small club in Boston to hear Chris Botti, the well-known jazz trumpeter. I love jazz and it had been a particularly demanding week at the church, so I was eager for this night out. The place was packed, but we had the best seats in the house, right next to the stage. When Botti took the stage and they began the set, I was transported. The concerns of the week seemed to recede to the vanishing point. Between songs Botti would talk some about the music and his relationship to it, but never so much that it detracted from the main order of business which, clearly, was the music itself.

Then Botti began to tell a story about the time, early in his career, when he auditioned for Frank Sinatra. It was a charming little story filled with self-deprecating humor. I was clearly following this story very intently, because I love Frank Sinatra. At some point I must have laughed or made a facial expression that brought me to Botti's attention. Suddenly he stopped and said to me, "Sir, may I ask your name?" This was the first time he had addressed anyone in the audience, so I was a bit startled, but I immediately responded, "I'm Martin Copenhaver."

"Martin Copenhaver," he echoed back. "The way you say that makes it sound like you are running for office. Are you?"

"No."

"Are you a lawyer?" I should have seized on that as an opportunity, but let it slip away.

"No," I said.

"Then what do you do for a living, may I ask?"

I was not about to have my evening out spoiled by having my pet peeve played out before a club full of people, so I said, "I'm not going to tell you that."

"Okay," Botti conceded. Then he went back to his story about Sinatra. But before he had gotten very far, he turned to me again and said, "No kidding. What do you do for a living? You really have me wondering."

I wasn't about to give in: "I am *not* going to tell you that."

"Really?" he asked, a bit astonished.

"No, I'm not."

People in the audience started to shout out their guesses: "He's an undertaker!" "Proctologist!" "Secret agent!" (I wish I had thought of that.)

Karen, on an errand of mercy, gestured to Botti to have him come to the edge of the stage. He bent down so that she could say something to him. Karen cupped her hand over his ear, as if to tell him a secret. He stood upright, with a look of good-natured surprise on his face, and said, "He is not." Karen nodded. Having gotten this far, I figured it was time to come clean. I took one of my business cards out of my wallet and handed it to Botti. He looked at it, paused to take it in, and then read, "Senior Pastor, Wellesley Congregational Church." The audience roared with a combination of laughter and applause. Botti stepped off the stage to shake my hand and then led his band in a rousing version of "Fly Me to the Moon."

After his final number, Botti again came off the stage, to shake my hand and to wish me well. He then waved to the audience and left the room. As Karen and I departed, a number of people made a point of saying something to me, more than one beginning, "So you're a minister . . ." I was grateful that, in the shuffle of the departing crowd, there was not an opportunity for much more conversation than that.

In the lobby of the club some of Botti's CDs were for sale. I stopped to get one and we joined the line of those who were waiting to have them signed by Botti.

A woman behind us in line said, "Excuse me, you're the minister, aren't you?" With a bit of dread I said I am. She then said, "Your church is in Wellesley, right? That's not far from where my brother lives. I'm going to suggest that he visit your church. He's had a real rough time with a divorce and he's got custody of the kids." We chatted for a bit and then I handed her one of my cards and said, "Please, suggest that he call me. I'd be happy to get together with him." And I meant it.

Someone from further down the line said, "My mother is in the hospital and she may never leave. Cancer. Her priest has been in to see her. But would you be willing to pray for her?"

"Sure, of course," I said. "What's her name?"

Then a couple of other people left their place in line in order to start a conversation with me. Mostly they wanted to share what was going on in their lives. They wanted to talk with the minister.

Eventually we got to Chris Botti, who greeted me as if I were an old friend who had come to see his show. He said he was a bit embarrassed by how the conversation in the club had unfolded. I assured him that I was fine — more than fine, actually — with how it turned out, which, at this point in the evening, actually was true. He, too, wanted to know something about my church, but he also asked about my love of Frank Sinatra.

And to think that none of those conversations would have taken place if I had said that I was a lawyer.

CHAPTER 7

I'm with the Band

LILLIAN DANIEL

When punk rockers grow up and get married in their forties, the celebration is bound to be a little different.

The wedding reception took place on the stage of a grand old theater in Buffalo, New York. Stylishly set tables, with crisp white cloths and bright crystal, were scattered across the wooden floor, with its stage markings and piles of ropes, velvet curtains swagged casually aside. We, the wedding guests, ate our wedding banquet up on that stage and looked out at hundreds of empty plush seats; we were a show with no audience.

Yet on that stage full of tables, there was a smaller stage for the wedding band. This was a revolving cast of musicians, who, according to a carefully planned set list, would get up from their guest tables at the appropriate song, and wander up to join the band for one number or maybe two. In between, one guitarist might hand her instrument to another, or a drummer might stand to make room for drummer number four of the evening. The lead singers changed, too, as different wedding guests took their turn at the mic. Two decades of friendship and musical history crossed the stage that night, as musical memories drew us into a wedding banquet like no other.

Thankfully this was not a karaoke affair, with amateurs torturing one another with spur-of-the-moment song choices and alcohol-induced confidence, nearly always misplaced. No, this was a carefully choreographed set list that took experienced, gifted musicians from many bands and pulled them together in odd combinations.

Some of the musicians were former bandmates to one another, now moved on to be lawyers, mothers, and businesspeople. But many of these wedding guests were still in the music business, playing in bands that record and play shows. Some had been in bands together that were now broken up into new combinations and adventures. But all of them wandered forward to perform and to celebrate the wedding of the bride, a singer, songwriter, guitar player, and punk rock music activist, and the groom, a journalist who loves music, thank God.

As a minister, I have learned that wedding receptions reflect the best and worst of people's pasts. Here, the past and the present of the gathered community, of the couple and their friends, were present in the setting itself, a huge theater. These were people who were comfortable on stages, whether on them as performers, in front of them as fans, or behind them as sound and support crew. So to have the wedding celebration take place there was only natural. As natural as the bride taking her turn at the mic to sing a few numbers at her own wedding reception.

The wedding ceremony had taken place in the theater's lobby, an ornate space, beautifully restored as so many old American theaters have been in recent decades, with plenty of nooks and crannies where guest chairs could be placed. The bride and groom had processed up a winding staircase to a high alcove from which they could look down to see all their guests, who looked like elegantly dressed theater patrons, frozen in the middle of intermission by the sight of something remarkable.

There at the top of the stairs I waited to perform my friend Jenny's wedding. It had been over twenty years since she and I had first met in high school, and it had been sixteen years since we had been locked inside another old theater, in another place and another time.

Sixteen years earlier, long before I was a performer of wedding ceremonies, I was a bass player in a punk rock band. Jenny was the singer,

Derek played guitar, and Steve was on drums. Sixteen summers ago, we had been on tour. It was in some ways our first big break, a trek of several weeks, and many shows, across the United States, with two other bands, Seaweed, from Seattle, and Superchunk, from Chapel Hill. But this big tour would also be our last, for that was the summer before I started my master's of divinity degree at Yale Divinity School. Our band was called Geek.

Not many bands can say that they broke up because the bass player went to seminary, but there you have it. I broke up the band when I followed my call to the ministry.

In the book of Revelation a bride and groom appear as signs of what heaven may be, stretching our imaginations with an iconic image. "*And I saw the holy city, the new Jerusalem, coming down out of heaven from God, prepared as a bride adorned for her husband.*" I thought of Jenny, coming up those bridal stairs so beautifully dressed, in a vintage-style white lace gown, her red hair cut into a soft bob, when sixteen years ago it had been a wild mass of waist-long dreadlocks.

In life, we are constantly moving back and forth in time, back and forth between what was, what is, and what might be. But the writer of Revelation never lets you get stuck in one time zone. After the bride, come these words. *And I heard a loud voice from the throne saying, 'See, the home of God is among mortals.*" God is right here, in the middle of ordinary life, no matter where you are. Or where you were.

Sixteen years ago, in the weeks before divinity school, and what eventually would become a ministry of three churches, and then an old friend's wedding, life had seemed very different. If God's home is among mortals, we mortals were leading very different lives back then.

The bands' tour had started in Asheville, North Carolina, where our first audience had consisted of three drunk men who had shouted at us to play softer so they could continue to have meaningful conversation. But it's hard to play electric guitars softly, particularly in our genre. The three men left the place annoyed, and we were left with no audience, but given that it was the first night of the tour, we were so excited that all three bands played full sets to a single bemused North Carolina bartender.

The crowds picked up when we played in New York City at a famous club where meaningful conversation was not on the agenda. But during that show someone broke into my car and stole all my clothes — a fact that explains why in almost every picture from that summer I am wearing the same t-shirt. It said "bagel eater," and it was all I had to remember a New Yorker who gave it to me out of pity at three o'clock in the morning as I picked through the smashed glass from my windshield.

Later we drove to Madison, Wisconsin, where along the highway two guitars fell off the top of one of the cars, so that we had to turn all the vehicles around and search for wreckage on the other side, until remarkably we found them, still safe in their cases, on the side of the road about forty-five miles back. Losing all your clothes was one thing; losing your guitars — that would be a disaster.

And then finally to Flint, Michigan, where we gasped to discover our venue, an enormous old theater that seated thousands, right in the center of town. Could this be right?

For punk rockers didn't usually play in venues that size. We played in crowded basement clubs, with black walls and grottos, rarely any actual seats. When we had to sleep, if we weren't tripling up in the very cheapest motels, splitting Subway sandwiches and 7-Eleven burritos, we were on the sofas of fans we had never met before, who politely inquired if we were vegan.

So for our motley caravan to pull up at this massive old theater was like the Beverly Hillbillies pulling up in their Appalachian jalopy at the California mansion. We had struck black gold — oil, that is. We could hardly believe this theater was for us.

But as we got closer, we saw that the theater was clearly in bad shape. Seeing our bands' names on the marquee had been exciting, but thick chains on the main doors did not bode well. We saw people waiting to see us at a side door and we were ushered in there, not to the theater, but to the lobby, which had been set up with a few folding chairs, plugs to use, and a stench that indicated that no cleaning had taken place in years. The lobby was our venue. As for the main theater, we were told it had been condemned.

Flint had fallen on hard times. Auto jobs had left the area, and the city's residents were struggling to support themselves on the industries that remained. (It was during these days that Michael Moore made the documentary film *Roger and Me,* about corporate greed and its devastating effects on the city of Flint.) So poor were the kids in Flint that many of them could not afford the show, listening outside until we insisted they just come in. There were no hotels around us. No one invited us over to their house that night, but when it was time to sleep, we were told we were staying in the old theater.

Apparently this was how they handled hospitality for all the bands. They simply turned off the lights and locked you inside. We did not sleep easy that night. Some of us snuggled near the lobby door, at least wanting to see who might burst in from the street, as we imagined our appropriately edgy end. (Killed in a condemned theater in Flint, Michigan? Sad, but that's so punk rock.) But the optimists among us sneaked into the condemned theater itself, and ran around on the main stage, dancing, singing, and imagining an audience in the dark and grim decay.

"I heard a loud voice from the throne saying, See, the home of God is among mortals. He will dwell with them; they will be his peoples, and God himself will be with them; he will wipe every tear from their eyes. Death will be no more; mourning and crying and pain will be no more, for the first things have passed away."

It was that vision that would call me to leave this life and pursue another, and yet still sense God in the one I had left behind. In the midst of a depressed city, artists danced around on a stage condemned, but with all the joy that musicians can bring to an impossible situation. In music, we transcend reality. In music, we imagine a better world. It's also what we do in the life of faith. We imagine in an empty condemned theater a show that will rock the world.

When I arrived at Yale Divinity School a few weeks later, I had no idea what to expect, only that it would be different. And different it was. From the bagel eater t-shirt punk rock tour of America's dirtiest places,

I now found myself at the new student orientation picnic at Yale, on a little green, surrounded by Georgian cloisters and peppy preppiness, being led in song by a throng of sincere yet ultimately bad guitar players. They were urging us to sing (I kid you not) "Kum Ba Yah."

It was a like a *Saturday Night Live* parody of what seminary would be. *Revenge of the Nerds* meets church camp.

"I've made a horrible decision," I thought to myself. "I'm surrounded by geeks, who will suck me into their geeky world, and I'll never be cool again."

And I wasn't.

Because of course, part of following a calling is giving up stuff like that. I came to divinity school that summer carrying a boatful of ego, attitude, judgmentalism, and insecurity — in other words, all the things that in the life of faith, Jesus calls us to work on. Naturally, I left divinity school with the same list of imperfections. But my feelings from that first day of divinity school, my fear of giving up one self-image for another, equally shaky, stay with me as a rebuking gift. The haunting words, "I'll never be cool again," remind me today, as a pastor, of how hard it is for people to step into our churches.

I remember to tell people what I always needed to hear myself, that when we enter into a community of faith, we're not graduating, we're matriculating. In the journey of faith, we don't cross the finish line at the new members' class, the seminary graduation, or the installation at the new church. We are always merely beginning a new lap of a race. The throne is always out of reach ("You mean we never were cool to begin with?"), which makes me particularly grateful for the reminder, "*See, the home of God is among mortals.*"

Back among mortals, sixteen years after my band's big tour, my own spiritual tour took me to a place I could never have imagined. Now, I had the privilege of performing the wedding of my old friend, the lead singer. Back in the days when we had been on that tour, the lines between cool and uncool seemed so much clearer, and what I was leaving to do put me into a social Siberia that made me wonder if I would ever see those music friends again. But today Jenny was in a white dress singing in her own wedding band, and on top of it all, she and her new husband had started attending church. "So you're a minister now?" someone said, adding words that sixteen years ago, I could not have imagined hearing. "That's really cool."

Sometimes in our lives, we think there are breaks, these moments when we make a big change. We move to a new church, we make a move to a new denomination, we form a new relationship, or we pick a new path. But really, looking back, we were always playing the same song, just different variations, and in different combos.

From the stage at the wedding banquet, I thought about how being a bass player is a lot like being a minister. You lay down the beat, trying to keep it solid and true. Sometimes your job is to keep it steady enough to allow others to shine, to sing, to play, and to dance. Other times, it's the bass that makes it funky, adding needed surprise. But the bass is just one part of the band, and alone it doesn't sound like much.

For people like me who are drawn to music, the mystery that draws us into the bands we love the most is that we know it's not just about playing alone. The notes and sounds come together, the different people play their roles, and what is produced transcends the individual parts. It's like when you join a church and become a member of the body of Christ. Where you join a band that is way better than you are, and the next tour is always just beginning.

CHAPTER 8

Made Better Than I Am

MARTIN B. COPENHAVER

Being a pastor has made me better than I am. That is because the pastoral vocation requires that I act in ways that seem beyond me.

Recently I came across a sermon entitled "The Pleasures Peculiar to the Ministerial Life," preached in 1728 by the Rev. Amos Adams at the ordination of Jonathan Moore at First Church in Rochester, Massachusetts. The sermon reads like an extended love letter from a pastor to his beloved vocation. The Rev. Adams commends to his hearers "the superior advantages found in the ministerial life." In one section he examines the ways in which being a pastor can enhance one's spiritual life. While granting that there are temptations in the ministry, he affirms that "ministers have superior and peculiar advantages for their own improvement in every branch of evangelic holiness." He wants his hearers to understand that, "I don't mean that ministers are necessarily eminently good men." Nevertheless, he concludes, "The ministry is, in short, a school of virtue." Reading this sermon is a reminder of how little has changed in pastoral ministry over the years. Update the language a bit and the Rev. Adams could have been writing about my experience of how pastoral ministry has formed me in ways that make me better than I am.

I began to learn how to pray when I was in seminary — not in a class, of course, but in a small prayer group of my fellow students that met weekly. It was only when I became a pastor serving a church, however, that my experience of prayer deepened. After all, the only way to learn how to pray is to pray. Or, as Thomas Merton put it, "If you want a life of prayer, the way to get it is by praying." And pastors are asked to pray a lot. In his sermon, the Rev. Adams makes a similar observation: "The continual exercise of prayer, to which we are called, in public and private, on a variety of occasions, and in a multitude of circumstances, can scarce fail of improving the spirit of prayer within."

In 1985, very early in my ministry, Tom Cullins, the son of members of the church I served at the time, was one of 152 passengers on an airplane that was hijacked and diverted to Beirut. There they were held by terrorists for seventeen days before being released.

When I first heard about Tom's captivity from the local news station, I went to his parents' house, where other members of their family had gathered. I stayed for hours as they made phone calls, watched the news, and awaited word. The situation seemed grim, to say the least. One of the hostages had already been shot by the terrorists and his body thrown from the plane. Sitting in the Cullins family's living room on that anxious first day I was keenly aware that I didn't know what to do. So, for the most part, I just sat there in silence, which might seem appropriate under the circumstances, but which also seemed entirely necessary to me because I didn't know what to say. Then, after the family received a few more frightening details of Tom's situation, his mother turned to her young pastor and said, "Martin, this is when you offer a prayer." It was part instruction and part demand. Everyone else in the room may find it difficult to pray on such a day, but for me that simply was not an option. I was the pastor and so I was expected to pray, which, of course, I did.

As a pastor you cannot opt out of prayer. You cannot say, "I'd rather pass, if you don't mind. I don't have the words today. Is there someone else you could ask instead?" At any given moment you may not be expected to feel particularly prayerful but, by golly, you are expected to offer a prayer anyway.

If I were not a pastor I am sure that I would still pray, but I am equally sure that I would not pray as often. I would probably be like so many people who find prayer difficult to fit into the hectic tumble of their days. The Rev. Adams described them sympathetically as "the greatest part of mankind [who], in the busy and active scenes of life, have scarce a moment to turn their thoughts to heaven." Although — God knows — a pastor's thoughts are not continually turned heavenward, it is also true that a pastor's thoughts are frequently reoriented in that direction simply by performing his or her pastoral duties. As a pastor, you are simply expected to pray "on a variety of occasions, and in a multitude of circumstances": with the Men's Fellowship at their breakfast, with someone who is ill in the hospital, with the youth group as they head off on a service project, with a committee before they meet, with a couple as they prepare to marry, with a family as they gather after the death of a loved one. But since the way to prayer is through prayer, the expectation that as a pastor you will pray early and often can be something of a gift. I may have begun to pray in all those settings because I was expected to, but, over time, I discovered that prayer was beginning to dip deeper into my soul. Over time, through one of the untraceable patterns of grace, the prayers of my lips became the prayers of my heart. Increasingly my life as a person has been shaped around the contours of the practice of prayer because, as a pastor, I was simply expected to pray and was given abundant opportunity to practice.

There is no escaping the pastoral role. It follows one around relentlessly. That is a good thing, I have concluded, but like many things that are good for us, this aspect of pastoral ministry doesn't always go down easily. Anyone who has spent time as a pastor knows what it is like to covet the "off duty" sign of the cab driver. Because we are not issued such signs, there is no such thing as slipping in and out of the local grocery store for a quart of milk. A simple errand like that is always potentially strewn with unplanned pastoral encounters.

And because there is no escaping the pastoral role there is no escaping the scrutiny of the people around you. The pastoral life is lived in the round. In a term used in the theater, there is no "blind side," no side where there is not an audience. As Garrison Keillor once observed, when you are a pastor, people are always reading you literally.

I know some pastors who have served in settings where the expectations of a pastor, and sometimes the pastor's family, can be unreasonable, even oppressive. I am grateful that, for the most part, that has not been my experience. I have not served in settings where I have felt hemmed in on all sides by the range of expectations people have regarding what a pastor should be and do. And what expectations there have been seem largely appropriate and even seem to draw the best from me. This seems to have been the Rev. Adams's experience as well, because in his sermon he testifies, "That government of our tongues and passions, and that form of religion to which we are obliged, must have a favorable influence on our own virtue."

This same dynamic became clear to me early in my ministry when I attended a high school reunion. I was eager to attend because there were many old friends I wanted to see. I had not seen most of my classmates since I had gone to seminary. Perhaps because my father was a pastor, no one seemed particularly surprised that I had gone into the ministry. Actually, at the time I think I wished that they had been a bit more surprised because I didn't want to seem so devoid of imagination or as if I were merely going into the ministry as one goes into the family business.

As is the way with reunions, everyone seemed to slip comfortably into the roles they played ten or fifteen years before, as surely as if we had picked up old scripts with our names on them when we walked in the door.

We had all thought of ourselves as so knowing and sophisticated when we were in high school. One of our favorite expressions was, "Of course," as if we had already seen everything there was to see by the age of sixteen, and so we were beyond the reach of surprise. Irony and sarcasm were the lingua franca. Humor tended to have an edge. Conversation was something like a contact sport, particularly among the males.

Gratefully, by the time of this reunion everyone had matured a bit, which mellowed the conversation, but the pull toward our familiar roles was sometimes too much to resist. As the reunion was concluding, a small circle of us were comparing notes on the evening. Someone mentioned having a conversation with someone I will call Paul Jameson, who in high school had been widely considered "obnoxious." One friend said, "Paul told me that he lost ten pounds so that he could look his best for the reunion." I quipped, "The trouble is, even ten pounds lighter he is still Paul Jameson." It is the sort of put-down that would have been part of our banter in high school, but my friend wasn't going to let me get away with it. She said, without a hint of sarcasm, "Martin, and you're a minister?" Another friend added, "Yeah, we're counting on you." I don't recall what I said in response, but to this day I remember well my embarrassment.

Even though these were my friends and not my parishioners, they were holding me to a higher standard because I am a pastor. My first thought in response was probably something like, "Can't I just take a break and be petty for one evening? Do I have to be a pastor even here?" But my embarrassment was a sign that these friends were not wrong to expect me, in the Rev. Adams's words, to "govern my tongue." They did not want me to forget that I am a pastor, which, in this instance, meant prompting me to do the right thing. They were challenging me to do something that I should do just because I am a person, but that they probably wouldn't challenge me to do were I not a pastor. It is telling that the old English term for person, *parson,* came to be used to describe a pastor, as though the person and the vocation were so completely integrated that they had become synonymous. As a pastor you can take a day off from your duties, but there is no taking a day off from your role. People rightly expect that the person they see in the pulpit will be the same person they run into at the grocery store or meet at the high school reunion. The pastoral life is an integrated life. There is another way to put it: being a pastor requires integrity. That does not mean, as the Rev. Adams reminds us, that "ministers are necessarily eminently good" people, only that we can be made better by a vocation that he described as "a school of virtue."

As a pastor I am expected to care about people I may not particularly care for. I remember, for instance, getting a phone call from one parishioner informing me that another parishioner, whom I will call Jim, had been taken to the hospital because he had chest pains. The person on the phone was an active member who knew very well that Jim had been relentlessly critical of my ministry. Most often I was able to let what Jim said to me or about me slide off my back. At times, however, when I was particularly tired or when for other reasons my patience was worn thin, his criticisms would get to me. Jim was the sort of person I would find myself talking with in the shower or as I was driving in my car. In these conversations, in which I played both parts, Jim would say something potentially wounding and I would have the perfect rejoinder — strong, not unkind, irrefutable — the kind of statement that would reveal to him the error of his ways and send him home duly chastened, to sin no more. I had a lot of conversations like that with Jim when I was able to play both parts. But, unfortunately, in real conversations, Jim always insisted on playing himself and seldom did it go well.

Anyway, when the parishioner called to tell me that Jim had been taken to the hospital, he assumed that I would go to be with him, to comfort him, to pray with him. And I shared the same assumption. When I got off the phone, I simply got in my car and headed toward the hospital. Because it's what you do. It is not something I would choose to do on my own, but it is something that is expected of me by virtue of my calling. You are his pastor. He has been entrusted to you, big pain in the ass though he may be. My wife, who is an attorney, can "fire" a client who is too difficult to work with. If a doctor's care is continually criticized by a patient, that doctor can refuse to offer further treatment and refer the patient to another doctor. A restaurant manager can refuse service to a recalcitrant customer. But pastors are expected to care for those they did not choose and perhaps would never have chosen under any other circumstances. The church, like the family, is a place where we try to learn how to live with those we are stuck with. Of course, we are not always able to pull it off. But in those times when we are able to live with, and perhaps even love, those we are stuck with, the church can still give us glimmers of the love of the God who is stuck with us all.

When I got to Jim's room at the hospital, I perched on the side of his bed. I learned that Jim had had a mild heart attack. He told me about the treatment options that the doctors were considering. For reasons that I can only guess, he sounded positive, almost cheerful, as he discussed his condition. He certainly sounded more positive than he did whenever he talked about church matters — which, thankfully, he avoided on this occasion. Then, when I asked Jim if I could offer a prayer, he said, "Well, I'm not sure that's necessary. It was only a small heart attack." I responded, "Well, I'd like to, if I may." So I offered a prayer for his healing. I asked that he might know God's love through the skill of the doctors and nurses, through the devotion of his family, in the care of the church. I went on to ask that he be given, grace upon grace, those gifts that we wish we could give him, but which he can only receive from God's hand — the gifts of strength, hope, peace. And then I prayed that he might nestle in the everlasting arms that we are assured are underneath it all. Underneath it *all.*

Given the nature of our relationship, one might expect such a prayer to ring hollow. But if it was hollow, it was with the hollowness of a cup waiting to be filled. And filled it was — filled with my own struggling attempts to love this one I was stuck with and, by the time I was finished, filled with a resonance and power beyond whatever I was bringing to this encounter. In my prayers for Jim's healing something in my own heart was healed. It used to surprise me when things like that happen. Now I look for it.

Here is how the Rev. Adams put it in his sermon: "The continual exercise of pastoral affection, in earnest care, tender pity, and affectionate sympathy with the flock in all their variety of circumstances, in trouble and in joy, hath a most powerful tendency to form in us those habits of goodness, that liken us to the angels of light."

It does not always work that way, of course, but it does often enough. I now think I understand why Jesus tells his followers to act in particular ways, regardless of how they feel at the time. He says turn your cheek, pray for your enemies, pray then like this. He focuses on actions, not because interior dispositions are unimportant but because most often we act our way into a new way of thinking and feeling, rather than the other way around. So I am grateful that the pastoral vocation requires that I act in ways that seem beyond me.

In Max Beerbohm's story "The Happy Hypocrite," he tells of a wicked man who loves a virtuous girl. The man knows that he cannot hope to woo her if he approaches her undisguised, so he dons the mask of a saint. Sure enough, the girl falls in love with the man — or perhaps it is more accurate to say that she falls in love with the saintly mask. Years later, when a spurned lover of the hypocrite discovers the deception, she challenges the hypocrite to shed his mask in front of his beloved and show his face for the ugly, repulsive thing it is. When, after considerable protest, he drops his mask, he discovers what he could not have anticipated: under the mask of the saint his face has become transformed. It is the face of a saint.

Beerbohm correctly labeled the character in his story a "hypocrite," for clearly it was the man's intention to deceive. When someone takes on the pastoral role, obviously it cannot be as a deceitful disguise. Nevertheless, the pastoral role can be donned in the hope that one might be inwardly transformed to its likeness. Or, as the Rev. Adams put it, we assume the role in the hope that "the continual exercise of pastoral affection, tender pity, and affectionate sympathy" might "form in us those habits of goodness."

Perhaps that is a lot like what Paul had in mind when he urged the members of the church in Rome to "put on Christ." He was asking his listeners to assume some of the qualities of Christ, to wear them as they would a new and perhaps ill-fitting set of clothes, in order that some day they might fit, and be fitting expressions of who they had become. Such an outfit may not fit snugly at first. It may balloon in just the places where it should fit smartly. It may be so bulky that it makes the wearer feel awkward. But as every child who has been fitted for shoes has been told, it is important to have "room to grow." What seems to cause you to trip all over yourself today allows for the possibility of growth.

Those who have experienced some form of transformation in their lives often exhibit a tendency to exaggerate both the before and the after. So let me add: If I had not become a pastor I don't think that I would have been a child of the darkness. In many respects, I probably would have been very much the same person. Just as surely, even though I have been a pastor all of these years, I do not think anyone would describe me as one of the Rev. Adams's "angels of light." But I do believe that, by donning such a role and by doing those things that are associated with such a role, being a pastor has made me better than I am.

CHAPTER 9

Crumbs from the Table

LILLIAN DANIEL

Like many recession-strapped cities in America, New Haven was willing to give away the store to get one. Where once the town's greatest fanfare was reserved for the opening of a new church, today the President of Yale himself announces the opening of a new J. Crew chain store, and a donut chain's willingness to open up shop is front page news. And so it was with great fanfare that the little city announced in 1997 that we were to get a new four-star hotel, through the makeover of an old one. And the chain was being given $9 million in tax abatements to do it.

It is an interesting commentary on our society that the term *hospitality* has come to be associated less with the Christian faith and more with an industry. With the announcement of the new hotel, the hospitality industry had arrived, and with images of filet mignon and round red wine glasses, perhaps we fantasized that our city's star would rise with the four shiny ones on the new hotel's door.

The workers inside the old hotel, from the cooks who diced carrots to the people who washed the stained sheets other people left behind, looked forward to being part of something a little nicer. Their small local union prepared for what was to be a friendly transition. This was the union that over the years had given them higher wages, health insurance, and, most importantly, a voice on the job, the right to speak up as part of a group. The incoming hotel chain had promised to recognize the existing union in a process called card-check neutrality, in which union members sign cards and have them counted when they reach a majority. It was a process that promised to be smooth in a workplace that had already been unionized under the old management.

But underneath the hoopla of the proposed grand opening came word from the kitchens and the bathrooms and the hallways of the made-over building that the hotel corporation had changed its mind. They would not recognize the existing union as promised, but would instead call for a National Labor Relations Board election. The idea of an election sounds profoundly fair and democratic to most people, but the laws surrounding labor elections are so slanted toward the management that they are nearly impossible to win, and so the workers in the union braced themselves as union-busting consultants were hired. Shortly after, the union workers were called into special meetings in which they heard veiled threats about the security of their jobs should they choose to stay in the union.

Ophelia, one of the chefs in the kitchen, had already been called to such meetings and her anger boiled. She told her story to a meeting of a group of pastors who were involved in local community organizing efforts. Ophelia was a long-term employee, an elected leader of her union, and a leader in her church; she was already known to many of the New Haven-area clergy who had gathered in the dilapidated chapel of a Roman Catholic Church that sat next door to the city's largest homeless shelter in one of the poorest parts of town. At that shelter next door, hospitality was no industry, but a labor of love performed by a people of faith. Perhaps that ongoing practice gave us imagination that night.

The old chapel had little carved wooden thrones around the perimeter, but the clergy were huddled together on folding metal chairs on that cold day, in the unheated room, waiting for weak coffee to percolate.

Ophelia told the clergy the story of what it felt like to be in those meetings with her new employer. "They don't call us workers anymore," she said. "They call us 'associates.' And they're trying to take away our union. When they got that $9 million from the city, they promised they wouldn't do that. Can they? And do you think that's right?"

The clergy looked weary. We were a small group, varied in our denominational affiliations. We had been through smaller struggles, such as efforts to close down liquor stores next to schools, or fights for a living wage, or attempts to call absentee landlords to account. But were we ready to fight with a national hotel chain, especially when we also had churches to run, services to plan, weddings and funerals to preside over, committee meetings to attend?

Ophelia insisted that we hear her story. She told us that the management had threatened to fire her if she spoke with other workers about organizing. And she knew that the management would hire new workers before any election took place, guaranteeing that she would lose her right to shape her working life. Ophelia did not want the crumbs from the table. She wanted the hotel chain to keep their word.

"It's just not right," she said again and again. "I've been a cook there for twenty years, and I've never been reprimanded before now. Now, just because I want the union, I'm suddenly a bad employee." We shifted uncomfortably in our folding chairs. I suspected this fight was not winnable. I wanted to fold myself.

Back at the Congregational church I served, the décor was plain, white walls, no stained glass. When we served the sacrament, our Puritan communion table seemed spread thin. Little square cubes of white bread were supposed to fill us up. We were supposed to be intoxicated by tiny cups of refrigerated grape juice in little shot glasses, made of old pewter, which were sent out to the pews, each individual drinking quietly and alone. And did I mention that those tiny, perfectly formed cubes of bread that we passed were always Wonder Bread? To call the New England Congregational feast "understated" is an understatement. Some would say we were feast-impaired.

This is certainly how I saw communion when I first came to this part of God's garden, for I had been raised in the more ornate tradition of Anglicanism. When I left the church of my youth for the church of my adult calling, what I missed most was communion. Once a week, grand and dramatic, the Episcopal Church called us to walk forward and receive bread from a gilded altar, from the hand of the priest. When you took your gulp of real wine, your head would spin afterwards for just a moment, as you pulled yourself from kneeling, to standing, to returning to your place both full and filled.

So when I became a Congregationalist, the little portions in tiny cups and white bread seemed to speak of a lack of generosity at the moment it was most called for. The heavenly banquet was offered grudgingly, on a monthly basis, with no hope of seconds, in a church with no stained glass, no sherry after worship, and no wine, even at communion. I worried that in my call to a new church I was being pulled into Puritan plainness. In New England, the land where a kilt and pearls can be considered a seductive ensemble, our communion table was about as full as we could handle.

We had a small room off the side of the chancel of the church called the deacons' closet. It was there that the deacons, the lay leaders responsible for the spiritual and community life of the church, prepared the communion feast.

Even though the silver trays came out to the table neat and orderly, with a complete absence of crumbs, the deacons' closet itself was a bit chaotic. On the trays there was perfectly cubed bread, but back in the deacons' closet there were wild crusts everywhere and crumbs falling from the counter to the floor. As we prepared for the sacrament in church, the cool sanctuary exuded calm, but the deacons could be back there during the communion hymn frantically cutting up extra bread and mopping up a messy spill.

I think God keeps those who prepare communion rushing around and busy because if we actually stopped to think in the midst of communion, we would be overwhelmed with our purpose: they are feeding us the body of Christ. They set a simple table so that the rest of us might actually feel the presence of God.

Over the years, it was the chaos of the deacons' closet that helped me to love the simplicity of the New England communion table. They needed one another. The perfectly cubed bread was the orderly, pristine vision. The closet was my messy, disordered life. And at the table, they came together. It wasn't about portion size or pewter cups. It was Jesus who made it a feast.

Back at the Catholic chapel, Ophelia spoke to the gathered clergy about covenant promises broken and a hospitality industry that was not hospitable to the people who made it run. Ophelia was willing to challenge her own pastor and a bunch of clergy who preside over holy tables where we claim there is enough for everybody. But she looked us in the eye and told us she wanted more. Who were we to tell her she ought to want less? She didn't want almsgiving or sympathy. She wanted a meal of justice. Were we clergy the ones who were feast-impaired?

Meanwhile, others ate well. The city chamber of commerce began to hold their monthly cocktail hours at the new hotel as a show of support to the management. The Yale University administration began to hold its banquets there, and allowed its name — "at Yale" — to be added to that of the hotel.

The unions held a small but loud picket line. Some members of our churches found this distasteful. They agreed that the hotel was breaking its promise, but we needed the hotel. Why couldn't that tiny group of workers disappear? In New England, they may take their food in small bites, but they do want it to go down smoothly.

Still, Ophelia's words rang in the clergy's ears. "It's not fair. The hotel got our city's money. They have to keep their word." As a Christian raised in a church based on covenants, she was calling us to be a covenant people, as one who had felt the power of the covenant herself. She didn't want alms, she wanted justice.

So we decided to hold a large community meeting of clergy and laypeople, to which we invited the new management of the hotel as well as Ophelia and other union members. By now, the increasingly regular requisite gatherings between supervisors and workers were being referred to as "captive audience meetings" by the employees.

Ophelia, who had never once been written up in her twenty years at that hotel, was now getting a thicker personnel file. On paper she was suddenly being reprimanded for poor job performance. She was told that she could not take work time to discuss the union. Ironically, this was a privilege management enjoyed at will. The practice of shaping communities can be misshapen by power and wealth.

So by the night of the meeting, Ophelia and the workers were nervous. They did not want to be there in the church hall when the hotel manager was to appear. They were worried they would lose the jobs they had held for years and be replaced by a younger, cheaper, weaker, non-union work force. By calling in the clergy, who in turn were now calling in the management, Ophelia and her colleagues were risking everything. When Ophelia, an elected leader of her union, spoke to the gathering of Catholics, Pentecostals, and mainline Protestants, she asked us to keep her identity a secret. Then, before the manager arrived, she stepped to the corner of the old church hall and secreted herself in the broom closet.

I have always wondered what it was like for Ophelia to hide in the broom closet that night. Was she feeling like a servant, or a person with a divine purpose? Was she a commodity in the hospitality industry, or the priceless currency of God's economy? The world had told her to be content to serve and then gather the crumbs. The gospel to which she had entrusted her soul told her that she was to have a place at the banquet table. Now she was in a broom closet.

The hotel manager arrived for the meeting in a dark blue company blazer. The hotel logo stood out like a military rank. His eyes swept the room, and suddenly, sadly, I saw the room as I imagined he saw it. What we had hoped would be the site of a powerful action was actually a depressingly dilapidated old church hall that was already scheduled for demolition, with peeling paint and a startling odor of mold. It stood in a neighborhood with too few streetlights and too many boarded-up homes. The hotel manager's eyes took us in and seemed to count us for little.

As he sat in the chair and answered our questions he grew bemused. "Why would clergy get involved in something like this?" he asked. "What on earth does this have to do with the church?"

I could see why he was confused. It occurred to me that the keeping of promises was indeed the work of the church, but it was a work we had shied away from in the messiness of public life. With our soup kitchens and our food pantries, an observer might suspect that we are called merely to help people survive our communities. But every now and then we remember that we are really called to shape them as well.

"The opening of this hotel will be nothing but good for this city," the hotel manager said, confident that we would hear the veiled threat of pulling out. "I want to invite you all to the grand opening," he said, "because we're investing in you. And we're not against unions," he continued. "We just want to offer our associates the chance to vote in a democratic election."

As the manager stretched back in his chair, he looked so confident among our ragtag group, in a building about to be torn down. I thought of Ophelia, who was still hiding in that closet, with the mops and the brooms, and the cleaning products, as he waxed on about the benefits of being an "associate" with his company.

Later, after he left, she burst out of that closet raging. "What he said about working there — how great it is — well, it's not like that at all!" she cried prophetically. "They never keep their word!"

A week later, we received word that despite the hotel manager's eloquence on the subject of his employer's generosity and goodness, he had been fired.

Our exploration was now becoming a campaign. Our community organizing group was faxing letters threatening boycott to the hotel's headquarters in Texas. To us New Englanders, Texas was a mythical place that was too big even to return our phone calls, until suddenly, word arrived that their top management was coming to New Haven specifically to meet with our group of clergy.

The day of the meeting, our small delegation stood in the lavish hotel lobby. It had been refurbished beautifully, with enormous velvet couches that invited lounging. Soft music scented the sterilized air. We were greeted and told to take the elevator to the very top floor.

We were ushered into a conference room that overlooked the New Haven skyline, with a table laden with sweet pastries and silver pots of coffee. Clergy, it is well-known, are genetically predisposed to eat any and all free food. I am someone who eats constantly and automatically. I am told I eat like a bird, but it is the hummingbird, who eats twice her weight in order to stay in the air. So naturally, I rushed to the table, but our community organizer, Pete, held me back. "Don't eat their food," he muttered. "In the middle of an action, we never eat *their* food."

Suddenly a group of three tall men entered the room, all in well-cut navy suits with elegant ties. Only one of them was shorter than 6'2". Perhaps he had misread the dress code and forgotten to add height.

Our own little group must have looked strange to them as we sat around the enormous cherry conference table. Pete had worn one of his nicer outfits, a stained yellow tie with a sport coat that looked like it had been rescued from a funeral home fire sale. The Pentecostal minister, dressed as he was in a sharp lime green suit with matching green lizard-skin shoes, seemed to glow radioactively next to the discreet blue suits of those on the other side of the table, but his face was a fierce and frozen blank. Louis, the Jamaican Catholic lay leader, slouched coolly in his chair as if bored, but we knew he was like a cat waiting to pounce. The hotel executives pulled out three matching yellow note pads, sat up in unison, and prepared to take notes like the smartest kids in the class they must have been.

The discussion began awkwardly. After they introduced themselves with their various titles of corporate management, we introduced ourselves with titles like "Organizer," "Outreach Minister," "Father," "Evangelist." We even had an "Apostle" in our group. When I, a woman in a clerical collar, introduced myself as a Senior Minister, they looked at me as though I were delusional. And I felt a bit like an impostor, given that no one in my church would recognize me in such an ensemble, given that the old collar only came out on such occasions.

As we began our discussion of a potential boycott, the president jumped in several times to ask us variations of the same question: "Why are you here?"

Why would church people be involved in something like this? As we tried to explain our own call to shape our community, he began to instruct us on economic theory. We were nervous, unable to make our case for all his quiet interruptions, offered with the tone of a patient teacher addressing a group of slow students.

Suddenly Louis sprang out of his slouch and stretched his lanky body across the table punctuated by a sudden smack of his arm on the polished wood. "Do you think we are ignorant?" he shouted in his beautiful Jamaican accent. "Do you think that we as pastors do not hear what goes on in your workplace? Do you think we believe that your elections would be fair? Do you think we don't know there's a multi-billion-dollar union-busting industry you've enlisted all over the country? Do you think that we do not understand our own community? How dare you speak to us as though we are . . . simple." The word *simple* popped out like a spark.

As Louis pounded his fist on the table and the other ministers laid out the principles of labor neutrality and the details of the city's business plan with the hotel, it became clear that this particular situation had not been covered back in business school. They still didn't see how the saving of souls connected to the saving of jobs, but to me it was increasingly clear.

Louis' anger hung in the air until the president turned to me, the woman minister, and the youngest person in the room. Locking his eyes with mine, he said, "Ma'am, you need to know something about me. And that is that I'm a Christian. In fact, we're all Christians, and you should know that we are all on the same side here. Let me tell you a little story."

The suits put down their pens and smiled at their leader as if he was about to retell a favorite bedtime tale that would bring comfort back into the penthouse conference room. "Our hotel chain was approached by . . . if you'll excuse me . . ." The president coughed gently in my direction, as if to prepare me for something necessarily shocking. "We were, at one point, approached by the purveyors of smut and pornography. And they offered to give us free television sets if we would allow them to broadcast their filth in our hotel. You know what I said to those folks, pastor?" he asked, looking solemnly at me as he shook his head. "I told them no. I said we would pay for our own television sets, at a cost of hundreds of thousands of dollars, just to keep out the purveyors of smut and pornography. What do you, as a pastor, *and as a lady,* think of that?"

I prepared to speak but he jumped in again: "So you see, you and me, we are on the same side. And I imagine most Christian pastors in this town don't even know that story," he said, "and if they did, would they be sitting around this table discussing a boycott?"

"Well, maybe this group of pastors is a little different from the ones you know," I began tentatively. "But we read the Bible pretty thoroughly, and as I read Jesus' words, he spends a lot more time on the gap between the rich and the poor than he does on the subject of smut and pornography."

"So as interesting as that story is," another minister chimed in, "we'd like to get our conversation back to the boycott, which is going to start in exactly one month from today."

"Or you could always give our city its nine million dollars back," reminded another.

With that we looked at one another around the table, and our mismatched little group stood up in one fluid movement. Together, we pushed our chairs into the sleek table and it was as if we were all suddenly one body. And in that moment, of course, we were.

Exactly one day short of one month later, the hotel chain agreed to accept the workers' union cards and the management agreed to the original terms of their agreement with the city. Our New Haven hotel became one of the only union shops in the chain, and Ophelia was the steward of her local once again, shaping her community as she had been called to do. For her, leadership in the church was leadership in the workplace, leadership in her tenant association, and no one would tell her where one world ended and the other began.

In the press conference called to announce the agreement, the hotel management praised Yale University and the mayor for brokering an agreement. The pastors' plans to boycott were never mentioned. When questioned by the press, the management stated that the fact that the settlement took place on the eve of the boycott was an insignificant coincidence.

Our little group from the penthouse meeting attended that press event. Spread out throughout the conference room were pastries and sandwiches, sculptures of fruit, and frosty, overflowing silver buckets of ice with every kind of soda.

As I looked across the room at the men from Yale, the city, and the management congratulating each other, they looked exactly as they had when the news of the new hotel had been announced almost a year ago. But while they looked the same, the rest of the scene looked different. Hotel workers were attending this celebration, not just working at it. And there were church members from all different congregations who had worked on the boycott. We had a new covenant. This looked less like a corporate banquet than a heavenly one, in which rich and poor would eat together.

I caught our organizer, Pete, in a corner, holding a little plate piled high with food. To my raised eyebrows Pete responded merrily from across the room. "Now, Lillian, *now,* we can eat their food."

Soon after that feast, I found myself at the communion table back at my church. As the words of institution reminded us that Jesus was at the table with the disciples, I found myself wondering who had been behind the scenes preparing the disciples' food that night of the last supper.

From the union leaders in their closets, to the deacons in theirs, from the chefs in the fine kitchens, to the hotel's businessmen eating airplane food on the way home, I knew that our eucharistic meal this Sunday morning trumped them all.

Without this meal, we would never have had the vision of how to shape our own community. We might still be asking some to eat the crumbs that fall from the table instead of grasping for that heavenly banquet, where everyone will be fed and no one will be left hungry.

The Gospel of Luke puts it more succinctly. *And their eyes were opened in the breaking of the bread.*

CHAPTER 10

What Shall I Call You?

Martin B. Copenhaver

All the pastors/ministers/preachers I know have distinct preferences for how they are addressed and how their vocation is described. There are titles we embrace and others that make us cringe. We may be able to interpret our preferences by using the most sophisticated theological analysis, but for the most part our reactions are shaped by associations we have with various titles, so that the preferences are largely impervious to the influence of reason.

For as long as I can remember, my father was known in his congregation and beyond as "Dr. Copenhaver." The association of that title with his name is so strong for me that, to this day, if someone mistakenly calls me "Dr. Copenhaver" (I do not have a doctorate), I almost have to fight the impulse to turn around and see if my long-deceased father has entered the room. Even if I were to obtain a doctorate myself, I am quite sure that if people were to begin to address me in that way I would feel forever like a young boy in the attic trying on his father's clothes.

I have never really settled on a title that works for me. *Reverend* — a title that is available to me by virtue of my ordination — can seem problematic for a number of reasons. For one, although *Reverend* is an adjective (meaning "revered"), some people are always trying to make it a noun. So if someone says, "Hello, Reverend," that person actually is saying, "Hello, Revered." It would be like saying to a judge, "Hello, Honorable." Likewise, because *reverend* is an adjective, it is improper grammatically to call someone "a reverend." To complicate matters further, because this adjective is also a title, it can be used properly only if it is accompanied by the article *the.*

Even if folks were able to negotiate the grammar, it sounds beyond egotistical to refer to oneself using that title, which is equivalent to saying, "Hello, I am Martin Copenhaver, the revered one." Then there are those who, by virtue of their office, are given additional honorifics that, when strung together, begin to resemble those medals given for Sunday school attendance that would drip down the chests of those who never missed a class, titles like, "The Very Right Reverend Doctor Julius W. ('Who Are You to Question My Authority?') Johnson, III."

Early in my ministry I got around this ambivalence about titles by asking that people simply call me Martin. After all, I reasoned, most of the folks in the congregation were considerably older than I was, so why should they address me in a way that sounds so deferential? This reasoning is an example of how our ambivalence about titles is a reflection of our mixed feelings about the sources and uses of authority.

Each title used for clergy refers to a different source of authority. Since the title *Doctor* is conferred in the academy, it points to academic status as the source of one's authority. *The Reverend* situates the source of one's authority in the esteem in which one is held. *Pastor* and *Minister* each refer in different ways to the authority that is vested in a particular office of the church. The title *Preacher* points to a particular, and in some ways defining, pastoral task. I just wanted to be called Martin.

Of course, being called by one's first name is not the perfect solution, either. If everyone is invited to call you by your first name, even when they first meet you, it can sound overly familiar, like the way people might introduce themselves at a sales convention: "Hello, I'm Martin." "Good to meet you, Martin."

Some of us may try to avoid titles like *the Reverend* because they seem to stress too much the ways in which the pastor is set apart from others. Nevertheless, when we seek refuge in our first names it can be an attempt to deny that which is finally undeniable: there are ways in which the pastoral role actually does set us apart. When I ask to be called Martin, it is a way of saying, "Hey, I'm just one of the guys." But there are ways in which, as a pastor, I am not just one of the guys. It is not that pastors are a different breed of person, of course, but the pastoral role is different from the roles others play. Titles can be a way to honor the role, rather than the person who plays that role. But people are not always clear about such distinctions and I am quite sure that I could lose sight of such distinctions myself. So, through the years, when people have asked me what I would like to be called, I have said, with a bit of aw-shucks awkwardness, "Just call me Martin." It is not the perfect solution, but at least I feel addressed when I hear my name. I know that the person is talking to me.

How one describes one's vocation is no small matter. Early in my ministry I described myself as "a minister." I was relatively comfortable with that designation, but then I began to see that description of my role as usurping a role that belongs to everyone. In the church I was serving at the time, my role officially was described as "the Minister." But what does such a title say about the role of the other members of the congregation? It seemed to imply that ordained clergy are the only ones with a ministry. But as everyone has a ministry in the world by virtue of their baptism, so we are all ministers. To be sure, some are called to a particular ministry within the church, but there is a different and differentiating name for such ministers: we are "pastors." To use this description of my role seemed like a way to honor the role of the laity by affirming the mutual ministry of all believers. Or so I became convinced. It all seemed reasonable, but because such matters are laden with association, they are never simple. (Case in point: As much as I was beginning to embrace the designation *Pastor,* I was determined not to be called Pastor Martin. To me, that made me sound like the host of a children's television program, perhaps because it reminded me of Beachcomber Bill, the host of a popular local television program when I was a boy.)

When the proposed change in the description of my role was brought to the annual meeting of the congregation, it sparked considerable discussion. Someone said that the term *Pastor* sounded "so Catholic." Someone else countered that in his days in the Catholic Church he had never heard a priest referred to as a pastor. Another person stood to say that he grew up as a Lutheran, so he was comfortable with the term. Still someone else muttered loudly, "I always thought it sounded Baptist." (Pick an association, any association.)

As the discussion continued, it was clear that at least one person was quite concerned that this change in the description of my role might be a power-grab on my part, as if I were angling for a kind of promotion at the expense of the laity. So I stood to speak for the first time in the meeting. I spoke about my understanding of the terms *pastor* and *minister,* and how using the term *pastor* in reference to me actually was a way to honor and support the role of the laity as ministers in the world. Then I said that I had rejected one of the titles that we were considering for my role, "The Most Holy Reverend Father." Gratefully, people laughed, and we moved on.

At other times, however, we can be reminded that titles are serious business.

For women in the ministry, the complications that come with titles can be even harder to negotiate. Female clergy are accustomed to hearing questions like, "Well, what exactly should I call you?" The manner in which the question is asked makes it clear that it is properly translated, "Surely you don't have the same title as a clergyman?" "Are you a reverend?" someone will ask as she exits the church after a funeral. "Can I say that?" Such questions seem to imply that a woman has to borrow a title that just does not fit properly.

Titles flow less freely for women in the ministry. With men, often the first response is formality, while with women, it can be assumed that the formal title does not apply. Most male Protestant senior ministers are not asked, "I know you're not a priest, but what *are* you exactly?" while this happens to women all the time. And in many churches, the power differential between male and female clergy can be played out in the relative formality of the titles used, as in, "Meet our senior minister, Dr. Smith, and his associate, Julie." When something like that happens, even those who claim not to care much about titles find out again that titles matter.

There are other cultural nuances in clergy titles. Our congregation has a very close partnership with the historic Charles Street African Methodist Episcopal (AME) congregation in Boston. Over a ten-year span I have worshiped there so often, and our congregations have taken part in so many shared ministries, that Charles Street Church feels like a second church home to me, and to many in our congregation. Early in our partnership I stumbled into the realization that different traditions have quite different approaches to titles. Since the members of my mostly Caucasian congregation were quite used to calling me Martin, they assumed that they could address Gregory Groover, the distinguished pastor of Charles Street Church, as Greg. At the time I was too ignorant to correct them, and Rev. Groover — as he is known within his African American congregation — was too gracious to do so. When I began to pick up on the different ways the two congregations used titles, I asked him about what is customary in his tradition. He explained that in the church he is addressed as Rev. Groover, except when he is among very close colleagues and friends. In such settings he is called Greg. He urged me to continue to call him Greg, and I do in private conversation, which now feels like a privilege.

Years later, before worship one Sunday when I was the scheduled preacher at Charles Street Church, as I walked through the fellowship hall with Rev. Groover to his office, I was warmly greeted by the members of the church, a number of whom said things like, "Welcome, Pastor" and, "So good to see you again, Pastor." When we got to Rev. Groover's office, he turned to me and said, "I don't think you know what just happened there." I had to confess that I was not sure what he was referring to. He went on to explain, "In the AME tradition, you can have many ordained ministers in the church — we have about twenty — and they are all referred to as Reverend. But in an AME church there is only one Pastor. And yet those members of Charles Street just called you Pastor. I just don't want you to miss what that means, because you might not know if I didn't tell you."

Of course, he was right. I did not know what it meant until Rev. Groover explained it to me. After all, titles mean such different things to different people in different settings. After he explained it, however, I realized that here, finally, is a title that means a great deal to me.

CHAPTER 11

"I Was Looking for the Pastor, But You'll Do"

LILLIAN DANIEL

I have had too many friends leave the ministry before they've even started. The large majority of these friends have left because they've had bad experiences as associate ministers, which is the role to which many clergy are first called.

On the other hand, though, some of the happiest ministers I know are long-term associates, individuals who know that they are in the right role for their gifts and who love specializing. These associate pastors also have — and this is key — rich relationships with their senior pastors.

In churches today, there are more models of associate ministry than ever before. In the old model, associates were generalists, apprentices in their first job, learning a new line of work. Some associates still function in this capacity. But others are specialists, bringing a certain expertise to their church that is valued and appreciated. Some are associates at a particular church for a short time, as it's understood that they are being groomed to go out and get their own senior pastorate. Others stay for many years, developing deep relationships in their congregations. When they leave, it may be to a senior pastorate, or it may be to another associate position, having determined that this is God's call for their life's work. These many models make for many options, but still the role of the associate is a delicate one.

Having served first as an associate minister, and now having served at two congregations as a senior minister, I look back on my first job as my most stressful. It was a time of happiness and excitement, but also of real tension. People are surprised when I say this. They assume that being the senior minister of a multi-staff congregation would be more stressful, but for me that has not been the case. Even in the best of collegial situations, the role of associate minister is a tricky one, and unless the church gives it serious attention, we remain in danger of losing some of our best leaders after their first job.

Some associate ministers in that first year buckle under the mundanity that is pastoring. Fresh from the rigors of study — the classics of theology, the newest biblical criticism, and the assurance from their professors that they are brilliant — they suddenly find themselves week after week in the basement, with the youth group, playing sardines. And they can't help but wonder, "For *this* I spent three years in grad school?"

But other situations break down in the delicate relationship between the senior minister and the associate. "The senior minister won't let me do anything," one friend told me. "She does almost every wedding, funeral, and baptism. And when I do get to do some little thing in worship, I feel like I'm still an intern, not a colleague. It's as if she is still in charge of everything, allowing me to borrow her role for just a minute."

I know of one senior pastor who, at the conclusion of the associate minister's sermon, would approach the mic and say, in a warm and encouraging tone, "Thanks, Rob," thus getting the last word, at the end of someone else's sermon, and once again establishing who was in charge. The senior probably had no conscious awareness of what he was doing. But his chummy "Thanks, Rob" was a way of restoring the balance of power right back to where the senior minister wanted it.

Other associates point to the frustration of simply being new to the role of clergy. Because they are learning on the job, they are not seen as having as much real pastoral authority as their senior colleague. Similarly, few associates stay as long at a church as the senior; consequently they are seen as merely passing through, no matter how many years they stay.

Most new associate ministers have a story like this: a parishioner walks in looking for the senior minister. Finding him gone, the church member stops by the associate's office and says, "I was looking for the pastor, but you'll do."

Associates are sometimes treated like the unsatisfactory stand-in for the "real pastor," whom the parishioner would rather see at the hospital, the meeting, or the social event. "But you'll do" becomes a phrase that delineates the line between the two roles in the worst way.

Yet in a healthy church, the associate role can flourish in its very uniqueness. All the things that make it different from the senior role can be embraced as offering a special opportunity for ministry. A smart senior and associate understand these differences and work with them.

When I arrived at my first clergy position, as an associate minister at a large suburban church in Cheshire, Connecticut, I was to be working with a senior who had been in the ministry for thirty-four years. Mine was the classic associate role that fit the stereotypes of a novice, a generalist, and an apprentice. At the age of twenty-six, straight out of divinity school, I was not surprised when church members commented that I looked like a member of the youth group rather than the clergy. I was also the first woman pastor they had installed, and I was replacing a male associate minister who was in his sixties.

While questions of pastoral authority were at the top of my mind, the parishioners were adjusting their expectations and commenting while they did it, thinking out loud, much to my dismay. "You look cute in your robe," one told me. I thought about those pictures of small animals dressed in human clothing, little kittens in elf suits, puppies with reindeer horns, and all sorts of other images that would be adorable on a junior high school poster but not taken very seriously in the pulpit. I was already counting the days until I could be the senior minister myself, and finally get some respect.

But a parishioner, in that very first week, made an appointment to talk to me. She entered the office, sat down, and poured out a melancholy tale like nothing I had ever experienced. Her husband's life-threatening illness had sent her back to work when all she wanted was to be at home with her kids. She wondered about her spiritual strength in the midst of fears for his health. She questioned her ability to succeed as a mother and an employee when she had medical issues of her own. At the end of her outpouring, this middle-aged mother of three turned to me and said, "Reverend, I just thought that you might give me some coping skills."

And the only thing that came into my head was this: "Your life stinks."

I did not say that, of course, but I thought it. It was the thought that swept through my mind, and still does, when people tell me about the pain that life metes out. Some people have desperately difficult lives. I had no advice that would cure her husband, no scripture passage that would provide health insurance for the kids, no magic wand that would return life to the way it used to be when they were all happy.

But I also thought to myself that the next time I needed coping skills, I was coming to this woman for advice. Her bravery and faith in the midst of it all were more than I could imagine. I had nothing to say at all, and yet simply by virtue of my role, she had come to tell her story, and asked me to respond. And I knew that "Your life stinks" or "You tell me" would simply not be enough. She was expecting more.

I wondered why she had come to me, the new associate minister, and not to the senior. There were many reasons I could come up with. Perhaps she wanted to speak to a woman. Perhaps the senior minister had heard her story before and she needed to retell it to someone with fresh ears. Perhaps I was the only one who had time on my calendar that day; she was looking for him, but I would do. Whatever the reason, God was using me, as surely as God was using her, and together we spoke and prayed for a day when things would be different.

Pastoral authority, I was learning, was a mixed bag. While I bristled at being told I was a "tiny little thing up in that big pulpit," I might have welcomed a little of that in this pastoral moment when I was given credit for possessing much more wisdom than I had.

Or was I? I have come to learn that when parishioners ask for answers, for coping skills, for theories as to "why God would do this to me," they are seldom actually expecting brilliance from us. Rather, they are seeking a place to tell their story and to hear that they are not crazy, not alone, and not unheard. I could give that to her.

Most of all, they want to hear a word from the Lord, and we are not the Lord. They hope that with our study and our training we will be able to refer them to a jewel in the tradition, some wisdom from the generations of God's children whose stories rest in scripture and the practices of the church. They ask far more from us than the paltry wisdom of our own individual experience. And because we clergy are shaped in God's community over time and place, we can deliver a word, on our first day at work or our last, and we can always deliver a gracious ear. That day, the woman and I spoke about faith and her church. We recalled some scripture and we prayed together. It was not all I wanted to be able to do, but it was enough.

I was finding my way. I was walking the delicate line between humility, in which I acknowledged how much of my learning would come from my parishioners and my colleague, and confidence, as I realized that God's grace through the church was also working through me, and my seminary training in rich theological texts and Bible verses was never wasted.

Yet in those early years as an associate, I had several friends from divinity school who were absolutely exhausted in their positions. They were not swimming in streams of God's grace, but rather struggling to stay afloat. There was little joy in the work, and most of them ended up leaving the ministry from that first job. While they now have interesting lives in the fields of teaching, publishing, counseling, and business, I still regret the church's loss and wonder what could have been different in that first associate job. I take these musings into my role as a head of staff and have tried to learn from their stories.

To a one, these unhappy associates served under seniors who worked constantly. They were expected to do the same. Sometimes, it was a clash of generational habits, compounded by the workaholic leader. The senior minister, usually a parent of older children or an empty nester, was oriented differently from the associate, who might want a few evenings free to spend time with a spouse or a child, or to go out and actually make friends in a new community, even meet someone to date. In these cases, for the senior the church was everything, willingly, and for the associate it had to be too, begrudgingly. Some young clergy tolerate this for a short time and then start looking for another, less life-consuming field.

Some of the tales had a profoundly sad quality to them. "The senior works late every single night because his family is so resentful of him that he really has nowhere to go. So they resent him for working all the time, and he avoids their resentment by working more." Young associates looked at this model, feared for their own family lives, and some got out.

A wise senior understands that the roles are different, and seeks to understand the demands of different life stages as well. And when we do not do this, we lose some of our brightest young clergy to other fields. They tell each other the stories and warn one another away from the pastoral life. Sadly, what they were warning one another away from was one bad associate position, but by then they had mistaken the part for the whole.

Before I took the call at that first church, there were many friends who warned me not to take the associate job. They had heard the stories of those who had gone before and made assumptions. "The senior minister is old. He's bound to be sexist. You won't get to do anything. Better to go somewhere where the senior has worked with a woman associate before, and the congregation will respect your authority." Their advice was sound, if generalizations are truth, but my call to that church took me into a senior-associate relationship that today, in many ways, I hold up as a model.

For one thing, a senior minister who has been at it for thirty-four years has very little to prove. I preached once a month. Despite the fact that people told me I was a fine preacher, attendance dipped slightly on my Sundays. I knew from my friends that other seniors used this as an excuse to have the associate preach less, but he took pride in leading a teaching church, where interns and associates were launched to great things. One of my predecessors in that associate role went on to become the president of the denomination, and that wasn't from being left in the basement to play sardines all the time. He had been mentored.

When it came to my job description, the senior had worked with enough people throughout the years that he knew how to let people rise with their callings. In those first years, I had a passion for two things I had learned nothing about in seminary: fund raising and church growth. I was thrilled when he "allowed" me to work with those committees. Years later I would discover that these are the banes of most ministers' existence, and certainly not areas he wanted to lead, but I felt in those early years that I had been given a gift. And I had.

Many of us from divinity school had landed in these apprenticing associate roles, generally at thriving churches in the suburbs, because those are the congregations who can afford associates. But some of them were not soaring. One explained, "The associate's job description is everything the senior doesn't want to do. Period. I feel like I have no control of my time, let alone a life. I am at his beck and call to do everything he hates to do, and no longer does, but remembers enough about to criticize me for doing it wrong."

It was a contrast to what I was experiencing. Certainly there were things I did not want to do, meetings I did not want to attend, and chores I wished would go away. But in our senior-associate relationship, we both were honest with one another about those things. It was not uncommon to hear either of us say, "I'll do this one, if next time you'll take it." There were times when he told me to spend time with my family, and there were times when I told him, "I'll cover it." And now, years later, I am also aware of how many times he protected me from work and lessons I was not yet ready to absorb.

Most associates will hear criticisms of the senior. I heard plenty, and so did my friends serving other churches. We would call one another up and share stories of our colleagues' incompetence, amazed that these large churches had survived their leadership. Some of the stories were appalling, for there is indeed much that does not bear up well under the inspection of a newly minted colleague. But there was also much we did not understand when we criticized our colleagues.

I had no idea when it happened to me, but I have since learned that associates always get swarmed by the people who have a grievance against the senior. It begins gently, and it feels good. "You are such a breath of fresh air," they would tell me, and leave me to fill in the blanks. Having seen me lap up some little bit of praise, they would offer more, perhaps with a little twist at the end. "You are such a breath of fresh air . . . and we need that around here." And then, I would start to hear the stories, the ways in which I was "not like him" and how much the church needed my particular gifts.

In any situation like this, some of these comments are old grudges that go way back and will endure long after the associate has left. You hear about them with shock and disappointment, sad to realize such animosity could brew, and glad to be the one to offer a listening ear, unaware that every associate before you has had the same conversation and the same thought.

But more troubling is when the grievances are legitimate. Not knowing that the system had tolerated such rumblings for years before my entrance, as an associate I wondered what to "do" with such information. Should I refuse to engage in such gossip, or listen to it as a pastor? Should I tell the senior what they were saying about him? Should I step in and try to right all his wrongs by being perfect myself? It was tempting to try to create myself in the image of these parishioners' ideal pastor and hope that I would never be complained about.

Finally, I tentatively brought it up with the senior minister, and he responded brusquely. "Every time your parishioners tell you that you are wonderful, and that one of your colleagues is not, or, for that matter, that your predecessor is not . . . take out a little index card and write this on it in great big letters: 'Me next.' Then take it and put it back in your pocket, so you can pull it out the next time someone tells you what a breath of fresh air you are compared to the other guy."

I remember being surprised that he knew that people complained about him and knew what they were saying to me. I was more shocked that he seemed to have a pretty accurate idea of what people saw as his shortcomings. Such criticism had not erased his flaws or allowed him to become the pastor they wanted him to be. But somehow, he, and also they, had learned to live with the ways in which he did not measure up. And I as an associate learned that my role in all that was significantly smaller than any of us understood.

Today, as a senior minister, I recall these moments prayerfully. I consider that the person I am working with as an associate is watching me closely, and at the same time deciding each day whether or not to continue in this odd and wondrous calling. It is not all up to me, of course. But if lay leaders in churches and clergy at all levels do not think hard about the lives of associate ministers, we risk losing some of our best clergy too early in the game.

Churches do well to examine a wide variety of associate ministry models. Some of the most gifted pastors I know are associates who have developed a specialty. These associates are not generalists being groomed to go out and serve their own church. They dig in deeply to an area like Christian education, or pastoral care, or adult spiritual formation, and stay for many years at churches that respect their unique gifts.

In some cases, an associate who starts out as a generalist will discover that she has a call to a specialty. Research has shown that churches benefit enormously from long-term pastorates, but many people assume that this applies only to the senior role. Yet in many churches, associates stay a long time. They are encouraged to try out different roles within the role over time. They are cornerstones of the church in that they play a role that no one on staff can play as well. Associates who find positions like this want to stay in them.

In an interesting recent development, some associate ministers are now staying longer than the senior ministers. One associate pastor I know has served with four different senior ministers; some of those were intentional interims while the others mistakenly thought they would be there for a while. He played no role in their comings or goings, but has been used by God to be an anchor in the church, and his parishioners know it.

Bi-vocational clergy will also become more and more common, studies show. Some of this has to do with what churches can do, but some of it has to do with how clergy want to work. Churches that cannot afford a full-time associate may call one to work part-time. Some congregations may create two part-time specialist positions instead of one full-time generalist spot. For multi-talented clergy whom God has called in more than one direction, an associate role allows them to pursue their call to Word and Sacrament while working for social justice at a secular agency, say, or teaching at a seminary. Some churches have been remarkably creative in using a part-time associate role to tap the talents of a pastor who might otherwise choose secular work. It was my pleasure to work for six years with a part-time associate whose other jobs included social work, community organizing, and teaching. He brought those passions and skills to his ministry at the church, and his bi-vocational call became our blessing.

Yet when I think of my time as an associate and as a senior, the job descriptions, the hours, and the contractual arrangements all take a back seat to the relationship. The relationship among clergy at the same church is profoundly intimate. When it works, there can develop something close to telepathy, as one finishes the other's sentences, or says, "I knew you were going to say that."

In the world of ministry, where the work never gets done, it is enormously comforting to have a colleague who shares that burden of eternal incompletion. No matter the complexity of the relationship, clergy who work with other clergy have been given a gift that solo clergy might long for. You do not have to be lonely in the work, but can talk to another who knows and loves the same people you do but in ways that are different enough to offer a much-needed shift in perspective. There are few major decisions that I do not run by my trusted colleague at the church I serve today, and when I don't, I often wish I had. But trust is absolutely essential to this relationship.

When the associate-senior relationship works, it is a beautiful way to do ministry. And when that relationship is broken, it can be as painful a rupture as the unraveling of a family relationship. The intimacy and intensity of this work make the stakes so high. Both clergy and the church at large would do well to pay attention to these roles, and strive to set both senior and associate ministers up for excellence in their callings.

By the same token, associates must take responsibility for their own longevity as well. When seminary graduates ask me for advice about their first call, and they are looking at associate positions, I tell them to first and foremost choose their colleague. Never mind where your fiancé is in graduate school. Never mind how much you loved the people on the search committee. Is the senior minister someone you will learn from and who will treat you as a respected colleague? These are the things you can tell in a one on one meeting, but over and over again, I see new clergy gloss over this point. They privilege the location, the church program, the job description, or the salary over the one thing that will make or break their experience.

Can associate ministers survive a rough experience with an insensitive colleague? As surely as good things can come out of Nazareth. And some of them use that time as instructive, allowing it to shape them into being the kinds of senior colleagues they wished they had had.

But how much richer the world of ministry would be if we paid more attention to this area, even trained clergy in how to work together in these intimate and complex pairings. Churches who nurture new associates and watch them blossom know the joy that such a ministry brings. Seniors who work with gifted colleagues know how important it is to keep them happy, challenged, and growing. As we seek to develop leaders who will last for the marathon and not drop out in the early sprint, we need to shift our cultures, so that instead of hearing, "I was looking for the pastor, but you'll do," the associate minister hears, "You're just the person I was hoping to see."

CHAPTER 12

What Kind of Strange Place Is This?

MARTIN B. COPENHAVER

In my first ministry, in the late seventies and early eighties, I served a church in Westport, Connecticut, a tony suburb of New York. At that time there were no homeless shelters in the area, so our congregation ran a kind of makeshift shelter in one of the church school rooms. It began when a homeless man came to the church on a cold winter's night and the senior minister couldn't bring himself to turn him away, and it just kind of grew from there. On any given night we would have between one and six men spending the night. One of the ministers would check in on them at the end of the evening, reminding newcomers that everyone was expected to leave the church first thing in the morning. If they didn't have a job they were expected to spend the day looking for work. The ministers on staff met regularly with these guests to coach, to encourage, and, if necessary, to prod them into doing all they could to find work and a more permanent home.

Looking back it is clear that I was spectacularly unqualified for this part of my ministry. I was in my mid-twenties. Most of the men I was working with were considerably older in years and many times older in life experience. I knew little about life on the street. The only times I had ever been hungry were when I had been late for dinner. I had led a well-paced life of privilege. For the most part, I had followed the rules and I knew how to negotiate my way through the relatively manageable challenges I had faced. But I did my best and I learned a lot along the way, often from the very people I was charged with helping.

On one occasion I was having a meeting in my office with one of our guests. Terry was a bright, well-educated man, a few years older than I. During my time as minister there Terry stayed at the church on more than one occasion. In between visits he would often stop by just to say hello. Life was a challenge for Terry, but he was very personable and easy to have around. Perhaps too easy. We were concerned that Terry had settled into the church and was not aggressive enough about finding work and a place to live. On this occasion it was my turn to give the Stern Lecture. I brought out all the phrases I had learned along the way: "This cannot be a permanent solution for you . . . it no longer seems to be working for you . . . looking for a job is a full time job . . . it is important that you take some responsibility . . . etc., etc., blah, blah, blah."

Then the phone rang. I picked it up and told the receptionist that I couldn't take a call because I was in conference. She said, "I understand. But I think you will want to take this call. It's from the police. It sounds urgent."

Thinking that the call was about one of our guests, I said to Terry, "Excuse me. I think I will need to take this call."

The police officer began by asking, "Are you Martin Copenhaver?"

"Yes."

"Do you drive a maroon Volvo?"

"Yes."

"Did you get gas at the Mobil station earlier today?"

"Yes."

"Well, you didn't pay."

As soon as he said it, I knew that he was right. I could picture the whole scene. I had gotten some self-serve gas and, in my hurry and absent-mindedness, I had simply filled up and then drove away. I said, "I'm so sorry. It was entirely unintentional, of course. I will go to the station and pay them."

To which the police officer said, "Well, we've had a rash of these crimes recently, so I'm afraid that I am going to have to arrest you."

"*Arrest* me? Wow . . ."

Then, for some reason, probably to check his assumption that I was one of the men who spent the night at the church, the police officer asked, "What is your connection with the church?"

I said, "I'm one of the ministers."

A long silence. Then he said, "My wife will kill me if I arrest a minister. Hold on." He covered the phone, clearly consulting a colleague or a superior about what to do. When he came back he said, "All right. Go to the Mobil station immediately and I will meet you there. And when you show up you better look like a minister." Under other circumstances I might have asked what he meant by that. But as it was, I simply said, "Of course. Right away."

Then I hung up the phone and turned to Terry. He had obviously listened to the entire conversation with interest, maybe particularly because it interrupted my lecture about responsibility. I said, "I'm sorry but we will have to continue this later. You see, I got gas this morning and it seems that I didn't pay."

Terry shook his head and, in an expression of newfound solidarity, said, "Yeah, I've done that a few times myself. I hate it when that happens." Then with a wry smile he added, "Well, nobody's perfect, I guess."

In Jesus' parable, when the shepherd finds the sheep that is lost, he puts the sheep on his shoulders and carries it home. He does not carry the sheep into the field next to the house. Rather, he carries the sheep right into the living room. Now that's a crazy thing to do with a sheep. But that is something like what we were trying to do when we welcomed homeless men to stay in our church school room.

I don't want to gloss over the difficulties. If you have six homeless men spending the night in a small church school room, you really have something. After all, if these folks were easy to live with, chances are that some friend or relative would have taken them in already. Many of the church members questioned the wisdom of what we were doing. Some worried that we were putting the church and its members at risk. Others doubted we were ultimately helping those we aimed to serve. In my preaching at that time I would make the case that our ministry to the homeless was part of our franchise agreement with Jesus that our church should reflect Jesus' own concern for those who are the least, the last, and the lost. But many were not convinced. And sometimes I was not convinced myself, particularly when listening to parents with concerns for the safety of their children or when I was aware of some serious difficulty with one of the guests that I hoped church members would not learn about.

There is no getting around it: taking in lost sheep can be a messy business. Sometimes this can be literally true. I remember the time I had to tell the men not to take their boots off until after the last church meeting was over because some of the good church folk meeting in a room down the hall were feeling a bit queasy. The Episcopal Church down the street always had the lingering aroma of sweet incense, but we had . . . smelly boots.

Welcoming the stranger can be messy in other ways, too. One of the men who stayed at the church for a time was a fellow named Bernie. Bernie was very bright and well-educated. And when Bernie played a Beethoven sonata on the piano in the sanctuary you might think you were in a concert hall. But he also had Tourette's Syndrome, a rare disease that causes those who suffer from it to burst forth with involuntary exclamations, sometimes obscenities or something similarly inappropriate. In Bernie's case, he would bark like a dog and very loudly. The sound he made was distinctively a bark, but Bernie had a way of letting the bark transition into a terrible coughing spell, which he probably learned to do to cover up the barking sound. So the first time you heard him, you might think, "Did he just bark?" But then Bernie would bark again, as he did frequently, and the sound was unmistakable.

Due to his unusual disability, Bernie could not hold a job. His family couldn't handle it and turned him out. Yet in spite of his affliction, Bernie was not one of the most difficult of the homeless men to have around the church. But then one day Bernie decided to join the choir.

I must confess that the first time I saw Bernie put on a choir robe and process down the aisle, my first thought was not, "Thank you, Jesus." No, it was more like, "Jesus, you've challenged us enough by sending someone like Bernie to us, but then you give us teachings like the Parable of the Lost Sheep that limit our options on how to deal with him." So Bernie sang in the choir — and he had a beautiful voice when he wasn't barking. (Perhaps that experience explains why I am not as disturbed as some people are by crying babies during worship. Once you've had someone bark periodically during your sermon, everything else seems to pale by comparison.)

As you can imagine, there was a lot of discussion about what we should do about Bernie, but in the end we decided to do nothing. He stayed with us and sang and barked for a couple of months.

But here is my favorite memory from that whole experience: After a few weeks members of the church became so accustomed to Bernie's periodic outbursts that they weren't as much of a disruption. So when visitors came to worship and they heard this strange sound from the choir loft behind the pulpit they would first try to see where it was coming from. Then they would look at the church members seated around them and notice that they didn't seem to be in the least disturbed.

When visitors noticed the lack of response from the church members they would get uneasy — almost panicky — looks on their faces that said, "What kind of strange place is this I've wandered into?" I have since concluded that this question is one of the highest compliments a church can receive.

CHAPTER 13

Casting Out Demons

LILLIAN DANIEL

I had always imagined that the first time I tried on the ministerial role I would be in a pulpit, but instead I was in a mental hospital.

On my first day of my first seminary internship, I walked into the Mental Health Center with a tentative step. After passing through locked doors, I found myself in the ward looking for my supervisor, the chaplain. "You're going to be working here as a chaplain?" a nurse asked, as if she could not believe it. "You seem too young." I was twenty-three.

She told me to wait with the patients. At this inpatient facility in a New England town, university professors sat next to the homeless in the common area, bound only by their shared struggles with mental illness. Other staff stared right through me, as if I were simply another graduate student recently admitted to the ward as a patient.

I was enormously relieved when the chaplain opened her office door and let me in. "I don't think anyone is going to take me seriously here as a chaplain," I told her. "A couple of the staff already said as much when I was waiting out there. I wish I were already ordained."

"What difference would that make?" she asked.

"Well, they all respect you when you're ordained," I explained. She gave me a hard look, but after twenty minutes on the job, I had some other important questions to ask her.

"What am I supposed to be doing in this internship anyway?" I asked. "Frankly, I don't see what I can do to help these people before their medications kick in."

"Just wander the floor," she told me. "Talk to the patients. Embody the loving presence of Christ. Make conversation."

I was horrified. Making conversation at church coffee hours is hard enough. The idea of making conversation in a mental hospital set my heart beating fast.

"Can't I lead a spirituality program or a worship service?" I asked.

"You'll get to do that eventually," she said. "But why don't you start by leaving this office and going out to talk to that gentleman?"

I looked out from the womb of her office window to see a lone man rocking back and forth on the couch, muttering and shaking his head, as if to disagree with his own last comment. The idea of making conversation with someone who was already making conversation with himself did not appeal to me, but I ventured out.

It turned out that he was more than willing to talk. I felt as if I were drowning in his agitated words about angels, an angry God, and the Central Intelligence Agency. I found myself correcting him but later I would learn that my role was not to point out the difference between fact and fiction. Instead I would learn to listen to conspiracy theories that made me laugh, to paranoid worries that made me sad, and to ideas about God that made me cringe.

At this facility, the staff met as a team to review cases. I learned as much about medical culture as I did about mental illness. While we called ourselves a "team," this hospital hierarchy made church hierarchy look like the work of amateurs. It was easy to see that there were tensions among the different healers, from the aides to the social workers to the nurses to the psychiatrist who shared with many of the patients the habit of wearing her dark sunglasses while indoors.

I suspected that the chaplains were at the bottom of this hierarchy, since some of the medical staff seemed to lump the delusional patients together with anyone who professed faith. After all, we both talked about and trusted in things that were unseen. I would complain to my supervisor that none of the staff listened to me. Her response was always the same. She sent me out to listen to the patients.

But at that stage in my life, I was consumed with my own calling, whatever it might turn out to be. If I got ordained in a year or two, what would my life be like? This was the early nineties, a time when very few young people were getting ordained. Second-career ministers were the norm, and they were praised.

"He gave up everything to be a minister," people would say of these people. "He was a partner in a law firm, and he gave that up to follow his calling."

"Look at the gifts these people bring to the ministry," we would hear. "The life experience and wisdom . . ." But for those of us entering the ministry in our twenties, there were no accolades, and much more confusion. Not used to seeing young ministers, people reacted to us as oddities. We young seminarians who were also female were even odder. "You're going to be a minister?" I heard it over and over again.

And it wasn't just coming from the voices around me. Some of those voices were coming from within me. Because I did not remind myself of any minister I knew, there were times when I doubted the call as well. The comments of others fed into my own insecurity, and the best response I could come up with was that the church and the world were sexist. Regardless of whether that was true — and for the record, I believe it is — it wasn't much of a call-sustaining answer. Fighting and raging against an anonymous "they" was exhausting. I wondered why my African American female supervisor, a trailblazer in her own right, wasn't more eager to reflect on this with me, and instead kept sending me out to listen to the patients.

Would anybody ever take me seriously as a minister? I didn't want to listen, particularly to crazy people. I wanted someone to listen to me. So determinedly I would knock on my supervisor's door each week with the same list of questions about pastoral authority. Apparently I didn't have any and I wanted to know where I could get it.

My complaints began the same way. "Nobody takes me seriously as a chaplain around here. The staff ignore my suggestions. The patients yell at me, and insult me, make lewd and sexist remarks . . ."

"Well, they are struggling with serious mental illness, Lillian . . ."

"No, it's not that. I don't think they'd treat me like a minister if they were sane either. It's sexism, the patriarchy, my gender, my age, my hair color." (Blonde, of course) "I wish I had a minister's collar like yours."

There was a long silence. She did not jump in as she usually did. Instead she said, "Okay, Lillian, then why don't you go out and get yourself a clerical collar?"

I was horrified. "I can't wear a collar. I'm not yet ordained. That would be fraud." I couldn't believe I had to explain this to a professional.

"Get a clerical collar, a black suit, and a black clerical shirt," she said. "I give you permission, special dispensation, call it whatever you want. Go out there and get yourself a collar and wear it all around the ward."

"I'm not wearing a collar before I am ordained," I said. And as the awkward silence hung, I felt a question arise in my mind that I was afraid to ask.

"Ok," I said. "Tell me. Why is it that you are telling me to go out and get a collar?"

"I want you to see what difference it will make," she said.

"I already know what difference it will make," I said. "They'll all take me seriously." She shook her head solemnly. "No?" I asked. "Well, what difference do you think it would make?"

"Here's what I think would happen," she said. "All those people you want to respect you . . . they'd look at you and say 'Who's that little girl and why is she running around the psych ward wearing a clerical collar?'"

I was devastated. "Well, what should I do?" I asked.

"Get out there and spend time with the patients." And like many stubborn servants before me, I was sent back out to a land I was afraid of.

In those weeks that followed, I wondered whether I really wanted these people to see me as a minister, with their rants about religion and their visions of angels. For when I did talk to the patients, when I told them I was preparing for the ministry, they may not have seen me as a pastor, but I still got an earful.

How cruel it seemed to me that people in the grip of delusion often turned to God, only to dredge up some punishing vision. How interesting it was that the deluded seemed to relate to the devil so much more strongly than those we call sane. In my mainline Protestant upbringing, I don't think I'd ever once heard a sermon preached about Jesus casting out demons, but that was the story they wanted to talk about on the floor.

As the patients grew more used to me in the role of student chaplain, they began to confide in me the things they could not tell the rest of the staff. "Whatever you do, avoid the water fountains on this floor. The water is poisoned," that rocking man told me. "I'm only telling you this because you're a woman of God." If this was pastoral authority, it wasn't what I had in mind.

After months of wandering the halls, making small talk amidst the bizarre talk, I finally got to lead my first worship service. This was not only my first time leading worship at the hospital, but my first time leading worship ever.

A small group gathered in a dark conference room. They were the usual lively mix you find in a mental health facility, professionals and parents, street people and suicide attempters, the addicts and the alienated. They were the people Jesus cared about.

One large woman had come into the room early and set up on the conference table an elaborate paper construction made of postcards and clippings, every photograph featuring Princess Grace of Monaco.

I took a deep breath and began to read my carefully prepared 25-minute sermon on Galatians. A man began to cough and then shake. Another woman shifted in boredom. A cocaine addict interrupted me.

"Are we allowed to ask questions?" he said in the middle of my remarks. I nodded, keeping my finger on my page so as not to lose my place in the sermon. "Exactly how long is this part, where you talk on and on, going to last?" he asked.

Now the large woman felt free to interject. "I'd like for us to pray to Princess Grace," she said.

"Well, certainly, we can pray for the world's leaders and we will pray for Princess Grace as well," I said, gently correcting her with a preposition.

"I don't want to pray *for* Princess Grace," she said, gesturing to her makeshift altar. "I said I wanted to pray *to* Princess Grace."

"Well, we're not going to," I explained. "We pray *for* Princess Grace. We pray *to* God."

"So give me one good reason for that," she said.

By now I had lost my place in my notes on Galatians for good. Theological narcissism took hold of me yet again, and I wondered what God was telling me about my future in parish ministry in this, my first sermon ever. The room was erupting into chaos as I began my sermon over again, this time with more volume, to drown out the theological hecklers.

And finally it hit me. This would be no different if I had a collar, if I had the title of "Reverend" or if Jesus Christ himself was sitting next to me with a big sign announcing me as God's gift to the world. These people were ill, they were suffering, and I should have been thinking about that all these months, not my own pastoral authority.

I put the sermon aside, to a few sighs of relief from the congregation. "Does anyone want to sing a hymn?" I asked, and they smiled. Finally, I was offering something they needed. We spent the rest of the session singing, interrupted by their spontaneous testimonies about devils, UFOs, the Book of Revelation, and other topics I had neglected to touch upon in my own remarks. But mostly we just sang.

Afterwards, they didn't want to leave. We had our own version of after church fellowship as we admired the photos of Princess Grace and helped the woman dismantle her portable shrine.

"Church was good today, Pastor," one man said on his way out.

"I'm not really a pastor," I explained to his back, and his shrugging shoulders. He was out the door, but in the interests of full disclosure, I had to keep talking to the others. "I still have to finish school, you know, do this internship here with you guys, pass through the denominational ordination process . . ."

"Whatever," the Princess Grace-worshiper said, patting me on the back. "We'll see you next week. Will you be a pastor by then?"

I have since decided her question was a rhetorical one. She saw through me. As surely as she wrestled with her demons, that year I was wrestling with mine. Was I called? Was there a place for me in the church? Would anyone ever respect me? My questions were not significantly different from the patients'. We are all in need of healing.

I did eventually become a pastor. It wasn't a one-and-only moment. It wasn't that week, or the next week, or even at the moment of my ordination, two years later. It was happening slowly, in all the weeks over all the years.

After ordination, I never took to wearing a collar. My supervisor's words rang in my ears. Not the ones about the collar, although today I smile at her wisdom.

What has stayed with me more is her advice in my times of vocational doubt. Every time she just sent me back out to listen to the people. They were the only ones who could turn me into a pastor.

CHAPTER 14

Expertise and Wisdom

MARTIN B. COPENHAVER

My wife, Karen, is an attorney with expertise in a narrow subspecialty of intellectual property law. For the most part her working life is kept at a distance from our family life, but occasionally she talks to clients from home. On one such occasion she was walking some clients through the draft of a long and complicated contract. I could not follow what she was saying. The language was technical and the concepts foreign to me.

What I was able to pick up, however, was the quietly authoritative tone in her voice. She spoke in the taut sentences of someone who knows what she is talking about and doesn't need to demonstrate that to anyone else. It is simply understood. As she read through the contract with her clients she would briefly explain why she made a particular provision, and then she would move on. Sometimes you could tell that her clients had asked a question for clarification, so she would offer an explanation in more depth. They were not questioning her expertise; they just wanted to understand.

At the conclusion of the conversation I could tell that the clients on the other end of the line were expressing their appreciation for Karen's work, praise that must have been rather effusive because her voice, which is usually low and husky, became lighter, supported by a full-throated laugh. It was a tour de force from a professional at the top of her game.

When Karen got off the phone, I said to her, "I want an expertise!" I realize that may sound rather peevish, but that is the way I felt. I went on, "It's incredible. You don't have to convince them that they should pay attention to what you have to say. They just listen and write it down. You don't have to defend yourself or your positions. You just have to tell them what you know. And no one says anything like, 'Well, let me tell you what *I* think about that.'"

Pastors don't have an area of expertise, at least nothing like Karen's. Pastors are generalists. In fact, we are among the last generalists in a culture that draws people into ever-narrower areas of specialization. And there is something wonderful about being a generalist. Certainly there is more variety in the tasks one performs, which is great for those of us with short attention spans. But more than this, a pastor's work does not consist of distinct tasks that simply are performed at different times. Rather, the various pastoral duties and pastoral roles relate to each other in dynamic ways, setting each one in a richer context. So, for instance, the preacher is aided by the work she does in pastoral care and preaching itself can be a form of pastoral care, and so on. So, much of the time, I revel in the ways that, as a pastor, I can be a generalist.

But I also recognize — and experience — some of the challenge of being a generalist because, for the most part, in our culture generalists are viewed as those who have neither the time nor the expertise to do anything particularly well. Coupled with that is the recognition that there was a time when the pastor was the most highly educated person in town, but now, in most settings, that is no longer true.

Pastors' lack of specific expertise may be felt all the more keenly because we are trained largely by experts. In seminary, we learn biblical interpretation from biblical scholars, pastoral care from psychologists, and preaching from those who may spend more time on the preaching circuit than in a local church. It is not surprising, then, that when pastors serve their first churches they can feel inadequate in virtually every pastoral duty. For example, it is telling that in many congregations psychotherapeutic terminology has virtually overwhelmed the language of the church in descriptions of the human condition. No wonder, then, that pastoral care can come to be viewed as little more than the ministrations of those who arrive first at the scene of an accident. The best that can be expected is to hold on until the experts arrive. Likewise, after having been trained in the scholarly tools of the academy, pastors often feel unqualified to interpret scripture without recourse to commentaries by scholarly experts.

In the congregation I currently serve, there is a theologian and a biblical scholar who know more about the Bible than I do. Also in the congregation are university professors who probably are better teachers than I am. We have therapists, counselors, and psychologists who probably know more about the vagaries of the human heart and mind than I do. We have people who, unlike pastors, actually are *trained* in administration; for some it is their life's work. We even have a former television news anchor who probably is better at public speaking than I am. Part of being a generalist is realizing that no matter which particular task may occupy you in any given moment, there probably is someone very close by who can do it better.

So perhaps it is not surprising that, when Karen got off the phone, I blurted out, "I want an expertise!" After all, twenty-first-century Americans can understand and appreciate expertise. In our time, expertise confers a kind of authority that is harder to find elsewhere. People may choose to rebel against any manner of authority, but not the authority that comes through expertise. Instead, we honor expertise and will pay handsomely for it.

A pastor's authority derives not from expertise but from other sources entirely. Some authority is conferred on a pastor by the church: through the recognition that this person has been called to such a ministry, by virtue of her ordination, and out of respect for the office she holds. But a good deal of pastoral authority is not granted by the church. It is earned over time. Such authority is earned, not through a demonstration of a particular expertise and, indeed, there are dangers in thinking of the pastor as "the God expert" of the congregation. Rather, authority is earned when people recognize that they can entrust the pastor with leadership of the church and care for the church. To be sure, a pastor must demonstrate a basic competence in pastoral duties. But for trust to reach full flower requires something more: the manifestation of qualities such as integrity, faithfulness, and wisdom.

This last quality — wisdom — may be the one distinguishing quality of pastors, because all people have an equal opportunity to demonstrate integrity and faithfulness, but pastors are given a unique opportunity to become wise. Of course, not all pastors are wise, God knows, and often the wisest people are not pastors. But the nature of the pastoral life is such that it gives a person an extraordinary shot at becoming wise.

Before going further with this, I need to pause to say a word about what I mean by wisdom. It has been called the woolly mammoth of ideas — big, shaggy, and elusive. Philosophers, theologians, and social scientists have all found wisdom notoriously difficult to define. In part, this is because wisdom is more than a single attribute. It is more like a cluster of attributes, including a clear-eyed view of human behavior, coupled with keen self-understanding; a certain tolerance for ambiguity and what might be called the messiness of life; emotional resiliency; an ability to think clearly in a circumstance of conflict or stress; a tendency to approach a crisis as an intriguing puzzle to be solved; an inclination to forgive and move on; humility enough to know that it is not all about you; a gift for seeing how smaller facts fit in within a larger picture; a mix of empathy and detachment; a knack for learning from lifetime experiences; a way of suspending judgment long enough to achieve greater clarity; an ability to act coupled with a willingness to embrace judicious inaction.

This cluster of gifts will be configured somewhat differently in the lives of the different people we come to think of as wise. Some are born with more of these gifts, which is why certain young people can seem uncommonly wise. At the same time, these gifts can be nurtured through one's life experiences, which is why wisdom is more often exhibited by those who are older. It is also why pastors have an extraordinary shot at it. Again, just as not all older people are wise, not all pastors are wise. Nevertheless, the kind of experiences one has as a pastor are just the kind of experiences that can help nurture whatever gifts for wisdom one may have.

For instance, as a pastor one has privileged access into the lives of people, an unparalleled opportunity to see them at their best and their worst, in a variety of circumstances, both as individuals and as part of a wider community, often over an extended period of time. It is a rare, if not unique, opportunity to learn about the complex contours of human life. Also, a pastor confronts the messiness of life on a regular basis. People are always confounding your expectations. Someone you thought of as upright confesses to something shameful, while someone else you might have given up on surprises you with an act of extraordinary generosity, and no one stays in the neat categories in which otherwise you would be tempted to put them. Then too, the loop-de-loops of congregational life are such that a pastor will not long survive without developing a gift for emotional resiliency. In fact, all the attributes of the wise person listed above are gifts that are used extensively in pastoral ministry. Even further, all those gifts can be nurtured through pastoral ministry in extraordinary ways (again, for those who have those gifts).

Unlike expertise, wisdom is lived out in community. One can become an expert by solitary study. One could, for instance, become an expert in the mating habits of turtles by reading every published study on the subject and doing one's own field study. Wisdom, by contrast, is not a solitary activity. Wisdom is formed in the ongoing life of a community and it is exercised in community. One cannot speak of wisdom without reference to human community. This is another reason why pastors, whose vocation is lived out in the thick of community, are given an opportunity to have their gifts for wisdom nurtured.

There is one other way in which pastors have an extraordinary opportunity to attain something like wisdom. Their vocation is situated at the intersection of the community and the biblical story in such a way that they are always having to interpret one in light of the other. Pastors do not need to make it all up as they go along. They can draw on the wisdom of the biblical story and Christian tradition, which are proved wiser than we are on a regular basis. As Goethe once observed, anyone who does not draw on three thousand years is living hand-to-mouth. By living and working at the intersection of the community and the biblical story, pastors have an opportunity to see both more expansively and more deeply than they might otherwise be able to do.

When I had been a pastor for about five years, I attended a large denominational meeting in another state. Also in attendance at the meeting was Al Cohen, someone I had known as a boy, but had not seen in about twenty years. I knew him because for a number of years he had been a young minister at the church where my father served as senior minister, so he knew my family well. When we saw one another early in the meeting, we expressed our mutual desire to get together, but Al was on the planning committee for the meeting, which meant that he was kept on the go the entire time. So we kept missing each other. The last night of the meeting I went to bed early because I had a very early flight the next morning. I was just drifting off to sleep when the phone rang. It was Al: "Say, I'm down in the lobby. Can we get together now? I would hate for you to leave before we've had a chance to talk." So I got up and got dressed and went downstairs to the hotel lobby.

It was late and the lobby was largely deserted, so we found two large upholstered chairs that were well situated for conversation. Al asked me some about my family and I told him about Karen and our new baby daughter, Alanna. Then he wanted to know something about the church I served. After that, he said, "Well, I want to tell you, I have thought of you so many times since your father's death. Those years I served with him were among the most formative of my life. I learned so much from him. He was a great preacher — everyone recognized that. But he also always seemed to know how to handle every situation that came along." Then he proceeded to tell me story after story about my father, mostly about how my father had brought deft pastoral skill to challenging circumstances in the life of the congregation. My father had been gone for a few years at this point, long enough that people no longer talked about him as much anymore. So I loved hearing these stories. What is more, I had never heard any of these stories before, so it felt like coming across a trunk filled with old family photos, letters, and journals that I had not known existed.

The last story Al told me that night was about the time when the congregation was considering whether to join the United Church of Christ. This newly formed denomination was the result of a merger between two predecessor denominations: the Evangelical and Reformed Church and the Congregational Christian Churches (the denomination in which my father had been ordained). The polity of the Congregational Christian Churches was such that every congregation could vote on whether to join the United Church of Christ.

Al told me that a large number of the more conservative members of my father's congregation were very vocal in expressing their objections to the move. They said that they feared that the congregation would lose its autonomy and come under strong liberal influences as a part of this new denomination. (This was 1957, a jittery time when some people were inclined to look under their beds every night before retiring, just to make sure there were no Communists hiding there.) My father had been senior minister of this church for less than a year and this was the most controversial issue that the congregation had faced in a generation. Complicating the matter was the fact that my father's predecessor had been very vocal against the congregation joining the United Church of Christ.

Considering all of this, Al was more than a little surprised when my father's first move was to appoint a committee to study the matter that included a disproportionately large number of vocal opponents. Among them was a man who was leading the charge in that congregation against the United Church of Christ, someone Al assumed my father would want as far from the center of the process as possible. My father explained, "Well, given the make-up of the committee, if the recommendation comes out in favor of the UCC, people will really listen." He also explained to Al that one of the reasons he offered to chair the committee was so that, in that role, he would not be expected to express his own opinions too early in the process. My father wanted to be sure that his leadership was — and was understood to be — even-handed. Between meetings he spent extra time with the opponents, mostly just listening, but after a time, also beginning gently to engage the issues. Al said, "He had a way of articulating the concerns of the opponents, sometimes better than they could themselves, which helped them know that their concerns were being taken seriously."

Gradually, the sentiment of the committee began to shift — not dramatically, but perceptibly. When it came time to present a report, my father offered to write a first draft for the committee to consider. Much of the report was a careful summary of all of the questions and concerns represented on both sides of the issue. Included was a recommendation that the congregation join the United Church of Christ, with a few provisos added that did not much change the substance of the recommendation. The committee adopted a slightly revised draft of the report.

A few Sundays before the scheduled vote, my father preached a sermon that addressed the issue. He spoke about the importance of both diversity and unity in the body of Christ and about how the essence of their ties as a congregation was in their covenant with one another, rather than agreement in all things. He told the congregation that he had been reluctant, as their new minister, to weigh in too soon or too heavily in a matter that had been the subject of considerable discussion long before he had arrived. He then went on to express appreciation for the fine work of the committee. Then he reported that there were many in the congregation who had sought his opinions on the matter, and that this seemed the appropriate time to share them. He said that he entirely supported the findings of the committee and went on to give a more eloquent case for joining the United Church of Christ than anyone had yet heard. He concluded his sermon by saying that he did not expect everyone to agree with him, but that he did hope that after this vote was taken, whatever its outcome, they would all reaffirm their covenant ties with one another. "And that," concluded Al, "is how the congregation joined the UCC. I am convinced that it wouldn't have happened without your father's skilled leadership and wisdom."

I listened to this story both as the proud son and as the young minister who felt like he should be taking notes. Al had given me something I did not know I needed, a gift that I would not have known to ask for.

After Al finished this last story, he said, "Hey, it's late. I need to go."

I responded, "But the whole time we have been talking about me and my family. I haven't had a chance to hear about your family or what is going on in your life."

"But that's as it should be. This is what I wanted. In my years as a pastor I've learned that people need to hear the stories, particularly after someone dear to them has died. All of us need to hear the stories. They are what give us life. And I wanted to do that for you." With that, we stood up, embraced, and he was gone.

I have reflected on that conversation often through the years. I particularly remember how much I loved hearing the stories. Indeed, as Al knew, I needed to hear them. That is, they were stories about one wise pastor told to me by another wise pastor.

CHAPTER 15

A Cast of Thousands

Lillian Daniel

At my daughter's elementary school musical, the printed program modestly explained: "This musical was originally written for 15 actors, but it has been adapted to accommodate our cast of 206."

You know what kind of show this was. It was the chaotic result of no-cut auditions, where no performer is left without something special to do. Each grade had a scene they had been rehearsing for months. They danced, they sang, they dressed up like archaeologists and Egyptian mummies. Somehow 206 children made their way across the stage that night.

It was not a short program.

Nor should it have been.

So many productions in life are competitive. The television talent show *American Idol* is popular as much for the failures as for the successes. Admit it. If no one got cut, would we really want to listen to these people sing? There is an excitement to seeing who makes it and who does not, and the winner does not just get fame and money. The winner gets to be worshiped, for that is what we do with idols in an idolatrous culture. Celebrity worship is not just a figure of speech.

Well, the world may operate that way, but the gospel has a response, mediated through the church. We're called to be like the volunteer geniuses behind the elementary school musical that took a play with 15 parts and creatively made room for 206. We take a few loaves and fishes and feed thousands, at the church potluck or at the homeless shelter. We take a task that we could simply pay someone to do, and we divide it into fifteen parts so that everyone has a job. Is it efficient? No. Not if all you care about is getting the job done.

But in the church we should care less about getting the job done and more about the people doing it. We are not in the efficiency business. We are in the business of making disciples. We want to offer as many people as possible the chance to know Christ in service and in community.

I have sat at church meetings in which the most unlikely person volunteered for the job. The woman I had envisioned on the finance committee chooses instead to join a team of church supper cooks. Yes, we want her excellent mind and her keen eye keeping track of our numbers. But that is what she does all day. "At church, I want to do what I love," she says, and until then, I never knew it was cooking. That church supper could have been catered, with much more efficiency, but instead the script was adapted to accommodate a person with a calling.

Sure, there are people we might not want on the program. Sometimes the accountant reminds us how grateful we are that cooking is not her day job. We have to adjust, to help her find the place where her gifts meet the world's needs. But in the midst of a bite of half-cooked quiche, or rubbery sausage, we recall that Jesus came for all of us, not just the star performers, or even the merely competent. The church is one of the last remaining homes of the no-cut audition. You have to want to get in, but once you are here, we will find a part for you if you want one.

When I give thanks to God for the church, my mind is awash in the sheer number of volunteers I have known, and the many ministry teams that keep the place humming. Some of them are out front, stars of the congregation. Many of them I have never met, because they have been behind the scenes, like the stage crew. I know them only as part of a greater production.

There are so many parts in this musical. It will not be a short program, but one that will last from generation to generation.

Sometimes we forget that the church, the early church of Jesus' day, started small. Jesus started this venture with just twelve disciples — but look where it went from there. The script was adapted.

One Sunday, I would like to add a line to our own worship bulletin a bit like the one from the elementary school musical. It would say this:

"Christianity was originally written for a cast of twelve men, but it has since been adapted to accommodate men, women, the talented, the untalented, the graceful, the klutzy, the rich, the poor, the wise, the silly, the brokenhearted, the joyful, the brave, the quiet, and the shy."

In other words, Christianity has been adapted to accommodate a cast of thousands. As a pastor, I am called to give thanks for every character in the show, and characters they may be.

At the church I first served in a small New England town, the ladies of the church had been putting on an annual strawberry festival for as long as anyone could remember. But this particular women's circle was growing older, and the younger women were not joining them. The younger women formed groups of their own that read books and had discussions, but their new callings did not include the mammoth task of hulling thousands of strawberries and baking shortcake for weeks.

Each year, the older women complained that they were tired and unless someone stepped up, there would be no strawberry festival on the church green. Finally they gave an ultimatum. Unless someone stepped forward to lead the effort, they were done. After all, they had been doing it for many decades and they were tired.

Finally, at the eleventh hour, someone stepped up. He was a lawyer, and a father of two school age children. In other words, he was the last person the ladies had in mind to succeed them. When asked why he had volunteered to take on the massive project, he said, "I felt like God was calling me to."

From that point on, the older ladies taught this young lawyer how to run a strawberry festival. They had to stick around to tell him when he was doing it wrong, which in many cases meant that he was doing something new, and as some of his contemporaries joined the project, everyone involved had to adjust the script. But as the season moved forward, so did the strawberry festival and it continues today. That production was originally written for twenty young stay-at-home moms, but it has since been adapted to include a cast of young fathers, older women, and whomever else God might be calling to minister among the strawberries, in a cast of thousands.

CHAPTER 16

A PK in the Ministry

MARTIN B. COPENHAVER

When my uncle, Paul Yinger, discovered that the church he served as minister counted a lot of PKs among its members, he thought it might be fun and interesting to get them all together. So one Sunday he put a notice in the bulletin: "PK's Reception: All PKs are invited to join Dr. Yinger in the Parlor after worship for an informal time of conversation and fellowship. If you do not know what a PK is, then this invitation is not for you."

Indeed, if you are a PK — a Preacher's Kid — you know it and, try as you might at times, you never forget it. People have quite different experiences of being the son or daughter of a minister. Some find it a burden, while others enjoy it, and probably most would describe their experience as a mixture of both burden and joy. But I have found absolutely no one who grew up as the child of a minister who would say anything like, "Oh, it really wasn't a big deal. I don't think it had much of an impact on me." My own father has been dead for twenty-five years and I have been an ordained minister myself longer than that, and yet, to this day, I still think of myself as a PK. It is not the primary way I think of myself, but it is an indelible part of my identity. And this is true of other PKs I know, including those who, as adults, make it a point never to go near a church. If you are a PK, you know it because it simply is part of who you are.

My family tree is so laden with ordained ministers that it veritably bends to the ground under the weight of us all. My grandfather and my grandmother on my mother's side were ordained ministers. They gave birth to eight children. Of the six boys, five were ordained (and the other barely escaped, becoming a professor of sociology with a specialty in the sociology of religion). My father, an only child, met my mother when they were both students at Union Theological Seminary in New York. When they married, my mother did not pursue her studies, but, in the manner of the time, she had something of a ministry of her own in the churches my father served.

When my extended family came together, my father and my uncles would roll up the sleeves of their starched white shirts and loosen their dark and narrow ties, as if preparing for some form of exertion, when in fact they were readying themselves for another round of church talk, which they obviously relished. They would talk about what was going on in their churches and what they were reading. I did not understand much of what my father and my uncles would talk about, but even as a boy I liked nibbling at the edges of those conversations because it seemed clear that they were concerned with important matters.

One night, when I was tucking my own daughter into bed — she was about eight years old at the time — she asked me what a pastor does. I described some of what my day entails, and then I heard myself say, "And I just think it is very important work." I am sure that my own words made more of an impression on me than they did on my young daughter, because suddenly I heard in them an articulation of an understanding that, in my family of origin, seemed so self-evident that it went without saying: the Christian ministry is a very high calling, indeed. I recognize that my family is different from some others in this regard. Let me put it this way: my older brother received something like sympathy because he did not have a call to the ministry. He had to settle for being a highly successful lawyer.

I did not experience many of the difficulties sometimes associated with growing up as a minister's child. In fact, in many ways I delighted in the role. I loved my father and, as his son, I basked in the overflow of respect in which he was held. I am sure I enjoyed the extra attention that I received in the church because I was the son of the minister. I was Little Lord Fauntleroy, sliding down the banisters in the palace, the son of royalty, given free rein, if not yet the reign of the kingdom.

I did have my moments of rebellion. When I was twelve years old or so, the director of Christian education came huffing and puffing into our third-floor church school room, demanding to know who had thrown a folding chair out the window. Unfortunately, at that point my brother had not yet become a lawyer. I could have used him. I remember bracing for the lecture my parents were sure to give me about my misbehavior, but the lecture never came because the director of Christian education never told them about my antics. Sometimes being the child of a minister has its privileges.

When I was a teenager in the late sixties, hair was a contentious issue to a degree that is hard to imagine today. In those days, the length and style of one's hair made more than a fashion statement. It also seemed to make a political statement. My own hair was rather middle-of-the-road for the time — not down to my shoulders, but well over the ears and long enough in the front to sweep over my eyebrows. Picture early Beatles. Anyway, during coffee hour after worship one Sunday, I found myself in a one-on-one conversation with Fred Kappel. Mr. Kappel, as he was known to me and to most other people, was a prominent leader in the church; he had been co-chair of the search committee that had recommended my father to the congregation. Mr. Kappel also was a public figure of considerable stature. He was CEO of AT&T when it was still a government-sanctioned monopoly and one of the two or three largest corporations in America. He was an advisor to presidents and his picture had been on the cover of *Time* magazine. Mr. Kappel was also famously conservative and his hair showed it. It was very closely cropped, particularly along the sides, which made him look more like a general in the army than like a captain of industry. His haircut was so distinctive that my brother and I coined a name for the style: "Kappel cut."

The fact that I would find myself in a conversation with Mr.

Kappel was not surprising. Church members of any age often would approach me with an air of easy familiarity that no doubt came from my being the minister's son. And I did not find this imposing figure particularly intimidating. Mr. Kappel was a friend of my father's who had always been kind to me. Besides, as a PK, I had lots of practice at interacting with every manner of person. But this conversation started out ominously. Mr. Kappel seemed to make a special point of looking me straight in the eye and then said, "Martin, you want to be a man, don't you?" I did not know where he was headed with that question, but I braced myself for what was coming. My heart began to race a bit. All I could think to say was, "Well, sure." Mr. Kappel came right back: "Well then don't you think you should get your hair cut?"

I do not remember what I said in response, or anything else about the rest of the conversation. I think I just slipped away as quickly as I could without coming across as impolite. I do remember the conversation I had with my father on the way home, however. I asked him, "Do you know what Mr. Kappel said to me today?" Then I recounted the story. When I had finished, my father said, "Don't worry about it. That's his hang-up." And then he moved on to some other subject. Since then I have thought back on that episode many times. I think it reveals something of my father's determination not to lay too many expectations on me because I was a PK, made all the more remarkable because he probably would have preferred that I get my hair cut as well.

The daughter of a pastor summarized the particular challenges of growing up as a PK by saying that in some sense you are expected to be a pastor yourself from the age of four on. I think she is right. As a pastor's child, I learned how to listen to people and something about how to pretend to listen to people when I was not particularly interested in hearing what they had to say. I learned the skill of responding to questions from those who want to know too much, never revealing too much in the process and also somehow communicating that there is nothing more to reveal. I learned how to keep confidences. I learned how to study human nature, comparing the stories I heard about members of the church with what I observed. I learned to live with something like the kind of loneliness that can come with being a pastor because, although I had many close friends, I sometimes confronted ways in which my life was different from theirs.

As a PK, I also had a chance to observe pastoral ministry at close range. Unlike most children, I did not have to wait for a "take your child to work day" to have a chance to observe my father live out his vocation. I could see him in action in a wide variety of settings on a regular basis. I could see him lead public worship, but also I could see his preparations late into a Saturday evening. I could observe him talking with parishioners at a church fellowship hour, but also I could overhear his pastoral conversations on the phone at home. Then, in the course of conversation within the family, often I would hear my parents reflect on aspects of my father's ministry, sometimes unpacking for themselves an encounter I had observed, so in some sense I got the benefits of the action/reflection model of learning.

I think my father was eager for me to understand the pastoral life, in part, because it was his life and he wanted to share that with me. To understand him necessitated understanding something of what it means to be a pastor. But then, too, it was clear that he wanted me to understand what it is like to be a pastor because the worst kept secret for anyone who knew my father was that he was eager for me to go into the ministry. He would later point out that he had never talked with me about it — scrupulously so, because he was eager for me to make my own decision. But if he did not say anything it was probably because he did not need to. His wishes in this regard were just so obvious that his silence on the subject was deafening.

One of the reasons that so many PKs go into pastoral ministry themselves is that we are given glimpses of the pastoral life from the inside that others are not afforded. This view from the inside is the best way, and perhaps the only way, to appreciate the allure of this vocation. After all, it is not the kind of career one would be expected to pick out at a jobs fair. Then again, there may be no way to prepare one fully for the challenges of this vocation, either, until you inhabit it, or at least in some way view it from the inside.

Another reason that a lot of PKs end up in the ministry themselves is that, from a very early age, many of us are asked questions about our vocations. Even the most clumsy (and, at the time, annoying) form of such questions — "Are you thinking of following in your father's footsteps?" — can prompt one to take pause. Those who are not PKs are seldom asked about a potential call to pastoral ministry with the same regularity.

At the same time, being a PK was the biggest hurdle I had to get over in order to be able to discern my own call to pastoral ministry. Whatever a call to the ministry might mean or not mean, I was quite sure that it was not like a generalized shout to an entire family. One does not go into the ministry in the same way as one decides to go into the family business.

Then, too, my relationship with my father complicated my own discernment about ordained ministry. He was a towering figure in more ways than one. He was tall, with a naturally deep and resonant voice. His words would flow as if he thought in complete paragraphs. He was quite reserved in some ways, but he also had a commanding presence. When he entered a room — even one crowded with people — everyone seemed to know it, although it is hard to explain exactly how because he would not call attention to himself in any obvious way.

To people outside the family, my father was rather formal, even a bit distant, but he and I always enjoyed an unusually warm and intimate relationship. From an early age I knew without needing to be told that he took particular delight in me. To this day, I attribute my own sense of self-esteem largely to my father's affection and appreciation. But he also was so obviously eager to claim me as his own. He loved to point out the similarity of our gifts and interests. Much of the time I recognized the truth of what he would say about the many affinities we shared, but, when I was a young adult, that did not make it any easier to have them pointed out. It may be in a father's job description to claim the son, but it is in a son's job description to claim a measure of independence from the father. Or, at least, that was true of this father and this son.

So, indeed, we never did talk about my going into the ministry. When I did decide that I wanted to go to seminary and become a pastor, the summer before my junior year in college, I wrote my father a long letter to tell him. That, in itself, is telling. I did not write to seek his advice. I was merely informing him of my decision. I did not want to tell him in person, not because I feared what he would say, but rather because I knew all too well what he would say. He would express his joy. He would say that he sensed all along that I was called to this work. He would point out that he had been careful not to express this conviction, as heartfelt as it was.

In my letter to him, I expressed my pride in him, saying, "I have seen the ministry at its peak in the hands (I truly believe) of one of the greatest ministers of our time." The warmth of our relationship also radiates through this letter. But also reflected is the struggle of a PK — or, at least, this PK — with sorting out a call to ministry. Even here I was so obviously eager to find some daylight that was not eclipsed by my father's shadow. I wrote, "Even though I recognize our many similarities and take pride in them, as you seem to, I don't want to be thought of as 'following in my father's footsteps.' I hope you can understand this. It sounds too much as if it is a thoughtless 'going along,' an embracing of the familiar because it is familiar. It indicates no individual thought or motivation in what should be the most individual of decisions."

When my father received my letter, he did not call me on the phone, probably because he wanted to respect the bit of distance that I desired, the kind of intimate distance that a letter can provide. So he wrote back a long letter in response, which he put in the mail the day after receiving mine. In that letter, he wrote:

> I have known in my heart, almost from the very beginning, that God wanted you to serve Him through the ministry. And yet, even as you have been wonderfully sensitive to the hazards of "following in my father's footsteps," so I have disciplined myself through the years to "underplay" the ministry so that my son would never feel parental pressure, indeed, not even know the deep personal sentiments of his father. The overpowering purpose of parenthood should be to let children go — free them, free them to be themselves and to achieve their own unique personhood . . . Thus it is,

> though I have seen in you the exceptional gifts that I have long believed God could use in His Church — if you desired and were willing — I disciplined myself to speak softly and let the whole matter be your concern, knowing that your life belonged to you and in the important areas of experience it would always be yours, and your ultimate accountability would be to yourself and to God — and not to your earthly father.

When I was ordained six years later, my father preached the sermon, tellingly entitled, "The Glory of the Ministry." It was rather formal in tone and, at the same time, a bit over-the-top in its effusiveness, a kind of tripartite love letter expressing my father's affection for his God, his vocation, and his son.

For eighteen months after my ordination, my father and I served churches that were less than an hour's drive apart. Once a month or so we would meet in between for lunch. Not long ago I said to my wife, Karen, "I wish we could have one of those lunches again." She replied, "I understand that, but just remember that you always found them difficult at the time." And she is right, of course. My father and I remained close and we could talk about just about anything, but, when the talk turned to ministry, the conversation was often sprinkled with a bit of tension, for me at least. I was both too cocksure and perhaps still too insecure at that early stage of my ministry to listen easily to the generous helpings of advice he would give me. And I would sometimes chafe under his assumptions that I would choose to do the various tasks of ministry in just the way he had. But I was right, also, in noting a deep and abiding desire for such times with my father. It is not that I have longed to do them over and differently this time. Rather, at this stage of my life, my desire is more simple than that: I would give almost anything to have one of those tense lunches again.

About two years after I was ordained my father died very suddenly. That was twenty-five years ago. It is an irony that years later, a time when I am better prepared to appreciate the ways in which we might be compared, fewer people who knew my father are around to make the comparisons. Each summer I am a guest preacher at a little seaside church where my father preached for years. One of the things that I love about preaching there is that there are people in the congregation who remember my father. I have been coming so many years that I get to be both Charles Copenhaver's still-young-son and something of a gray eminence myself, somehow both at the same time. If, after worship, one of the old-timers says, "You remind me more and more of your father," or even, "Someday you might even be the preacher your father was," I receive those comments as gifts to treasure. And today you might even hear me quote my father, something I never would have done while he was alive and would shrink from doing even for some time after his death.

In the church I currently serve, one of the scripture passages that is read every Maundy Thursday and Christmas Eve is the magnificent prologue to the Gospel of John. Each year I ask a variety of people to read other passages, but I always keep the John passage for myself because, to this day, I cannot read it without hearing my father's voice — much deeper and more resonant than my own — echoing through the sanctuary. I do not lose sight that these are words of scripture with a larger meaning. But when I read those words, "In the beginning was the Word, and the Word was with God and the Word was God . . ." I cannot help but feel as if those are my words with which I am reaching out to my father and he is reaching back to me. Even twenty-seven years after my ordination, standing in the pulpit addressing my own congregation, I am still the preacher's kid.

CHAPTER 17

Recall Notice

LILLIAN DANIEL

Growing up, the church was my one constant in a changing world. I was six months old when my father, a foreign correspondent with United Press International, was called to cover the story that would dominate the next decade, the Vietnam War. My mother and I flew from South Carolina to join him in Tokyo, then in Thailand, India, the Philippines, Hong Kong, and London before finally returning to the United States when I was in the ninth grade. By that time I had already lived in seven countries and attended eleven schools.

I loved the church as a child because it was steady. In all those countries we worshiped as Anglicans, and the ritual and rhythms of the Book of Common Prayer let each new church be old again, and as dependable as lukewarm tea, sherry, and sandwiches with the crusts cut off after services. Church was a port of comfort in the stormy seas of expatriate life.

When people ask, "What made you want to be a minister?" my first response is "I didn't." I didn't want to be a minister because I hoped to be rich. After four years of capitalist reeducation at high school in the U.S., I wanted to be a political science major with an economics minor; I also registered for Mandarin Chinese. I was going to take my international upbringing in a much more lucrative direction. As the 1980s stock market soared, I believed not only that my plan was impressive-sounding when parroted to my parents' friends at cocktail parties, but that it really would make me rich. But just for fun, I allowed myself one history of religion course. Just one.

By the end of college, I was a religion major with an acceptance letter to Yale Divinity School. There had been no thunderbolt, but there had been the nurture of my church over the years, a church that had encouraged me to think and to ask deep questions of God and the world. I'd been stimulated by courses on the history of Christianity taught through the lenses of feminism and Marxism, and by bright students of all faiths and no faith duking it out with intellectual rigor. A rich undertow toward social justice in every class echoed the Sunday school lessons of my youth. And the more I got caught up in that undertow of social justice, the more I seemed to be pulled back toward theological education.

I knew I wanted to study the church, but I had no inkling what it might mean to lead one. I could barely put together the words to name a call to ministry. The best I could articulate was a rather vague "call to divinity school." Still, that acceptance letter gave me a new talking point at my parents' cocktail parties.

That summer I had a summer internship at a national news magazine. As the editor of my college newspaper, I expected a plum assignment in the news section. I was shocked to hear that my spot would be in "advertising and marketing."

"You mean, *writing about* advertising and marketing?" I asked.

"No, you won't be doing any writing. You'll be working in advertising and marketing, on the business side of the magazine."

"I can't believe you're working with the bean counters," my dad, the lifelong journalist, grumbled. In my romantic vision of myself, I wasn't a bean counter but instead a summer sojourner in a strange land, like Jesus, who ate with the tax collectors and sinners. My father and his journalist friends were the Pharisees who grumbled, "This fellow welcomes sinners and eats with them." By now, you can guess who, in all my humility, I was in this narrative.

At the end of the summer, I spoke to a new interim priest at my father's church and told him of my plans to attend divinity school. He responded with very little enthusiasm, pointing out that I had advanced upon all this without the help of my church, that I was venturing out to divinity school alone, and that I had skipped the ecclesiastical steps toward ordination. He asked me about my call to the ministry and I could tell that what I said left him unimpressed. After our conversation, I called up Yale Divinity School to inform them I wasn't coming. "Not coming?" the woman asked. "But what is your reason?"

"I realize I don't know anything about real life. I've been in an ivory tower at college, and this summer I did work that I never knew existed except to disapprove of it. Furthermore, I have no idea what I would do after those three years at divinity school, and I've skipped all the appropriate ecclesiastical steps, and my priest hates me."

"Oh, you don't want to cancel," she said. "In cases like this, one simply defers."

"Defer? You mean, come later?"

"Of course," she said. "We hold your place. For up to two years."

"Ok, put me down for that. But I can tell you right now, I'm definitely not coming."

"Very good, dear," she said. "All the best, now."

From that decisive move, I launched into a week of lying in bed, eating potato chips, and watching one game show after another. It felt good to have made an adult decision and finally taken charge of my life. After a second week of this, my mother informed me I needed to move out and get a job.

The phone rang about that time, and it was the news magazine. "We heard you didn't go to school after all. Would you like to take a job here?"

And I agreed. After all, if my summer work experience had been miserable enough to provide with me with this much adult wisdom, imagine what a permanent position might bring.

It was indeed my shot at the young urban professional lifestyle. I got a new car, adopted three cats, and acquired a working woman's wardrobe. I was a grown-up.

A committee of lay leaders from my church, pulled together by the priest, agreed to meet monthly with me to discern my call. I met with the bishop, met with a psychologist to take some tests, and decided not to tell either of them that I was in a band. In this period of discernment, it became clearer and clearer to me that I had a real call to the ministry.

Yet I was never very good at expressing it, at least in ways that the committee understood. I would talk about social justice and they would talk about the Eucharist. I would talk about the prophets and they would ask me about the prayer book. It was as if we were all having conversations with someone else, not with one another. They asked me why I wanted to serve a local parish; I responded that I wasn't sure that I did. They asked me about obedience to the bishop; I said, "You're kidding? We have to do that?" because that really was news to me. It was only after I'd left that I would realize what it was that I should have said. I realized for instance, that when they asked me about my call to preside over the sacrament each week, my answer of "Sure, I could do that" was wrong.

The chairperson delivered the news at the final meeting. Reading aloud from her notes, she said that the committee would not recommend me to go further in the process. I could not hear the sentences, but the phrases came through with clarity. "No discernable gifts for ordained ministry whatsoever." "No appreciation of the sacramental ministry of the church." "A thrill seeker." "Issues with authority." "Immature."

When I asked them what they thought I should do with my life, they were surprisingly direct. Get an MBA, work in the nonprofit world, and serve the wider church as a lay leader committed to justice in the world. The chairperson even offered to serve as my mentor.

I actually gave their words authority. I quit the magazine job and took a job at a nonprofit organization that helped at-risk and homeless teenagers in Washington, D.C. My job was to recruit volunteers, but I begged for a caseload. In a typical nonprofit compromise, they agreed I could do both.

In my new work, I learned how to work with families in crisis, and discovered how hard life was for my fellow citizens in the nation's capital. The people who worked at this agency came from every background. Some had lived hard and in poverty; others were like me, recent college graduates fresh from the ivory tower. Social work veterans schooled us and we bonded with one another in our lack of training and our desire to help a hurting world. We used secondhand desks crammed into shared offices and ate lunch on the run. We learned our way around public housing projects and police stations, and discovered where kids hid on the way to becoming homeless. I was downwardly mobile, but I was on the highest learning curve of my life.

It took a while before I discovered that three of my coworkers were Howard Divinity School students doing internships in theological education. I was shocked. "How can this be your divinity internship?" I asked. "Shouldn't you be working in a church, performing the sacraments and all that?"

"This is preparing us for the ministry," Roxanne explained.

"What kind of church would consider this preparation for the ministry?" I asked.

"What kind of church wouldn't?" she retorted. It was the first notion I had that there was more than one way of being the church.

The Episcopal Church had been so constant in my life that I had mistaken it for the whole. In fact, if you had asked me which was the largest Christian denomination in the world, I would have told you it was the Anglican Communion, simply because I had known no other. My conversations with the Baptist divinity students rocked my world. They listened to my story about cancelled divinity school and having no discernable gifts for the ministry, and I listened to their stories about missionary appointments in Rwanda and preachers who could make you fall down.

Then, toward the end of my year at the agency, Roxanne pulled me aside. "We've been praying for you," she said, speaking for the small group from Howard. "And something has come to us from the Lord." I listened eagerly. Nobody had ever told me anything like this before in my life. I felt myself blessed just to have been prayed for, and it could have stopped right there.

"You are meant to go to divinity school," she said. "The one you deferred. You're meant to go."

"But I like working here," I said. "I may get an MBA. Or maybe law school. I've been turned down for the ministry. I have no idea now what I would do with a divinity degree."

"You're meant to go. It came to us that when you get there, God will open the doors and the windows."

"But my church told me not to go," I said.

And Roxanne, who had never stepped away from the church of her childhood, said, "Maybe you're in the wrong church."

And in my heart, I said, "Okay, God. I'll go," because, suddenly, God looked a lot like Roxanne.

So far I had felt as if 99 people had told me no, and I had taken them at their word. I had told myself that the majority ruled. But when just one person told me yes, that was all it took. And in that moment, I felt that finally someone had sought me out and brought me back.

True to Roxanne's vision, I had no idea why I was in divinity school that first year. I worshiped at smells-and-bells Episcopal churches that cared for the homeless with the same dignity with which they worshiped, and represented the best of the tradition of my upbringing, but it was a miserable time. I often considered dropping out. I was ashamed to have been turned down for ministry by my church, and I carried that secret with me everywhere.

But then I wandered to the plain white walls of New England Congregationalism, a United Church of Christ church with large clear windows where the concerns of the world were always visible from inside the church, and where the gospel light could always shine out on the struggles on the streets.

When I joined my first UCC church, the pastor said that he thought I had the gifts for ministry. I told him the truth. "I don't want to be one of those people who gets bounced from one church that has standards, and then tries to get in to one that doesn't."

Remarkably, he did not take offense, but suggested gently. "Maybe you were in the wrong church."

Looking back now, I believe there are no wrong churches. There is only one church. But sometimes one wing says no so that another may say yes.

My story of being told no by the church of my upbringing gradually worked its way up out of my locked box of secrets. First I shared it only with those who knew me best. Then I found I was able to share it more easily once I'd been ordained, and when I had achieved something that looked like "success" in my calling, if there can be such a thing. To be honest, I also hoped that it would get the response that my lingering insecurity craved. "How *awful*," close friends would say. "But look at you now." Such responses brushed up against the empty hole inside me, but never filled it up.

Only after ministering and living as a pastor over time did my story emerge from its secret box on its own terms. A realization came gradually, rained upon by the rhythms of preaching, by visiting parishioners, and even by performing the sacraments.

Gradually I came to know this: the Episcopalians were not wrong. Their ordination process actually worked. I wasn't called to ordination in that tradition and they saw it when I could not. I was immature. I do have issues with authority and obedience. I choke in hierarchies and thrive in independence. I love to preach long sermons and I hate homilies. I would have made a lousy Episcopal priest. But I was richly blessed by the Episcopal Church.

When my mother died, the priest from her church asked me what I wanted to do in the funeral service, because now I had been in the ministry for a good while. When I answered "Nothing" I realized that I trusted him. I trusted him as her pastor, and in that sad moment, as mine. The things I had left behind, from the wordy prayer book to the sacrament being served, were not things I would have chosen. But on this occasion I did not need to be the chooser. The church had taught me that.

At the service, I could be embraced by a tradition that had embraced her. I could delight in watching her priest do exactly what he was meant to do, and then return to my community of faith, and do what I was meant to do.

Just a few months ago, the phone rang at my church and it was the wonderful old priest who had kept me engaged in the suburban church of my high school years. He sat in my mother's living room when my grandmother died. He defended me as a Sunday school teacher when my nursery kids ran wild. He took our three-person confirmation class on a beach trip where we thanked him by breaking a motel television. And later, he said the prayer at my ordination into another denomination.

He calls me periodically to check in on me, to see what I am up to. I count it as precious whenever he seeks me out. It is as if I am the one sheep he does not let get away.

There are no wrong churches.

CHAPTER 18

Laying On of Hands

Martin B. Copenhaver

The scripture had been read, the sermon preached, the vows of ordination exchanged. I was then invited to kneel for the laying on of hands and the prayer of ordination. All the years of discernment about vocation, all the long and searching conversations, all the prayer, all the study, all the examinations by church bodies, had come down to this one moment, the epicenter of the ordination process. When the prayer was completed and I stood up, I would be declared an ordained minister.

The laying on of hands is a ritual that, through the centuries, has been enacted in a variety of settings and its meaning has been interpreted in various ways. The priests of the Temple in Jerusalem would lay their hands on an animal about to be sacrificed. They would pray that their sins and the sins of the people might be transferred to the animal, so that when the animal died, their sins would be eliminated as well. Jacob laid his hands on his grandsons' heads to confer God's blessing. Moses laid his hands on Joshua to transfer some of his authority, so that Joshua might lead Israel. Jesus laid hands on the sick, as a means of healing. In the early church, hands were laid on certain individuals to confer upon them the gifts needed for ministry. It was also by the laying on of hands that the church commissioned people for their ministries. When the apostles selected the first group of deacons, they blessed and authorized them by laying their hands on them and offering a prayer.

There are echoes of all of these meanings when hands are laid upon a candidate for ordination (well, maybe not the sacrificial animal part, although even that image might come to a pastor's mind at a time when he's feeling particularly sorry for himself). It is a symbol as ancient as a kiss, and it can mean just as many things. And, like all rich symbols, it has meaning beyond all the variety of meanings that can be enumerated. That is part of what makes it so powerful.

In the church parlor before my ordination service, Ted, the senior minister of the church, gave the leaders of the service some instructions. When he came to the laying on of hands part, he told me where I would kneel, and then he added, "And, Martin, just to warn you, you will feel as if you have the weight of the world on you." There was a bit of knowing laughter from the ordained ministers in the room. I didn't know what he meant by that, and if there had been time, I might have asked. I went into the service assuming that he meant that, in that moment, one can sense the weight of responsibility that comes with ordination.

When it came time for that portion of the service, I knelt on the first step of the chancel. Members of the congregation were invited to come forward and lay their hands on me. In some traditions, it might be an individual in authority — say, a bishop — who would lay hands on a candidate for ordination. But in our tradition, ordination is conferred by the gathered congregation, rather than by any one individual. So all were invited to come forward, beginning with those who were leading the service. The first ones to get to where I was kneeling — Ted, my wife Karen, my father, my divinity school professor, my colleagues at the church, and others who were leading the service — put their hands on my head. Others who came forward were able to touch my shoulders or my arm. One young child crawled under the arms of her elders and got a hold of my ankle. Those who couldn't get their hands on me put a hand on the shoulder of the person in front of them. Everyone was standing much closer to one another than people normally do, closer than if we had all been stuffed into a crowded elevator. On this warm June day, I could feel heat radiating from the bodies of those closest to me.

So many of the people who mean the most to me were joined together in that moment: my family, friends from various stages of my life, teachers, mentors, ministers from other churches, members from my home church, members of this congregation which had nurtured my growth while I was in seminary. There were people who had believed that I was called to ministry before I did, a few friends and family members who had told me that they wondered why anyone would go into the ministry, and others who only got to know me after I became a candidate for ministry and so couldn't think of me in any other way. Even my wedding had not brought together such a representative cross-section of people from every stage and setting of my life. And this moment brought us so close to one another that we could hear one another breathe.

Before I closed my eyes for the prayer, I took a glance around me to see who was standing immediately behind me. But once my eyes were closed, in most instances I couldn't tell whose hands I was feeling on my head or my body. I thought, "Is that Karen's familiar hand there? That hand that is shaking: whose is that? And that hand on my head that feels particularly heavy, is that my father's? Or, on second thought, is that Jesus' hand? After all, his presence has been invoked several times in the service already. About time he showed up."

My friend, Jim, was only a few phrases into his prayer when I realized what Ted meant when he warned me that I would feel "the weight of the world." I had thought he was speaking metaphorically, and perhaps he was, in part, but now I was beginning to understand that he was also speaking quite literally. Those hands were heavy. How could they be so heavy? After all, they were still attached to other people's bodies. It felt like they were bearing down on me. Were they doing that intentionally? And were there people who, in an effort to reach across others, couldn't keep their balance unless they supported themselves with their hand on my head? My neck felt strained. I stopped being able to concentrate on the prayer. I wondered why no one told them to keep a light touch. After all, this was an ordination, not a hazing.

Part of me wanted to interrupt the prayer to protest, "Hey, take it easy!" but I also knew I couldn't do that. Whether it was intentional or not, whether people were trying to impress something on me or it just felt like it, whether they were looking for support or just didn't know any better, there was no escaping the weight of their hands. Nothing in the entire service brought home to me the momentousness of what was taking place more than the physical sensation of feeling the sheer weight of those hands.

When the prayer concluded, people took their hands off me and one another. I felt so light that it was almost as if I could now float to the ceiling like a helium balloon. A number of people stopped to greet me before taking their seats, their hands now either shaking mine, or patting me on the back, or holding me in an embrace. Many of them had tears in their eyes, as if they had been present at a birth, or a commencement, or a wedding — and all of those are images that might be used to begin to describe what had just happened.

Even at the time, however, I wondered what the tears meant. Did the tears mean that they were happy for me? Or, for those who had known me since I was a boy, were these, in part, tears of sadness because this was another sign that I had grown up? Or were these the same tears that some people shed whenever a passage is marked? Or were they a silent testimony to the intimacy of prayer and how prayer can dip deep into one's soul in ways that summon tears? Or were the tears simply prompted by the rare experience of gathering so closely with our fellow human beings?

Any one of those could be an explanation for the tears, in part, at least. But now that I have attended dozens of ordinations myself, I think those present would say that, in addition to those reasons (or perhaps underneath and within those reasons), in ways they could not describe or account for fully, they sensed something holy in that moment.

I have always had, and still do have, a rather modest understanding of ordained ministry. Most often, I emphasize the ways in which all baptized Christians are called to be ministers — "the mutual ministry of all believers" is the way some people put it. And I still believe in that. But it is also hard to deny that something powerful happens in the laying on of hands. It is not about me, or others who are ordained, but something much bigger. It is bigger than the congregation that was gathered on that day. It is bigger than Moses and Joshua, too, bigger than the apostles and the first deacons, bigger than the long chain of people who have had hands laid on them through the centuries. When you experience something holy, it seems too big to explain. You can only point to it. And some weep.

As for me, when I stood up from the chancel step, my head was spinning, mostly with questions. Did something in me change in that moment when hands were laid on me? Did I feel like a different person? No, not really. Did I feel more like a minister than I did before I was ordained? Well, not yet. But had I changed in ways that I cannot yet sense? I would have to see. What exactly happened there when they laid hands on me?

In anticipation of my ordination, I was required to write a paper that laid out my personal convictions about Christian faith and practices. One of the subjects I was to address in that paper was the meaning of ordination. I was expected to be articulate and precise. I did the best I could. But when hands were laid upon me, I could see that any accounting that could be called articulate or precise would be something of an irreverence.

Not long ago I attended the ordination of someone dear to me. She had grown up in the congregation I serve, returned to the congregation as an adult, and it was there, in our midst, that she had discerned a call to ministry. As the participants in her ordination service gathered in the church parlor in the buzzing minutes before the service was to begin, a colleague was giving us instructions. When she came to the part about the laying on of hands, I interjected, "And, Pam, just to warn you, in that moment you will feel as if you have the weight of the world on you." The ministers in the room laughed. Then another colleague said, "Pam, it's true. But I am going to do for you what someone did for me at my ordination. As other people put their hands on your head, I am going to put my hand under your chin to support you. I found that made all the difference." Of course. Why hadn't I thought of that? Every minister needs someone to keep her chin up.

When Pam knelt on the chancel steps, all those hands piled on her head and one under her chin, I felt something like the awe that I was not able to experience fully at my own ordination, but had seen in the eyes of those who had surrounded me on that day. With our hands upon Pam's head, flesh upon flesh, all of us were gathered so close that I could hear those around me breathing, like a hushed amen to the prayer that was offered. When the prayer concluded, people took their hands off the candidate and one another. I could see that at that moment, Pam felt so light that she might float up to the ceiling and join the mighty cloud of witnesses who had borne the weight of hands, or placed hands upon another, in a ritual as old as time.

CHAPTER 19

The Calling Church

LILLIAN DANIEL

It seemed to happen rather suddenly. It was as if one day we woke up and suddenly saw they were everywhere, surrounding us. But later we realized they hadn't just sprung up, rootless, out of nowhere. Looking back, we realized that all along, they had been growing in the dirt under our feet, watered by the same water we drank, preparing to pop up their heads, and bask in the sun.

What were these creatures, the source of this sudden infestation? Seminarians, of course, and future seminarians: people discerning a call to ordained ministry. Suddenly, at a church with 225 members, our congregation had eight of them, all needing to meet with pastors and deacons to determine their fitness for the ministry. What was going on? We were a calling church.

One church I know of was well known for producing Presbyterian ministers. "What was the church's secret?" people wondered. After they interviewed staff, pastors, and the candidates for ministry themselves, an extraordinary theme emerged. Each of the young men (and at that time they were all young men) had been approached by the same elderly lady, who told each one of them the same thing: "Young man, I think you have the gifts for ministry." And such was the pastoral authority of that lady that the young men promptly went to seminary, and in good number. So what was going on at that church that produced so many ministers? Someone was asking people to consider the call. They were a calling church.

Sometimes, in our careful attention to the state of seminary education, to the latest classroom texts, or to trends in denominational training, we forget to consider that most important pipeline: the local church. If the local church is not producing future ministers, the seminaries will have little to work with.

Full of saints like that lady, local churches call, rebuke, and recall the explorers, and sometimes do so overlooked by the institutions that accept their recruits. Yet recruitment efforts led by educational institutions can only go so far. The real gift to theological education is that precious calling church that somehow seasonally sprouts up seekers and sojourners, ready to give seminary a try, all because some attentive gardener took the time to say, "I think you have the gifts."

Or in other cases, "Don't quit your day job."

The local church that produces people with a sense of call takes upon itself an enormous responsibility, both to discern the call alongside or to discern a different call to a different path. Smart seminaries do well to weight the call that comes mediated over time through a community of faith more heavily than a mountaintop experience between God and a midlife crisis.

That would have sounded like heresy to some of the first-year divinity students I studied with. They had arrived at seminary in order to find God, skipping the local church altogether. They had had their mountaintop experience and sent straight off for the application forms. In a perverse turn around the ecclesiological Monopoly board, they did not pass go, they did not collect $200, and they did not stop first in a calling community of the church. Instead, they went directly to jail. Or at least to a Master of Divinity program and its accompanying debt load.

In my own case, I had come to seminary against the advice of my church. I had a church; they just didn't think I was called to the ministry. But that was a church I stumbled into late, after college and already planning to attend seminary, turning back to get a visa for a country I already longed to visit. You might say they were not a calling church, but other people from that church went into the ministry. I have since decided they were indeed a calling church who simply did not call me.

The church that called me, when I look back, was the wider church, all the congregations we had been a part of wherever we lived. From the Anglican church in Hong Kong where I sang a solo with the children's choir, and had my first taste of standing up in front of a church full of people and liked it. There was the Baptist church in South Carolina where I joined my cousins for summer vacation Bible school each year, and noted for the first time that theologies could be fascinatingly different.

Mostly, I recall the church I attended in high school, the church where the pastor appointed me to a wider church committee that studied nuclear disarmament. I sat at that long table full of adults, amazed that I had been sent here. But my confidence at the table came from the notion that my church had called and sent me there. It was the same confidence I called upon when my Sunday school class of six-year-olds turned every biblical theme I presented into bathroom humor. I would fall back on the idea that my church believed I could do this work, and so I stepped out to face another fart joke.

Yet by the time I went to seminary and began to discern, through a new denomination, a call to the ministry, I had lost that confidence that coming from a calling church brings. I was unmoored, rejected even, and so I became much like the people who enter seminary education with shaky church grounding. And there I was met, as others have been, by these calling churches located near seminaries, willing to take on the seeking, wandering misfits, and to teach them a thing or two about discerning a call.

There, some seminarians encountered church for the first time in a long while, through an obligatory parish internship. Even then, when the order had been switched about, there were patient churches, ready to reclaim their role as calling bodies.

These churches were working with people whose call had thus far been between the individual and God, a direct two-way walkie-talkie without benefit of ecclesiastical eavesdropping. Faithfully and patiently, these teaching churches taught such interns the value of the conference call.

I remember sitting at the back of the sanctuary, reviewing my notes for my very first seminary-intern sermon. It was to be a mighty word from God that would correct all the hypocrisy, greed, and faithlessness of the local church that was, nonetheless, supporting my education as they had supported that of so many others. As I mustered my courage to sock it to them, I overheard one woman lean across her walker and whisper loudly to her pew mate, "Ah, our new intern is preaching. I see it's time for our annual scolding."

Later, I would pastor a church near that very divinity school, and hear for myself a few "annual scoldings." But more importantly, I would experience the enormous gift that being a teaching church brings. I came to realize that being a teaching church is related to being a calling church. And as to what caused that infestation of future ministers, some of whom ended up at the divinity school down the road, I have a few theories.

First, churches that are geographically fortunate enough to teach future ministers through seminary intern programs have a leg up. They are constantly sending the message to their members that God calls a rich variety of people to the ministry. Rather than week after week projecting one model in the pastor, or perhaps a few models in a staff team, interns stream through the church in all their quirky eccentricity to remind us of the wideness of God's mercy, and the delightfully disturbing idea that any one of us could be called to this work.

Second, calling church members recognize one another's gifts, in all areas. As such, they have the nerve to point out, one disciple to another, that strange set of symptoms that may lead to seminary. In sales terms, calling churches have the courage and the vocabulary to ask for the business and to close the deal.

Third, calling churches house happy ministers. Is it too simple to say that when we look like we're having fun, other people want to join in? A minister who obviously enjoys the call, who is treated lovingly by the church, and who seems to live a satisfying life, helps create a climate of calling. And conversely, churches in which the minister is disrespected, or churches that tolerate ministers who disrespect themselves and the church, may reap what they sow by producing no future leaders, or worse, leaders in their own image. Can a congregation like this still produce gifted leaders for the church? As surely as good things can come out of Nazareth. But it is still worth pointing out the powerful witness of churches and ministers who are having fun, even frolicking.

Perhaps because my own call experience was not neatly received by one church at the moment I felt it, I have a passion for nurturing calls in the congregations I serve. I search for those wise lay leaders who will pull aside the people and tell them they have the gifts for ministry. But at the same time, I know that I must do my part. I tell my own story of calling to this ministry. I speak realistically about disappointment, but, more importantly, about the delights of this work. I used to worry that this would be dull to people, or at worst appear self-centered. Yet in speaking to church leaders over the years, I have learned that the people who love the church the most share my deepest fear: that we will not have the right leaders for the next generation.

Laypeople see the crisis whenever they search for new clergy or struggle with incompetent staff, and we ministers are naïve to think they miss what we too see. So when I shamelessly recruit future ministers from the pulpit, they know that I do not do it for myself, but for my children, who may need to hear a good sermon one day. As calling churches, we band together not to lift up ordained ministry, but to lift up the church that deserves fine leaders.

The local church is more than the seedbed for seminary. It is the place where disciples are nurtured, grown, called, and sent out. Some of them may serve the church in a lay capacity, and calling churches honor these people as much as they honor those disciples who feel called to do this work full time, and for a lifetime.

Some of those Christ followers get sent out to sojourn in the strange land of seminary, and then into ordained ministry. When those leaders are asked to reflect upon their theological formation, I hope they remember their calling churches; the childhood classrooms, seminary internships, adult Bible studies, and youth fellowships through which God beckoned.

I hope that pastors recall their first teachers, the ones who long before a class in practical theology, sat them down and said, "You have the gifts for ministry." Or as I was once told, "If you'd just pull that hair out of your eyes, stand up straight, and speak up, you might just be a preacher."

Perhaps it happened on a confirmation retreat at the campfire. Perhaps it happened over coffee, after a long and difficult deacons meeting. Perhaps it happened on the flight home from the mission trip. Perhaps it happened after they read the scripture in church so beautifully, or painted the basement so patiently. But somewhere, someone in the body of Christ called another forward. They claimed the high calling of being a calling church.

CHAPTER 20

The Twin Impostors

MARTIN B. COPENHAVER

As a boy I always had a rather sunny disposition and, for the most part, the people around me reflected back to me warm affirmation in return. My parents communicated to me, each in his or her own ways, that they loved me as a son and liked me as a person. I was the child they did not plan on having, much younger than my brother and sister, so I grew up as if with four doting parents who enjoyed my company and delighted in my accomplishments. The home in which I grew up was largely free from conflict. I cannot remember a single instance when someone in my family raised his or her voice in anger. I always had a close circle of friends and, although we would often tease each other, we all knew without needing to be told that, for the most part, it was done with affection. So I approached the world with an openness as wide and trusting as the outstretched arms of someone anticipating an embrace.

In other words, I was completely unprepared to deal with the criticism that comes with being a pastor. Nothing like that had ever happened to me before. It had not occurred to me that when you approach the world with outstretched arms, sometimes you do not get an embrace, but rather something more like a kick in the gut.

During my first year of seminary I served a small church in a rural corner of Connecticut. One Sunday, as I was leaving the church, an usher handed me a note that he said had been left in a pew. The envelope had my name written neatly on the front. It was small, the size that might contain a card for a thank-you note. In fact, that was my first thought. This must be a thank-you note expressing appreciation for a sermon or a pastoral visit. So I opened the envelope immediately. On the note card someone had written these words: "Why don't you cut off that beard and be the nice, clean boy you were when you came here?" That was it. Nothing more. It was unsigned. I was stunned. I stood there at the back of the church, unable to move, reading that single sentence over and over. I did not want anyone to see how upset I was, so once I was able to pull my eyes away from the page, I put the envelope in my pocket and headed directly back to school.

Who could have done such a thing? And why? I concluded from the handwriting that the author was, most likely, an older woman. I tried to imagine her going to her desk and sitting down, taking out her stationery (perhaps the same stationery that she used for writing thank-you notes), pausing to choose just the right words to communicate what she had to say, and then scratching those words onto the paper. I pictured her looking at what she had written with satisfaction, closing the card, slipping it into the envelope, and sealing it. Then I pictured her writing my name on the envelope and slipping the envelope into her purse and taking it to worship.

I wondered what she had hoped to accomplish by writing such a note. I wondered if she had any second thoughts about leaving it in the pew. I also wondered if she had any idea that it hurts to receive a note like that, particularly when you are too young to have yet learned how to let such things roll off your back. But most of all, I wondered who wrote it. For a number of weeks, as I led worship, I would survey the congregation with the focus of a detective trying to ferret out a criminal — which I knew was not the best posture from which to lead worship, but I could not help myself. Eventually my preoccupation with the matter faded. Some time after that I shaved off my beard. In a sense, however, I never again would be the "nice clean boy" I was before I got there. There is something about being the object of criticism — even about something as inconsequential as facial hair — that makes you grow up. Or, at least, I think that was true with me.

Nevertheless, given my personality and background, I still do not find it easy to be the object of criticism. Dozens of people may offer a word of appreciation for a sermon, but if one person offers a criticism, that is what I will remember. I will keep going back to it, like the sore tooth that I cannot keep myself from touching with my tongue, even though it hurts each time. I have a file devoted to letters of criticism I have received over the years. When I confessed this to a colleague, she replied, "Oh, I have one of those, too. But I found a way to keep it in the back of the drawer. It's labeled, 'Yucky.'" Most pastors are like this and I wonder why.

Clearly, it has something to do with the kind of work we do. In our preaching we do more than just communicate our ideas, we share ourselves — our experiences, our feelings, our convictions, the things that mean the most to us — in ways that can make us feel extraordinarily vulnerable. Our relationships with parishioners are not like the interactions between other professionals and their clients. Pastoral relationships are lived out in a variety of contexts and settings, usually where there is less formal structure than in relationships between, say, doctors or psychotherapists and those whom they serve. A pastor's relationship with parishioners is lived in the round. So there are more opportunities for one's weaknesses to be exposed and there are always folks around who will not hesitate to do so. Besides, people can have such unrealistically high standards for clergy in every aspect of their ministry, not to mention as human beings. And often people will expect incommensurate things — like that you will have a healthy family life and also that you always will be available to parishioners, or that you will get out to see folks in their homes and places of work and also be in the church office when someone calls. Mixed up with all this are the ways people sometimes can project onto us their feelings about parents, other authority figures, or even God. So there are many reasons why pastors are the object of criticism. Oh, and besides all that, the gospel requires that we take a stand on many matters that will not endear us to others. That is, sometimes when we are criticized it can feel like confirmation that we are doing our job. But those times can seem rare. More often one can feel like the unfortunate fellow with the sign "kick me" pinned to his back.

A number of years ago the moderator of our church told me that he had received a letter that he needed to share with me. Before letting me read the letter, he apologized for bringing it to my attention, but, he explained, he felt that he should at least let me see it. The unsigned typewritten letter was from someone who described himself or herself as "a neighbor" of mine who, apparently, was not a member of the church. The author was writing to complain about the way I walked my dog. He or she described the scene that prompted the letter: "The Reverend stopped and shook the dog several times rather harshly. I was upset seeing this, but not inclined to do anything. Most of us seem to want to look away when bad things happen." Whoever wrote this had it right. It is an accurate description of what I had been taught to do by a dog trainer as a technique for handling an alpha dog who would become dangerously aggressive at the sight of another dog. The author went on to say:

> You might say, what is this compared to Bosnia and the many atrocities that are perpetuated daily. However, I think that here is an opportunity to look at a small "evil" occurrence in our own neighborhood and a need to not let it go unnoticed even if it only involves an animal. The reason for this is that this man is in a position where he is a leader, a model to his congregants. He more than any other person has a responsibility to emulate caring, human behavior, which he so blatantly abused.

The author of the letter then concluded by saying, "I realize that it is a cop out to remain anonymous, however I feel that I have to live with this man in my own neighborhood and frankly I don't trust him."

When I finished reading the letter, I responded with a swirl of reactions:

"This is so unfair! That is what I was taught to do. And I don't even know who to explain this to."

"For crying out loud, only a minister would be subject to this kind of treatment. No one would write to a bank to complain about the way the branch manager walks his dog."

"That bitch!" (Our dog was a female.)

Fortunately, the moderator, a person with whom I have a strong working relationship, did not seem to be taking these complaints too seriously. And, in truth, they did not bother me all that much, either. It helped that whoever took offense at my behavior was not a member of my church and it also helped that I knew the accusations to be quite absurd. So I was able to shrug off the entire episode rather easily.

Some criticism is harder to shrug off because, well, to a certain degree, on occasion, under some circumstances at least, it might be a tad legitimate. Possibly. I have said something insensitive. Or I seemed distracted at just the moment he finally opened his heart. Or I forgot to follow up with her in a time of need. Or I neglected to thank the people who had given so much of their time. Or I made too many changes too soon to the worship service. Or I failed to take up an important social issue. The possibilities are endless. Needless to say, I take full advantage of many of the manifold opportunities to mess up that the ministry provides.

Perhaps more than any other vocation, the ministry has an uncanny ability to expose one's weaknesses, whatever they may be. That is another reason why the ministry is not an easy fit for those who are particularly sensitive to criticism. But, in my experience, it is just such people who are called into the ministry in inordinate numbers. A person who is particularly well tuned in to what the people around him are thinking and feeling is just the sort of person who is likely to be told, "You ought to think about going into the ministry." Indeed, most pastors are the kind of people who care a good deal about what people think. With the exception of one dear friend, a fine pastor, who grew up playing ice hockey in Detroit, most of us are not the sort of people who relish the prospect of mixing it up.

So for someone to thrive — or even survive — in the ministry he or she has to figure out how to handle criticism. Here are some of the things I have learned:

Often it is not about me. I am — and need to be — a relatively safe place for people to bring their disappointment, or grief, or anger, even when I am not the original source of that emotion.

Sometimes it is about me. When criticism seems well founded, usually I am grateful for the chance to clarify, or to apologize, or to reconcile. Sometimes the voice of criticism is the voice of the Holy Spirit, speaking the truth, seeking to correct. But even when the criticism is well founded, that does not make it easy to hear. In fact, legitimate criticism may be the most difficult to hear because it cannot be as easily dismissed.

I let myself value the opinion of some people more than others. One way to sort this out is to ask myself, "Would I seek out this person's opinion?" If not, then why would I give it much weight? One minister of my acquaintance retired early because he was weighed down by his critics. Reflecting on his decision with the perspective that a bit of distance and a few years can bring, he said ruefully, "It was only when it was too late that I realized that I had spent all that time listening to the wrong people."

That is one reason why I put little stock in anonymous criticism. Does it come from a crank or from someone whose opinion I have learned to value? Since I don't know the source, I don't know how to assess it. In response to one form of anonymous criticism — variations on, "I know many people who feel this way" — I have learned to say, "Please tell them that I would be very willing to hear from them. But I don't know how to evaluate opinions that are offered anonymously." Then, too, when the criticism is anonymous, you don't know to whom you need to apologize or with whom you need to be reconciled.

I have learned that there are times when I am better able to receive criticism (like say, between 1:00 and 1:30 on Tuesday afternoon), and there are other times when it is more difficult. I relate to the experience of one pastoral colleague who says that, immediately after preaching and leading worship, she feels as if she doesn't have any skin on. Obviously that is not the best state in which to receive criticism. So, like Scarlett O'Hara, she says to herself, "I'll think about it tomorrow." She has learned that by the next day she will be more rested and she will have a new — even if still not thick — layer of skin and so she will be better able to hear the criticism.

Pastors not only receive criticism, of course. We also receive praise. Praise can play as prominent a role as criticism does in shaping one's ministry. In fact, for many people, praise played a role in their initial call to ministry. After leading a worship service, a young person is told, "Your words were so beautiful and wise. You should think of being a minister." Or, someone is told, "You are a terrific listener. Have you thought of going to seminary?"

Most ministers continue to receive a lot of praise. In fact, pastors are frequently praised for doing things that are just not all that remarkable — like showing up, for instance. As a pastor, if you just show up in the right place — say, at someone's side during a time of need or at a school event where a young person from the church is performing or playing — that can be enough to prompt abundant thanks and even praise. Another example: At a reception following a funeral, I was standing next to a friend, a pastor who had officiated at the service. One person who had attended the service offered lavish praise for how my friend was able to talk about the deceased "as if you knew her," even though, as he indicated in the service, they had never met. When the person offering the praise moved on, my friend turned to me and said with a smile, "Please don't tell anyone." He didn't finish the sentence. He didn't have to. As a pastor, I knew how it ended: "Please don't tell anyone that it is just not that difficult, if you ask a few questions and listen carefully."

Everyone likes to be praised, at least every once in a while. But beware the pastor who needs too much praise.

When I was a young boy, my mother would hold a Christmas tea at our home for the Women's Fellowship of the church. I always liked the attention that was poured over me on such occasions. Then one year — I was about five years old at the time — one of the ladies asked if I would sing a song. I did not have one prepared but, of course, I did not let that stop me. I sang "Away in a Manger," before an audience hushed with admiration. I don't know if I sang it well. I just know that they loved it. They were full of praise. I was proud.

The next holiday season, I was prepared. I was ready with "Away in a Manger," and "Silent Night" would be my encore. During the Christmas tea, I walked through our home, greeting the ladies, waiting for the invitation to sing. I walked through those rooms many times, with the confident expectation of a fisherman trolling through waters that had always rewarded him in the past. But the request never came. Why didn't they ask me to sing? I did not know. I just knew that I missed the praise.

When I started out in ministry, I think I was a lot like that, wanting and needing praise. In my own way, I probably signaled my need for praise as unmistakably as the acrobat who, after finishing a maneuver, thrusts his arms high over his head, palms open, smiles to the crowd and says, "Ta-da!" I imagine that, at times, I received compliments with an eagerness that was a little too obvious. At other times, I probably brushed aside compliments with what might seem like an "aw-shucks" humility ("Really, you think so? I wasn't sure that I got it right."), but was, in reality, a pitch for more praise.

Early on I used to prize the compliments I received, as if they were glittering gifts. These days I am more likely to question their value. Now when someone says something like, "That was a wonderful sermon," I want to hold on to their hand for an extra moment and ask, "Yes, but what did it do?" I remember one of my seminary professors saying, "We have too many preachers who want to hear their parishioners say, 'What a great preacher we have,' and not enough who long to hear them say, 'What a great God we have.'" I think I'm finally getting it.

A while back I received a letter on business stationery from a parishioner I deeply respect, a soft-spoken man of sagacity and integrity. "Dear Martin," he wrote, "As I currently struggle with the business issues related to my firm, I realize how important my faith has become to me during my time at Village Church. Hence, this is a letter to thank you for being my pastor." He went on to enumerate the various ministries of the church that had helped him grow in his faith. Then he asked, "So what do these activities have to do with my faith journey? A great deal. Each of the activities in which I participated challenged me to reflect upon my beliefs, to have conversations with others about faith, and have caused me to more overtly proclaim the Gospel of Jesus Christ." It was a letter of praise, of course, but the object of that praise was not his pastor, but his God. This letter was his testimony. When I finished the letter, I stared at it, not exactly reading it, for a long while, before putting it down. My response was something like awe. When I got home, I showed this letter to my wife. She said, "Be sure to keep this. You work your whole life to get one letter like this." And she was right, of course. That letter gets its own file, filed in the front of the drawer, under "A Letter of Encouragement," to be re-read whenever I begin to wonder why I accepted the call to ministry or forget what it is really about.

It is striking, and something of an irony, that I am not free from the need for praise in general. If, for instance, I have given a loved one a gift, I will ask, without shame, "Do you like it? Do you really?" If I have just cooked a meal, after my guests have eaten a few bites, I will look around the table, as if to say, "Give me some love here, people!" (and if they are good friends, I might actually say it). In those times, and others I'm sure, I can still resemble the boy who just sang "Away in a Manger" for the Women's Fellowship Christmas tea. So why do I need, and sometimes shamelessly seek, praise for doing these things and no longer need or seek as much praise for what I do as a pastor? The only way to assess whether a gift is a success is if the person receiving the gift likes it. There is no other criterion. If I have prepared a meal and one of my guests says, "This tastes disgusting," I will not respond, "Well, that's not the point," because the other person's pleasure precisely is the point. That is how a meal is to be judged. By contrast, in ministry, the ultimate object is not to do those things that will please other people and prompt their praise. The object of ministry is to be both faithful and effective in carrying out one's pastoral tasks, regardless of whether one is praised for doing so.

So I no longer need as much praise for what I do as a pastor. Perhaps that is because through the years I have become more confident in my gifts. But I think it is also because now I am clearer that this ministry business is not about me. More often now I feel like the cello that knows that it cannot accept much praise for a sonata. After all, I don't make the music. I am just the instrument. Then, too, now that there are more years in ministry behind me than in front of me, it no longer seems enough that people would think well of me. Not nearly enough.

I have become convinced that, in the ministry, it is important not to take either the criticism or the praise too seriously. In fact, that may be the only way to survive. If you take the criticism too seriously, you can feel as if you are being "nibbled to death by ducks," as one person has put it. Or you will be only as happy as your most unhappy parishioner. Or you will avoid speaking the truth. Or you will try to please everyone, which — news flash! — has been found to be impossible.

If you take the praise too seriously, you may find yourself doing more of whatever gets you praise, regardless of whether it is what you need to do to be a faithful and effective pastor. Praise may be a fitting reward, but it is a misleading motivator. And if you take praise too seriously, you are putting yourself in danger of forgetting this key tenet of ministry: it is not about you.

Not taking criticism or praise too seriously reflects a certain paradox of ministry. The ministry requires that one care deeply about God's people, including what they think. Otherwise, why would one go into this work? At the same time, the ministry also requires that one not care too much about God's people, particularly what they think. Otherwise, how can one survive in this work?

For the pastor, criticism and praise are twin impostors. Both are to be approached warily, because both can deceive and both can mislead.

So what did you think of this chapter? Tell me honestly. And give me some love here.

CHAPTER 21

Married to the Minister

Lillian Daniel

"You can be a journalist. Just don't marry one." These were words I heard over and over again in my childhood. My mother, who was married to a journalist, spoke them.

In her mind, she was being playful and a feminist all at once. In her day, it was assumed that the man would be the journalist, particularly among the foreign war correspondents who made up our expatriate world. Admittedly there were a few women reporters in our social circle, and in fact my mother would go on to do journalistic work herself. But back then we all knew that while she had a series of jobs, my father had a career. And he was the journalist.

So she was urging me to take the man's role, to not let my ambitions be limited to the choice of a husband, to not hitch my wagon to someone else's. She was urging me to do what perhaps she wished she had done, to have more agency.

But when she said, "You can be a journalist. Just don't marry one," she was not only telling me about my own life. She was telling me about hers. She was telling me that it was hard to be married to a journalist. And even if she had not said it as often as she did, from everything I saw, I knew it was true.

There were the long hours my father worked, his trips in and out of war zones, the constant socializing that was also work, and the sense of being on call for the story at every hour of every day.

I recall a quiet family vacation in Tennessee when my father jumped up from his father's soft recliner in front of the television news and ran to the phone. A convict had escaped from a nearby prison, and he was calling the local bureau to see if they needed him to cover the story. He was the foreign editor of the entire organization at the time. This local story was hardly his job. But wherever he was, the story seemed to be more compelling than everything else.

"You can be a journalist. Just don't marry one." My mother's words stayed with me when tempers rose around our house. In the aftermath of another marital spat, they rang in the frosty silence left behind a slammed door as he left to follow his call to pursue a story or perhaps just to escape from the more dramatic story at home. That story ended in divorce, and a daughter who wanted her own life to be different.

So it was with surprise that I heard myself saying to a little girl in my church, "You can be a minister. Just don't marry one." And I wondered where it came from.

In this case, I meant it as a compliment to my own husband, who was standing nearby. Perhaps I had been short-tempered, as I sometimes am on Sunday mornings, fueled by the adrenaline of a strong sermon or the anxiety of a weak one. Nevertheless, my comment to the girl was really a comment to my husband, my way of saying that I know it is not always easy to be married to a minister.

Yet, having recognized that, I must also confess that I cannot imagine being a minister without him. My husband Lou and I met before seminary. He has watched me study for law school tests when I wanted to drop out of divinity school. He has attended church interviews with me, knowing he was being watched as closely as I was. He has read drafts of sermons, drafts of newsletters, and even drafts of funeral bulletins. And it was he who discovered the denomination to which we now belong. I am certain that I would not be a minister today if it were not for Lou, who saw gifts in me when I could not see them, and who loved the church at times when I could not.

Lou is a PK, but not a preacher's kid in the usual sense. His father was the dean and later the president of a Presbyterian seminary. The language of church and theology were his native tongues. But by the time I met Lou, when he was in his early twenties, he was sick of church, church talk, and church people, and ready to enjoy a little time away from that world.

After a few months of serious dating, I finally got up the courage to tell him I was planning to go to divinity school. I worried about announcing this, well aware that it was not the most glamorous of plans. "All right, God, I give up," he said. "I'll come back to church."

His seemingly perfect response was later mediated by reality, as I later noted that he had said he would come back to church, but had not specified which church. In those early days, I had been dragging him to high-church Episcopal services. There was tension on those Sunday mornings. This was not his church, and he knew it.

Usually a healthy runner, in church Lou seemed to develop all sorts of physical ailments. He fell to his knees too late and with a groan, and coughed and hacked as the incense came by. He critiqued the homilies the whole way home. He attended on the grounds that it was more important to me than it was to him, but it came with a certain malicious obedience.

Once he suspected that I too was restless with our arrangement, he began to investigate. We had long talked about the idea of finding a church home that would be new to both of us, but what I really had in mind was a church that was new to him. It never occurred to me that there was another church for me than the one I had been raised in. I figured as long as I did nothing, we could stay where we were and he would eventually come around. I have since come to learn this is not an uncommon assumption among seminarians in love.

By then he was working as a labor union organizer. He wanted a church with a commitment to justice, and he found it in a local United Church of Christ congregation, where the minister joined Lou's union workers on the picket lines. But I, now a divinity school student and the resident expert on religion, refused to go. I had my reasons.

"Why won't you at least *visit* one of these churches?" he asked.

"Because I've heard they have tacky worship," I explained. And today I lead such a church.

I think our callings do not always come to us directly. They can come to us through other people, and sometimes, remarkably enough, through our spouses.

I would have blanched at that idea when I was younger. My mother's words haunting me, I would have said that we each have our own callings, and to hitch our calling to another person's is just another way of giving up. But eighteen years of marriage has humbled me out of such certainty. These days, as I look back upon the adventures of both ministry and marriage, I find that for me they have become like strings in a rope, almost impossible to unravel, for better or worse.

I am aware that for many clergy the role of spouse is not simply one of support and affirmation. I know that many clergy are married to people they love but with whom they do not share a love of the church. I am aware that many who marry clergy begin by loving the church and end up hating it. I do not minimize these experiences. I have at times shared some of them.

The minister's wife has long struggled around issues of role. In the old days, she was expected to play the organ, teach Sunday school, and be another staff person around the church. I know of ministries that would have failed were it not for the diplomatic skills of the minister's wife. I know of churches that would have gone under had it not been for her unpaid service. But as we honor that role and service, we must recognize that today clergy couples do not, and should not, represent a two-for-one deal.

The clergy husband, a relatively new character on the religious scene, gets a break from some of that. If there are role expectations, they are so new as to have less power. In some ways, the clergy husband gets treated like a man who does something generous yet against gender type. Like the dad who shows up at school to volunteer, surrounded by volunteer mothers, he stands out and receives special attention for doing what women have done for years.

So while a clergy wife misses church and people wonder where she is, the clergy husband shows up and hears, "How wonderful that you are so supportive." When a clergy wife chooses not to participate in a role that previous clergy wives have enjoyed, she runs the risk of disappointing the church. The clergy husband seems to get to choose. Given that most people do not know what to expect of a clergy husband, any interest he has in any aspect of the church is greeted with delight. "Your husband is really something," they tell me over and over again.

And then there are cases of two ministers being married to each other and pastoring different churches. I know a couple like this. When they were hired, both churches understood that they would see little of their pastor's spouse, for the most obvious of reasons. Both churches continue to honor this and seem to get it. However, when the female minister's husband shows up for a special event at her church, he is greeted like a rock star, with comments like, "How wonderful you could make it. We know you must be so busy!" And when the male minister's wife attends an event at his church, the members take on the air of, "Well, it's about time," or "Finally . . . we were beginning to wonder if you existed." It strikes me that two-clergy couples have the greatest of challenges, of holding both the role of minister and minister's spouse all at once. But at least they both understand one another's worlds.

In most clergy families, though, the minister partners with what I have come to call a "civilian," a term that speaks to the foreignness of the clergy role in our society, sometimes even foreign to the spouse. I have heard from many clergy friends that they find themselves unable to convey the wonderful oddness of this role to their spouses, unable to explain the life in a compelling enough way. "So just don't answer the phone," the spouse will say during dinner, only to sit angry and confused as her husband interrupts yet another meal to respond to the ring. "You're not that important, you know," she mutters to a husband who is conversing with somebody else.

Over the years, the tension in the family grows, until the pastor, who was once dashing out of the house to tend to church emergencies, is now dashing out of the house to avoid the emergency at home. If we are to speak honestly about the pressures that church work can put on a family, we must also admit that some pastors hide out in their church work rather than deal with the hurting people at home.

There are families in which the roles of clergy and spouse have been negotiated so poorly that the struggles within the marriage get passed down to children, who end up not wanting to enter a church as adults. For these families, the church has become a jealous mistress, and what family member would delight in spending quality time with their parent's mistress?

The future of church leadership depends upon us looking honestly at this issue. Clergy can be single or married. But if they are married, we must not, in our desire to be politically sensitive and inclusive, pretend that these marriages play no role in the calling. To look at ministry without considering the role of minister's spouse ignores a factor that could make or break a pastor's leadership. And to turn a blind eye to the struggles of the clergy spouse may ensure a future generation that resents and abandons the church.

One of the great struggles for clergy couples is that our marriages are so public. Like it or not, the clergy spouse is always being watched. Our smallest interactions, from who is driving the children home from church to where the potluck dish was lost, all take place onstage. Families all around the parish hall could be having similar moments, but ours will be the most closely observed.

Ministers are used to this scrutiny, but clergy spouses move in and out of that spotlight. In their daily lives or at work they are treated one way, and then at church they find themselves being paid attention to in a different way. Given that they move back and forth, they are not always aware of the dynamics that the minister knows inside and out.

My husband claims to have a permanent bruise on his foot from all the times I have kicked him under the table for saying something I deemed inappropriate. He may refer to something I consider private about me, himself, or another member of the church, and my foot flies out like a heat-seeking missile bent on destruction. (My theory being that sometimes you have to blow a thing up to save it.)

The next morning we parse it all out and review the conversation.

Often he remains baffled at my reaction, thinking that I have been oversensitive, or too concerned about what others think. He may comment that I have lost my edge, which infuriates me because it's what I worry about too.

But I will be just as baffled that he does not see it my way. Could he not read the confused expressions on their faces? Does he not recall the church conflict that arose out of just this sort of misunderstanding?

Sometimes I have to remind myself that most people get to attend church events without getting kicked by the minister. They get to say what pops into their head. Being married to me changes the way my spouse gets to experience his community of faith, and not always for the better. So I am grateful that despite our differing analyses the morning after, when I give him that look, or that kick, he usually yields to my instincts, and stops telling the story. He changes the way he acts because he is the minister's spouse.

His swearing is another issue entirely.

Lou works in the labor movement. I work in the church. You can see where this is going.

I learned the hard way that it is impossible to be a swear-word user on a part-time basis. Back in seminary, I thought I could pull it off. I swore with my divinity school friends (yes, we did, and yes, they still do) but in my work in local churches I was careful to choose my words more carefully. That is, until, with a car full of youth fellowship members, I accidentally ran a stop sign. As I swerved to avoid a crash, I yelled out . . . well, you can imagine. From that point on, the kids called me Pastor Potty Mouth, and I deserved it.

So I tried to stop using foul language in general, so that when the brick fell on my foot at church the wrong word would not come out. And that works pretty well for me.

But if Lou *didn't* use salty language in his work world, it would appear odd. So he is still struggling to be bilingual, a curser during the week, and a non-curser at church and home. You can imagine how well that works. When Lou's conversation at a church party heats up, so does his language. And I have learned to live with it.

In clergy marriages, we have to pick our battles. Where will we ask our spouses to yield to our standards and when do we rejoice in letting them be themselves? While we might want to say that we want our spouses to be themselves, most of us live in that more complicated middle ground. I have seen clergy couples for whom the weight of expectation from the minister reduced the spouse to a bland and bored partner, someone who dreaded church events because he could not be himself, and therefore could never have any fun. I have heard clergy spouses say that all the expectations of the role prevent them from even worshiping. On the other hand, I have seen cases in which the clergy spouse is the one who applies the hardest standards to himself, trying to be perfect but ending up isolated, a perfect clergy spouse with no real friends in the church.

I hold out hope that the clergy husbands of the world may be making the church a better place for the clergy wives. I pray that this new breed of spouse will be able to love the church on his own terms, and to find there a real worshiping community as opposed to an unpaid part-time job. I pray that all our spouses will be able to follow their own calls to volunteer or not to volunteer, and that they will make friendships that are deeper than a role or a job.

I am aware that in some ways my husband is actually not a new breed of clergy spouse. After all, he participates on Sunday mornings. He is a great support to me in my work. But he and I have learned many things the hard way — for example, that I may not accept invitations or volunteer requests on his behalf. We have learned that he should not serve on church committees. We have learned that he should not be asked to critique sermons, either before or after. While some clergy spouses offer helpful sermon feedback lovingly received by the pastor, we have learned that in our relationship the question, "How did you like the sermon?" is a lot like the question, "Does this dress make me look fat?" There is only one good answer and it may or may not be truthful.

There are times when Lou and I struggle with the fact that we both have demanding and potentially draining jobs. In both of our work settings, most of our colleagues have couple relationships in which one career takes precedence over the other. In some cases, one spouse may work part-time or not at all. We both have noted that our colleagues, either other ministers or union organizers, for the most part do not have spouses that work as many hours as they do. So by putting together two equally demanding careers, both of which could use the support of a spouse with more free time, we hit tensions along the way in our family life.

When I was asked to preach at my denomination's national gathering, I simply assumed that the whole family would attend. The event was to take place at a convention center in Minneapolis, during the summer. In the year that led up to the big event, the idea of speaking in front of five thousand people grew both more exciting and more nerve-wracking. It never occurred to me that I would be there without Lou, but it turned out he had to work toward an impending strike, so he and the children stayed home.

My dear father attended in his stead, quite ill, armed with a walker, a sleep machine, multiple medications, and boundless enthusiasm. His frailty and determination made me miss my husband's presence all the more.

After the sermon, as I wandered the convention center, everywhere I went people asked after my husband and children and wondered if they were proud of me. I felt sad and embarrassed by their absence. It seemed pathetic to say that they had watched it streamed over the Internet on the computer back in our dining room. I avoided answering such questions, allowing people to think he was there when he was not. But the fact was that the big event in my professional life did not trump the demands of his. It remains a painful memory for both Lou and me to this day. We both wish it could have been different. In cases like this, it seems impossible to make the right call.

Indeed, one of the thorniest issues for clergy couples is the sense of call, not just in small instances but in big ones. When a minister considers a call to a new church, she is also considering a new church home and perhaps a new location for her family. The minister may feel called. (Or in appointment systems she may simply be sent to a new ministry setting. Two-career couples are particularly strained in those appointment systems, and the church is losing gifted pastors because of it.) But the spouse plays a role in this process, too. Lou has come to every serious job interview I have ever had. This would be preposterous for a teacher, a plumber, or a surgeon, but in our tradition, when the search process between a church and a candidate gets serious, they bring out the couple to interview and spend a weekend driving around the community, looking at schools, houses, and parks. On these weekends the spouse is under as much scrutiny as the pastor, no matter what anybody says.

Lou has spent many a car ride being told about the sports leagues of a given community, or the joys of a particular park, well aware that this may become our new home. When the cell phone rings with a call from the children, he picks it up, dealing with a medical issue hundreds of miles away so that I can make small talk with a potential employer, all the while wondering what he is dealing with back home, but trying to give the impression of total attention to the church. This is a strange way to look for a job, and certainly not how he looks for one in his field.

And I in turn look at how these church people treat him. For God doesn't call one member of the family to happiness and fulfillment and leave the others to be miserable.

Many clergy families can be broken apart by a new call that only the minister feels. I have heard of marriages that have ended after such a time. In one case, looking back, the spouse said, "At our old church we were so happy, but after we moved, it all changed." Did the church end the marriage? I would not like to assign such blame to a congregation. But accepting a call that only honors one person can do great damage. A fresh set of demands, the loss of friends, a new community with different expectations — all these just pile up on top of a spouse's resentment. In cases where the spouse has noticed that his wife's call to the church is somehow more important than everyone else's, that resentment may spread to the church.

Even the most considerate of couples will have times when they perceive the call differently. When Lou had an opportunity to take a job down South, the two of us went to check it out. I suppose it was all those church interviews that made this seem like a natural way to do things. I did not want to move at all, but I also knew that to rule this opportunity out would damage our marriage. I had to be open to God's call in his life.

As that weekend unfolded, it was obvious that Lou could make a great difference in this job. But it also became clearer and clearer that there would be no work for me in this part of the country. Over dinner, he suddenly developed some kind of food poisoning that left him weak and incapacitated. As the hours of the wretched illness took their toll, he finally said, "I don't think God would be calling me to go somewhere where you could not be a minister." I look back upon that as one of the most loving things anyone has ever said to me. These were not sentimental words of affection, just the straightforward statement of someone who held me and my calling dear.

But I also worried about what he was giving up. I even wondered if he really did have food poisoning, or if this was a gut-splitting physical reaction to the loss of a long-held dream. In a marriage, these deep disappointments make for resentment, and so they should probably be shared equally.

Shortly after that trip, I realized that while I didn't want to move, I had to. I didn't have to move to a place where there was no work for me in my field, but I also could not insist upon staying somewhere where he was unhappy. So I agreed, very reluctantly, to look elsewhere, in fits and starts, and in between many late-night you're-ruining-my-life arguments.

Later that year, at a church interview in a very wealthy community, the search committee members wined and dined us. They asked Lou about his upbringing, his schooling, and his work. He answered the questions with good humor, but the conversation only continued around the two subjects of his schooling and upbringing. Clearly his work as a union organizer was not something they wanted to talk about. I tried to imagine my husband, whose work is his passion, living in a community where no one wanted to hear about it. I couldn't, and we did not end up there. To be honest, though, that was because they did not choose me. So even now I am left with the lingering question: would I have had the good sense to say no to them? I hope I would have. But I imagine the decision would have come hard and with my own bout of "food poisoning."

At the church I currently serve, the search committee took us on a similar weekend jaunt around the community. At the dinners and brunches of that exhausting weekend, I observed Lou. His hands were waving as he spoke, a sign that he was talking about the things he cares about. Some people challenged him on the subject of unions, but he enjoys that. I heard him putting forth his strong political views in a community that I suspected did not share them. But he was being himself. There would be no kicking Lou under the table on that important discernment weekend.

The search committee seemed to understand that as well. In debating with Lou, they were also being themselves. We were not pretending to be perfect. We were not pretending that we were all of one mind. When that happens in the midst of a job interview, you begin to suspect that this really might be the body of Christ.

Today, when little children come up to me and ask me about the ministry, I will not tell them again, "You can be a minister, just don't marry one." Instead I will pray that their callings will lead them to be themselves in all their glory.

Should they choose a partner one day who follows this particular odd and wondrous calling, I might warn them that it will not be easy. But I also hope they will not be scared away. We clergy need all the help we can get.

CHAPTER 22

Married to a Pagan

Martin B. Copenhaver

Karen caught my eye early in our freshman year of college, and no wonder: she had long dark hair, blue eyes that cannot be described without resorting to clichés, long eyelashes, high cheekbones, and lovely fair skin. In short, she was, and still is, beautiful. I have since learned that compliments about her looks don't mean much, if anything, to her. She would much rather be told that she is intelligent or funny. If I had been attentive in college, I would have been able to guess that. Even then she carried herself with an unselfconsciousness that is rare in people who are beautiful.

Perhaps as much as her looks, I was taken with her speaking voice, which is surprisingly deep, and a bit husky, reminiscent of Lauren Bacall's voice, but without the world-weariness. I have always been particularly sensitive to voices. In the fall of our freshman year, Karen was in a one-act Chekhov play, her only foray into acting. During many of the rehearsals, I would sit in the back of the theatre just to listen to her voice and to watch her move across the stage in a long flowing dress the color of a red rose.

During the early years of college we were both "seriously dating" other people, to use the nomenclature of the time. Karen and I were friends during those early college years, although we never spent much time together. We went on our first date early in our senior year, after both of us found ourselves single at the same time. Yet later I learned that, when Karen returned to her dorm after that first date and her friends asked her how it went, she replied, "It was great. But the relationship isn't going anywhere. He's going to be a minister."

In the days that followed, we took many long walks and talked late into the night. I was reveling in the company of a young woman of warmth, intelligence, and substance. I felt completely at ease with her. In truth, she didn't seem to mind that I was going to be a minister. She would have had reason to, however, because her own relationship to religion had been quite complicated. Her mother is Irish and was Catholic. In her early years, Karen attended a Catholic church and had her First Communion there. Then her mother read an exposé on the financial operations of the Vatican that greatly disturbed her. She left the church, taking her five children with her, and none of them ever went back.

When Karen was in high school she began to attend an independent "Bible" church with a friend and eventually became quite involved. Over time, however, she became disillusioned when she began to learn that many of those who had talked about their faith with such fundamentalist certainty were not nearly so certain after all. At the time, Karen's own faith was still a tender shoot, so she relied on the certainty of others, and even then she insisted on integrity in matters of religious faith. She left that church before heading off to college, so when I met her she was without any active religious affiliation.

Karen's own unsettling experiences with religion did not prevent her from being drawn to religious people. Her best high school friend had always talked about wanting to be a priest. She loved and greatly admired her aunt, who is a nun. So I think there were ways in which Karen actually was intrigued by me, in part, because I planned to be a minister. She was not dismissive of religious faith. In fact, she talked about wanting to have a faith that was not inherited or based on the faith of others, but her own. And I sensed, or perhaps wanted to sense, a strong religious yearning within her. So I think I assumed that her faith would grow over time. I thought she had just had bad experiences in the "wrong" kinds of churches.

So, ten intense and joyful days after that first date, I said to Karen: "You know, I think you're perfect for me, and we ought to talk about getting married." Karen laughed. She did not say a word in response. It was a long time before she was able to come up with anything remotely like a response to my sudden — and, to her, premature — declaration. Months later, she finally said, "You know, I think I might be in danger of falling in love with you." Now it was my turn to laugh. I said, "Okay, let's count the qualifications in that statement. It's not, 'I think I am falling in love with you.' It's not, 'I might be falling in love with you,' or, 'I am in danger of falling in love with you.' No, it's, 'I think' — one — 'I might be' — two — 'in danger' — three — 'of falling in love with you.' You're really taking a wild step here." Then we laughed together.

Somewhere along the line, when we talked about the future, it was simply assumed that we would be together. After graduation, I went off to divinity school in Connecticut and she stayed in Pennsylvania to go to law school. During that first year after college, we got engaged. When Karen visited me, she would go to worship at the church I was serving on weekends and, if she were there midweek, she would join my prayer group at the divinity school. And, during those years, the two of us would sometimes pray together.

We were two years into our graduate studies when we got married and moved to Connecticut. Karen continued in law school and I continued to prepare for the ministry. Karen became quite involved in the church I was serving as an intern and volunteered to teach a fourth-grade Sunday school class. She was horrified, however, when the first lesson in the curriculum was on the stoning of Stephen and asked, "How am I supposed to teach that terrible story as if it has some meaning for fourth-grade children? Or for anyone?" She decided that it would be better for her to work with younger children, whose classes were much less focused on content and where she was less likely to have to teach things she didn't believe in.

In anticipation of our first New Year's as husband and wife, we bought an elegantly bound book with blank pages. We intended to start a new family tradition. Each year we would pause and look back at the year just past and write down our "thanksgivings." Then we would look ahead and write down our "covenants" for the coming year, things that we would resolve to do with the help of God and one another. For this, our first year, the lists were long, written in Karen's handwriting. Under thanksgivings, in addition to "our marriage," "our health," the birth of a nephew, and things like that, we offered thanks for "our church," and "Karen's growing faith."

Under covenants, the first thing on the list is, "Pray and read the Bible more together." Today I can't remember what it was like to put that list together, so I don't know this: Did I just jump in right away and make this suggestion and Karen simply wrote down my words? These were supposed to be things to which both of us were committed, so perhaps those words actually expressed her own intention at the time. Or perhaps it was more like a wish. Or perhaps she did not think that this was the time to start articulating her hesitations and questions. Anyway, there were other things on the list along the same lines. We covenanted to "giving more time and money to the church," and to "making decisions in a more composed manner, praying about our decisions." Today, I read these lists as if they are historical artifacts, almost as if they were written by and about other people. As wistful as it makes me to read them now, I am also grateful that they exist. It reassures me that, no, I hadn't just imagined that these are the kinds of things we talked about at the time.

It may be telling that that was the only year we followed our "new family tradition" of writing thanksgivings and covenants. In any case, during the following year or so, Karen began to lean more strongly toward the conclusion that, even if she believed in some kind of God, she could not accept basic Christian teachings. The faith claims that Christians make about Jesus — about him being the Son of God, or at least something more than just a wise teacher — seemed quite unbelievable to her. The Bible is just another book, she began to conclude, and so cannot be granted any particular authority and, in fact, in some ways it is dangerous to do so. She wondered whether she could continue to attend church. Initially, this stirred a bit of panic in me. I would tell her to be patient and not to draw too many firm conclusions, that the church is a good place to bring your questions as well as your convictions. I also told her that many people in the church have the same kinds of questions. But she was also clear that her experience of church was different from other people's. She was not just Karen. She was the minister's wife. She was concerned — and, in some instances, rightly — that people assumed all sorts of things about what she believed or did not believe, because she was married to me. This was especially problematic for Karen, because integrity is the characteristic she most admires in other people and most wants to have reflected in her own life. So if she seemed to be affirming something — perhaps just by her presence in the church — that she could not affirm, it was particularly uncomfortable for her.

About a year after that first New Year's, I had an interview for the position of senior minister of First Congregational Church in Burlington, Vermont. Karen accompanied me as we met the members of the search committee, as they hosted us over meals and gave us a tour of the city. When it came time for the formal interview, there was something of a logistical glitch. No plans had been made for where Karen would be during that time, so the chair of the committee said, "So, Karen, would you be willing to sit in on the interview?" This is not something we anticipated but, after we exchanged a quick look, she readily agreed.

As the interview was winding down, the president of the congregation turned to Karen and said, "Karen, we probably should ask you one question: What do you see as the role of the minister's wife?" Uh-oh. Not only did this question tread on a delicate matter in our still-young marriage, we were also aware that the wife of the previous senior minister had been extremely active in the life of the congregation and we thought that there was a good chance that they might expect the same of Karen.

So for the first time in the interview, I was more than a little bit nervous. Karen seemed perfectly calm. I have since learned that when Karen is particularly nervous, she comes across as even more poised than usual. With a smile, she said, "Well, thank you for asking." And then she went on to describe some of the demands of the ministry, which she had seen firsthand, and how important it is to have a supportive presence at home. Then she concluded, "So I would say that the role of the minister's wife is to be a good wife to the minister." As she was talking, I was trying unsuccessfully to read the still countenances of the Vermonters around the table. When she finished, the president said, "Well that's good, because we don't have any special expectations, either." Whew. The next day they called and asked if I would become their new minister.

It has been only as the years have unfolded that I have learned from Karen how reluctant she was to make that move. Her response in the interview had been smooth, but there was a lot that was churning underneath. She loved me, but she had real misgivings about how she could inhabit the role of minister's wife. And, particularly, she worried about letting me down, that I would want something or someone she is not, and that she would have to live with my disappointment. She would say, "I think you should have married a good Christian girl." And I would say in response, "I didn't want to marry a good Christian girl. I wanted to marry you."

My mother had been the minister's wife in the more traditional mode. She was very active in the life of the congregations my father served. This came quite naturally to her, in large part because she was the daughter of two ministers and the sister of five ministers. That is, as the minister's wife, my mother was swimming in familiar waters. But she was also temperamentally suited to the role and seemed to delight in it. For instance, I have not known anyone who could work a fellowship hour after worship like my mother could. She would move effortlessly through a group, lighting up one face after another as she went, as if she were turning on lamps in a darkened house. Sunday dinner after worship always included conversation between my parents about what had happened at church that morning. They would reflect together on how the sermon went, whether the music was particularly good, who was there, what news was garnered about folks in the congregation. They were full partners in this work. It is telling that when I meet parishioners from the churches my father once served, often they are as eager to share their memories of my mother as they are to share their memories of my father.

If what I wanted was, in the words of the old song, "a gal just like the gal that married dear old Dad," we were going to be in trouble. But, thankfully, what I wanted was Karen. So we set out to try to find a different way of being minister and minister's spouse. It was uncharted territory for both of us. We had no models to work from.

During the years we were in Burlington, Karen did attend worship, first to be supportive of me, and then, when our children were born, to support our children's participation in the church. But there were some dicey situations along the way. When it came time for our children to be baptized, we faced a problem. Karen was willing to have our children baptized, but she did not feel able to make the public declarations of faith that parents are asked to make as part of our baptism liturgy. Since I was the officiating minister for the baptisms, however, I was able to craft the service in such a way that, instead of both of us responding to questions normally asked of parents, I was able to make statements about our commitment to raise our children as Christians. Those statements were worded so carefully that I don't think anyone in the congregation could tell that Karen avoided making any faith statements, spoken or implied, in the liturgy. I think both of us felt a bit compromised by how we handled the situation, but perhaps that is inevitable when what you have to come up with is, indeed, a compromise.

When our children were young, I wanted to find a family grace. The challenge was finding one we could all say together. Then our daughter Alanna rescued us by coming home with a grace she had learned in pre-school: "Blessings on the blossoms, blessings on the fruit, blessings on the leaves and stems, and blessings on the root." Alanna couldn't wait to teach us the grace. "Lovely," I told her, "just perfect." From then on we said that grace every night.

In the kitchen after dinner on the night Alanna first taught us the grace, I said to Karen, "It's a pagan grace, you know."

"Sure," she replied. "But that's fine by me. I am a pagan."

"Yeah, and you're my favorite pagan."

"Should have married the nice Christian girl."

"I'll stick with my pagan."

Neither of us were using the term *pagan* in a technical sense, of course, but it became a lighthearted way for us to talk about something that was difficult to talk about. One day I gave Karen a button that says, "Born again pagan." She never wore it, but she did put it in her jewelry box, alongside other items that she treasures.

After both of our children were confirmed in the church, during their mid-teen years, Karen began to find ways to share with them that her beliefs differ from mine. Up to that point, she had not said anything that would lead them to think that she and I were on the same page, but her mere presence in the church might have led them to believe that we were. As a parent it is often hard to know how much to share with your children, and when. Karen wanted to wait until they had both made their own faith commitments — or chose not to — before making her own beliefs known more fully. At the time we were not confident that this was the right approach, and I don't know that we are even now. In retrospect, at least we did avoid the outcomes we most feared. Our children were remarkably accepting of the fact that their parents do not share many of the same religious beliefs. They have said that they did not feel caught in some kind of bait and switch when they learned more about what their mother believes and does not believe. And both of them, as young adults, continue to have their own positive relationships with the church and with their own budding faith — something for which both Karen and I are grateful.

About the time Karen started sharing with our children more about her own beliefs, and disbeliefs, she also stopped going to worship. And she is not involved in other aspects of the church's life, either. That is so much of an established pattern for us now that I am sometimes startled by other people's reactions to it. Friends of mine who are pastors — and who are devoted to Karen — as well as other pastors who have not even met Karen, can have very similar responses. They will say things like, "I don't think I could handle that." Or, "That would be hard for me."

Their responses remind me that other people's marriages are always a bit of a mystery. Come to think of it, sometimes even our own marriages are.

So before I attempt to explain why it works for us — or how we have made it work — let me admit that, indeed, there are ways in which it is hard. And, of course, I can only talk about what is hard for me.

The most difficult part, for me, is not being able to share that part of my life with my life partner. But even putting it that way does not get it right. Being a Christian is not a part of my life. It is my life. Being a pastor is more than my job. It is who I am. How it is that I can feel so close to someone with whom I do not share these profound commitments is something of a mystery, even to me. At the same time, not having a shared spiritual life does feel like a deep loss and my own response to that reality is akin to grief.

There are times when I miss having a shared involvement in the church. I will talk with her about what is going on at the church, much as she will tell me about her work as an attorney. But Karen is perhaps the most perceptive person I know. So there are times when I would particularly love her firsthand take on things, her reading of people and situations. That is, sometimes I wish that we could sit down for Sunday dinner after worship and have the kinds of conversations my parents used to have.

I have drawn the difficult conclusion that being married to me may have prevented Karen from developing her own spiritual life. She would not draw that conclusion, but I still wonder. The role of the minister's spouse may be too confining and too public to allow for the kind of generous and gentle space that is required to grow in faith.

It has been hard to experience Karen's anger, sometimes even scorn, toward the church, which surfaces on occasion. When the news carries a story of religious intolerance or abuse of religious authority, her Irish temper, which rarely makes an appearance, can burn hot. Of course, often I share her outrage. In some instances, however, those become opportunities for her to offer more sweeping indictments of religious faith and religious institutions, which can cut a bit too close to home for me. Earlier in our marriage, Karen read *Trinity,* the Leon Uris novel, set in Ireland in the nineteenth century. A major theme of that book is the ways in which religious leaders — both Catholic and Protestant — would foment hatred in order to increase their power.

Karen is largely of Irish descent, so she felt a particular association with the story. Each night she would read that book before going to sleep and each night it made her angry and sometimes it seemed like she was angry with me. I couldn't wait for her to finish that book. And it is a very long book. The longest book ever written, I eventually concluded. Today, now years later, we can joke about it. But not at the time.

I have learned that I can't complain much about anything that may be going on at the church because Karen will be quick to say, "Well, then why don't you just quit?" For her, it is not a rhetorical question. Because it is such a pointed question that I would rather avoid, I think I end up giving her a rosier picture of the church than I would otherwise.

Sometimes it is just hard to explain why I keep at this crazy work, except to say that I am called to it. I love the story of the man who works in the circus, spending his day cleaning up after the elephants. At night he comes home and complains about it to his wife. Every day the same old mess, every night the same old complaints, until finally his wife says, "Well, why don't you just quit?" The man, a look of shock on his face, replies, "What, and give up show business?" That is not unlike the conversations Karen and I have sometimes. I have not found ways to talk about why I feel compelled to do this work, except by using the language of call. But what can the notion of call mean to someone who does not have the religious convictions on which it is based?

Indeed, one can be called to work other than ministry. Some people are called to be math teachers, or soccer coaches, or full time mothers or fathers, or singers, or social workers. The ministry is different, however, in at least one regard. Certain professions — law and medicine come to mind — are sometimes referred to as "a jealous mistress" because they demand so much. But the ministry is more than a mistress because, when you are ordained, you actually make vows of fealty and faithfulness to God and to the church that are not unlike the marriage vows. I have made vows both to my wife and to the church. Gratefully, most often those vows are not in conflict, but sometimes it can feel as if they pull in opposite directions, and that may be even more the case when the minister's spouse does not share a commitment to the church.

I have found, however, that there are ways in which I benefit from Karen's religious skepticism and lack of involvement in the church.

For one, I think being married to Karen has made me a better preacher. She keeps me honest. When preparing a sermon, I imagine Karen reading over my shoulder, and occasionally pointing to certain passages and asking me questions like, "How do you know that? Aren't you presuming a lot here? That may be your understanding of the truth, but on what basis can you claim that it is the truth?" Imagining Karen's questions has helped me speak to the skeptic that can reside in any listener.

Also, because Karen is not involved in the church, my relationship with her provides some much-needed balance in my life. In my case, this is particularly welcome because, when it comes to the church, I am a true get-a-lifer. My family tree is festooned with as many ordained ministers as a Christmas tree has ornaments. I have been on the staff of a church since I was nineteen years old. Most of my best friends are pastors. If Karen were active in the church I think I might end up so completely immersed in the life of the church that it would not be healthy. As it is, there are ways in which Karen is what every pastor I know yearns for: a close friend who is not in the church.

At the risk of sounding clichéd, in the end, what makes it work for us is something very basic: mutual respect. Karen is the best person I know. She may not be a Christian, but she is more honest, caring, and selfless than most Christians I know, including me. And because her integrity is, indeed, so integral to who she is, it is almost hard to wish that she professed a Christian faith and were a more traditional minister's wife, because, given who she is, that would entail compromising that integrity.

And, for her part, Karen lets me know that she has respect for me. One evening, I was telling her about something related to the church and I was speaking in overtly religious terms — that is, in language she would never use herself and might be even a bit wary of if used by others. I paused and said, "It's interesting: you hear me talk this way and you don't make me feel like a hypocrite." She replied, "That's because you're not a hypocrite. If I were to talk that way, I would be a hypocrite. But you're not." Coming from her, that meant a lot.

Given her lack of any commitment to the church per se, sometimes it amazes me to consider all that Karen has been willing to do in support of my ministry. Twice Karen has moved across the country and essentially changed career paths in order for me to respond to a call to another church. And, perhaps it goes without saying, there were some tense moments along the way. Because we have moved a number of times, Karen has had to take bar exams in six states, something that is unheard of in the legal field. She didn't do that because she loves the church, God knows, which makes it all the more clear that she did that because she loves me.

A couple years back, we started a new weekly worship service, in a more open space than our sanctuary is, to allow for more innovation. Chris, one of my pastoral colleagues at the church, aware that Karen has an artistic gift, asked me if she might be willing to make banners to decorate and, in some way, define the space. Long ago having learned that I dare not speak for Karen, I said, "Well, you're going to have to ask her directly." When Karen got off the phone with Chris, I asked her how she had responded to the request. She said, "Well, you know, I really like Chris and making banners is something I can do. I just said, 'You've got to promise that there will be no public mention of the fact that I made the banners.'" Almost immediately, Karen began to develop a vision for what those banners should convey and what they would look like. She spent much of the summer making those banners. Rather late into the night the Saturday before the first worship service in that new space, she had her sewing machine at the church, making last-minute adjustments and helping others hang the banners. Driving home, I thanked her for all the work she had done. "Well, I love you, babe," is all she said in reply.

The next morning she was not in the congregation for the worship service that was so enhanced by her vision and handiwork. In the intervening years, she has never attended one of those worship services and, in fact, I don't think she ever again entered that space where her banners still hang. When I consider that, as I do on many Sundays as I sit in that space, I find it both remarkable and sad at the same time.

I am often at the church late into the evening, either teaching a class or, more likely, attending a meeting. Sometimes Karen will already be in bed when I get home because she has to catch an early train in the morning. It is not one particular night that I remember, because it has happened so many times that the memories overlap:

It is the third evening in a row that I have arrived home rather late after a church meeting. The light is off in our bedroom, so I pour a glass of wine and flip rather mindlessly through a magazine that has just arrived in the mail. Then I tip-toe upstairs, turn off the light in the hallway, and gingerly open our bedroom door. Karen, who has been asleep and even now does not stir, asks, "How did your meeting go?"

"It was fine," I say.

"I'm so glad," she will say, and then drift back to sleep.

And then I crawl into bed and we lie beside one another in the shared darkness.

CHAPTER 23

Money Off the Shelf

LILLIAN DANIEL

I remember the day I decided that I would never be a tither. I was sitting in the pew as an associate minister, listening to the senior minister preach. The senior minister, who was a tither, was telling us about it. He was explaining that being a tither meant that he had always given the biblically commended tithe, ten percent of his income, to the church, then still more to other causes, and that God had blessed him for it. This wasn't hypocrisy. He really did it, and he believed that financial peace had come to him as a result.

But I couldn't stand to hear it. I was paying off massive student loans, paying for full-time day care for my first baby, and to be honest, even though I lived in a lovely parsonage, I was seriously underpaid by the church. Newly married, my husband and I had discovered that we were no different from most couples in that the major stress in our nascent marriage was money. In fact, we had just had an argument about our spending the night before that had ended without answers but with no shortage of hurt feelings. I was in no mood to hear about tithing.

I felt that my colleague, a widower whose children were grown and whose house was paid off, had absolutely no understanding of my situation. It seemed unimaginable to me that I could be a tither when I had so little to begin with, and the idea of giving such a large sum to an institution that wasn't paying me enough seemed absurd.

My anger was intense around these issues, but there was no place, in my vocational life, that I could express it. In fact, I was called to project to the congregation an entirely opposite affect and I attempted to do it. I preached generosity and grace while inside I felt worry and resentment.

In some ways, I came to this bipolar ministry of money naturally, for I was behaving as I had been taught as a child. When it came to money, you did not tell the truth. I remember my parents fighting late into the night, always about money, and in particular my mother's spending. Now, what fell into the category of "her" spending was just about everything, from groceries, to car payments, to my school supplies and clothes. And because of this, my father was basically unaware of what anything cost. Yet every now and then he would see a bill or a receipt and become irate.

So to avoid such scenes, I was taught never to tell my father what anything cost. If I had a new coat, I learned in my early childhood to say, "I've had it for years." When I needed movie money, he would give me enough for a ticket ten years ago, and my mother would surreptitiously slip the difference into my pocket on the way out. "Why can't we tell Daddy what the movie really costs?" I asked. "Why can't we tell him I needed a new outfit for the dance?"

"Shhh . . . it will only upset him."

I remember as a little girl delighting in my brand-new blue coat, but being afraid to wear it out the door past my father. From an early age, material things elicited in me both inordinate delight and misplaced shame.

But we don't have to carry every bad habit from one generation into the next. As a young adult starting out in both marriage and parenting, I longed to break that pattern. And when I saw myself carrying it into my new ministry, it gave me pause. I decided it was time to start telling the truth about money. There was no way I was going to be a tither, but I could at least be honest.

So when it came to stewardship sermons, I confessed to the congregation that I loved cars, clothes, and restaurants; that I wanted to travel everywhere in the world and not worry about what I spent; that when I gave money away, it actually was a sacrifice, because I really wanted the things I saw advertised on television. I learned, of course, that I didn't need to tell them. Congregations can read our lives pretty well. But in telling the truth, I got a strong response. We started talking together about money. I did not need to be a perfect, altruistic role model for God to use me in a ministry of money. We were all there to work on each other, and telling the truth, being authentic, was just the beginning. I even got a raise.

But when I moved to be the solo minister at my second church, in New Haven, I backslid into silence and avoidance. I hadn't been there long before I saw that each Sunday we collected the offering with awkwardness. This was a congregation that had not heard anyone talk about tithing in decades, maybe ever, or even really about money. There was an embarrassed fanfare around the offertory that seemed to suggest that while we needed money to exist we found the enterprise of asking for it somewhat distasteful.

The fanfare came from the outstanding choir, who saved their biggest anthem for the offertory moment. Yet I came to suspect that the anthem was not there to draw attention to the offering, but rather to distract us from it. The plates were passed apologetically, as people tried not to see what others had put there. Then those plates were shuffled forward, along with the weekly canned-goods offering which was held up much less self-consciously. It cost less.

Our offertory prayers of thanksgiving praised God for many things metaphorically but seldom for the actual dollars and cents in the plate. Those plates were in fact scurried away during the doxology, but not to an altar or a communion table. In that church the plates ended up on a tiny, specially constructed shelf behind the organ, around a doorjamb, completely out of sight.

Congregational lore had it that this little shelf was the invention of an atheist church treasurer. The story was that he had so little taste for worship that the shelf was placed out of view in order to enable him to sneak the offering through the door into a tiny room and count the money during the sermon.

Later I discovered that the architectural plans of the church actually included this little shelf from the very beginning. The congregation had at that time prided itself on the theological reflection behind the shelf: the communion table was so "highly" regarded that they decided it should never be "soiled or sullied" with something as crass as money.

At the time I served there, this congregation, which once boasted a large membership of wealthy business and civic leaders, had declined over the decades to paltry pledging levels and low attendance, supported by an endowment that allowed the church to exist longer than it would have otherwise. The message within the congregation was that financial matters were taboo in the church, and the effect was low giving and unspoken anxiety around money.

Yet when I arrived, the knowledge of their two church splits and the ousting of my two ministerial predecessors made me wary of speaking about money. I was afraid to look like I was singing for my own supper to a crowd that might not be interested in cooking.

This is the classic ministerial dilemma around stewardship. We are called to preach generosity, particularly toward the church, but we, through our salaries, will be among the beneficiaries. Add to this a history of conflict between pastors and congregations, and it is no wonder that I felt nervous to broach the topic. As a new pastor, ordained just four years, I was being pulled into a church culture that began long before I was even born, and it was a culture of keeping the money out of sight and on the shelf.

In my early days of ministry at that congregation, my own financial pressures had not gone away. (Do they ever?) Now, I was the parent of a toddler and a newborn, both of whom were in full-time day care that cost as much as community college tuition. My husband was a labor organizer in a local union that had a policy that when the workers were on strike, the organizers also gave up their pay. And the workers were on strike. I wasn't underpaid, at least not for clergy, but I wasn't making enough to support our family. There were tense conversations late at night about which bills to pay first, and whether our three-year-old son would get a tricycle for his birthday. Sometimes, in a moment of stress, I would find myself doing the very thing I ought to hate: shopping. A new pair of shoes I did not need would be discovered in my closet ("What? I've had these for years . . ."), and my husband would look at me dumbfounded ("But they were on sale . . .") as we wondered how to pay the day care bill. It was no wonder I was not particularly emboldened to challenge my new church on their money issues.

Wise mentors have told me that in many churches the congregation's issues with money can be traced to those of the pastor. But sometimes we clergy can also be shaped by the congregation. Most often, I suspect, we find each other in the night, like two star-crossed lovers who shouldn't get together but are oddly drawn to one another's neuroses.

When it comes to anxiety around money, the church and the pastor share something in common: our sin. We are all shaped by a world of greed and materialism, and, from deep within, the worst part of us participates. So together, sometimes, we may make a silent pact not to talk about money, and spend time in church thinking about more pleasant things. As a church, we weren't ignoring money. We couldn't, because we needed it to survive. But we collected it and put it quickly on its own little shelf.

But then I learned that not everybody in church wanted to put money on the shelf. I remember in those years, there were times when people in my church would come to me and recommend the best-selling book *The Prayer of Jabez*. Or they might tell me about preachers they watched on television who promised financial wealth as a result of prayer. These proponents of the "prosperity gospel" certainly had taken money off the shelf, but what were they doing with it? I took the time to read *The Prayer of Jabez*. While encouraging prayer, it mostly encouraged "enlarging one's territory," something the little-known biblical figure Jabez prayed for and got. While enlarging one's territory may have been important to Jabez, I remain convinced it was not very important to Jesus. But clearly, in reading these books and watching these preachers on television, my parishioners were looking for something they were not getting at the church that put money on the shelf. And I needed to step up. Not so much because they needed it, but because I did.

In the preaching moment each week, clergy are given the privilege and the challenge of engaging money through the eyes of the One who provides for us in more ultimate ways. I believe our work as clergy actually shapes us, and makes it impossible for us to believe the simple theories and easy answers. We cannot help but wrestle with money in complex ways, given a typical workweek.

One Sunday we preach about Jesus saying, "Woe to you Pharisees! For you tithe mint and rue and herbs of all kinds, and neglect justice and the love of God" (Luke 11:42). Then we go home to unpaid bills, and prepare the next Monday morning for the upcoming pledge drive. Any pastor who delivers the easy prosperity answers can't really believe them. Paying attention to our lives does not permit it.

Yet there is no denying that as clergy we often find ourselves living in economic disconnect with our neighbors and parishioners. Sometimes the clergy are the poorest members in a wealthy community, allowed to live there geographically by virtue of their position, but not really able to live like others. Our children may associate with the wealthy, but they cannot afford to go on the same ski trips, drive the same cars, or attend the same colleges that many of their friends do. In places where Christendom is still hanging on by a golden thread, some clergy have free memberships to clubs that they could never afford to join. But everyone knows how and why they got there. They may be taken as guests to restaurants they could never afford, or perhaps loaned the vacation homes of parishioners. In other words, they are in the community of wealth and privilege but not of it. This is a tricky place from which to proclaim good news to the poor.

In other communities, the minister may be one of the wealthiest members of a financially strapped congregation, able to have a nice car when others do not. In some faith communities, the people insist that the pastor live well as a mark of pride for the church. They make sacrifices so that the pastor can live as they might want to. There are churches where the pastor may call for one offering for the church, and for a "love offering" for himself, and all this is accepted practice in the congregation. But once again, the pastor sits in an economic community but is not entirely of it.

The reality that runs through these seemingly opposite situations is that pastors are often called to serve in communities that do not represent their own economic or educational status. We live not where we deserve to be but where we are called.

My sense is that God uses this complexity and this distance to prepare pastors to do the very job they feel unprepared for: getting money off the shelf that is hidden from view. The fundraising aspects of our work, the issues around clergy compensation, and the disconnect with our communities all force us to look at money in ways that others might be able to avoid. And then most weeks in church, even on our highest attendance Sundays, we have something like this to work with, a few choice words from a teenage mother who will change the world: "He has brought down the powerful from their thrones, and lifted up the lowly; he has filled the hungry with good things, and sent the rich away empty" (Luke 1:52). For Jesus, the money issue was taken off the shelf in utero, and every new year in the church we get that Advent wake-up call.

The clergy whom I admire most deal with money honestly, and they acknowledge the complexity, as well as their own brokenness. They read their economic landscapes through the lens of the gospel and then attempt to tell their congregations the truth. These clergy are not always popular for doing so, but rather, through years of pastoral care and integrity, they have earned the right to ask questions: While the adult education course on "affluenza" might compel the wealthy to live more simply, how much do the poor actually benefit when the wealthy clean out their closets? While a home built in Honduras is certainly a blessing to those who will live in it, and an even greater blessing to those who get to go there and build it, do these blessings distract us, or absolve us, from a clear analysis of injustice in our backyards?

The Apostle Paul, who never shrank from asking the hard questions about money, offered his donors in Philippi "thankless thanks." Paul refused to see himself as a supplicant or a debtor to the rich. Rather he saw himself as a participant in God's own redistribution of the wealth, for the purposes of a kingdom greater than our imaginings.

To make a claim like Paul's requires a rock solid sense of vocation. Perhaps some clerical discomfort with money is related to a greater discomfort with call. A minister who is uneasy in the proclamation of the good news in general is certainly not going to proclaim the good news for the poor. Put another way, where your treasure is, there shall your heart be also.

In my own life, my heart was transformed around economic justice issues long before it was transformed around personal giving. I was quicker to point out a materialistic society's evils than to look at my own habits. If it had been left up to me, I doubt I ever would have gotten around to it.

But a few years into my ministry at the New Haven church, I was sitting in a traffic jam on the highway, on my way back from a meeting in Hartford, late to pick up my children from day care, a mistake that would result in a fine. It was a small fine, but a bigger reminder that I had tried to pack too much into a day that had no margins. It was a good metaphor for my financial life. I tried to put far too much into a budget that had no margins, and the overflow had ended up in serious credit card debt. There is nothing like being late, broke, stressed out, and in a traffic jam to turn a person to prayer. I prayed for a way out of the cycle.

Suddenly, the view from my stuck car changed. Hartford, not usually beautiful from the highway, appeared to be gleaming, as if bathed in gold light. The ordinary buildings were shining, and the sky seemed to drip into them in an embrace. And then suddenly the heavenly veneer disappeared and it looked just like Hartford again.

Let me take a moment to clarify that I am not a person who regularly has visions. And that the last place I expected to have one was on the highway outside of Hartford, Connecticut. Furthermore, in the circles I run in, when you speak to God in prayer you are considered religious, but when you say God speaks to you people suspect that you are psychotic. Particularly if God speaks to you about money. But this is what I saw, and I was amazedly baffled.

So I closed my eyes tight, and then opened them again. Gleaming, and then gone. Heavenly city, and then Hartford again. I did this several times, until the traffic abated and I had to pull forward. I could not recapture the vision.

Stunned, I prayed again. The car was once again stopped and I closed my eyes, and saw in my mind's eye three things, none of which were very difficult to interpret. The first was a credit card, being cut up into pieces by a giant pair of scissors. The second image was a present, gift wrapped with a flamboyant bow, the sort of package one would delight in seeing under a Christmas tree. And the last image was the figure 10%. Then the traffic moved, my eyes were opened, and I was on my way.

I got home and told my husband the news. "I've just had a vision from God. We're meant to cut up our credit cards and start tithing."

"I've been waiting years for you to walk through the door and say that," he said. And here I think he was referring less to my vision and more to the financial plan. After all, he wasn't the one who liked to go shopping. "But just how are we going to pay off the credit cards?"

I told him about the three-part vision, with a special focus on part two. "We're going to get a present," I said. "A big gift, a financial windfall. Now, is there anyone in your family who might be planning to send us a check?" He shook his head, and I knew that no one in my family was planning such a thing. But I was sure at the time that I had the correct interpretation of the vision. I was going to win some kind of lottery. We cut up the credit cards, sent in our church pledge form, and started giving ten percent. I waited for the gift.

The windfall check never arrived. I would check the mail daily, and there was nothing. Do you actually have to buy a lottery ticket to win? Apparently so.

I felt both disillusioned and foolish for even imagining that such a thing would happen. I felt naïve and wondered if the vision was nothing but my latest self-help scheme destined to last as long as the average diet.

But God had made the city of Hartford look heavenly on a hot day in a traffic jam, and that was a scene I would never forget. We kept tithing, and somehow, in time and in ways that I cannot fully account for, we started getting rid of the debt. And since the gift, the big financial windfall, never came, we decided to meet with a financial planner.

He arrived at our house with a folder full of plans about what a young family should be thinking about: saving for college, retirement, and life insurance. He looked at our pay stubs, our credit card bills, and then asked about our charitable giving. I worried as I was telling him about our tithing plans, because once he had seen our situation, he might point out that it made no sense at this time.

Instead he responded, "Is that ten percent before or after taxes?"

"After taxes, of course. We're religious, but we're not crazy."

"Well, that's fine," he said, "If all you want is an after-tax blessing."

If it had come to me from a minister, I would have found it preachy, but coming from a financial planner, it struck me as miraculous. He went on to testify about his church, his own pre-tax tithing, and how it all fit together with his current line of work. We promised him we'd work toward a pre-tax tithe, and after a few years we got there, and got rid of the debt as well.

I have come to love the stewardship work of the ministry. Sometimes I think it is the most important work clergy do. We talk about money not because it shouldn't mean anything to us, but because it obviously means so much. So I preach about money all year round, not in order to raise funds for the church, but because I need to hear God's word on the subject.

To this day, I still tithe, but I'm also still materialistic. I still find ways to justify that new pair of shoes I don't need, and believe me, my feet stopped growing long ago. Yet I also know the ways in which a longing for things can corrupt my life. I preach to remind myself, and others like me, of a better way.

I later came to understand that the second part of my three-part vision had actually come true. The big gift had arrived after all. It was in the wise words of one Christian to another, amidst spreadsheets, insurance forms, and tax returns. It was in the generosity of my parents and in-laws, who had stepped in over the years to cover camp fees and instrument lessons for our children. It was in the health of our kids, the kindness of friends who covered for one another in lean times, the countless little gifts that come our way all the time.

But most importantly, the gift was Christ, in whom my debt had long since been paid.

Because I have known the joy of giving, I am at ease sharing the good news with others. I now stand in a long line of followers of Jesus who say things about money that make no sense — at least, as the world calculates such things.

I know there may be people who listen to me the way I listened to my first senior minister, with a sense that this stuff simply does not apply. I stand in the pulpit to preach on giving and I consider my old self, sitting in the pews. It is humbling. Today may be the day that as a result of my preaching, someone decides she will never be a tither.

And fortunately, God can work with that.

CHAPTER 24

The Ministry of Angels

MARTIN B. COPENHAVER

I was in a deep sleep when the phone rang. I am convinced that phones use a different ring in the middle of the night. More urgent and more menacing. When I picked it up, I heard my mother's voice: "Honey, your father has had a heart attack and it doesn't look like he's going to make it." I was twenty-seven years old.

I left immediately, driving as if in a fog, taking extra care to make each turn in the road. Looking back, that drive was the longest I have ever taken, not knowing for sure the whole time if my father were alive or dead. But, actually, it didn't seem so long at the time. In fact, in a sense, it took no time at all because it seemed as if there were no time. It was as if I weren't traveling on a road at all, but rather through some long, timeless tunnel, from one world to the next, from one reality to another.

I was two years out of seminary at the time and I had lived in Burlington, Vermont, for just three weeks when I got that phone call. My wife, Karen, was still in Connecticut, finishing up her work there before she could move to Vermont. My parents had stopped for the night in Hanover, New Hampshire, on their way to visiting me. It was to be the first time they would see our new home and worship in the church to which I had just been called as senior minister. But then I got that phone call.

When I got to the hotel room in Hanover my mother was sitting on the bed. She stood up and we embraced. I had to ask her if my father had indeed died and she told me that he had. It was then that I noticed that someone else was still seated on the bed. My mother introduced us. I did not carefully note the woman's name and cannot remember it now. But I do remember sensing that her presence was a comforting one for my mother, and was also for me, in our short meeting. She also embraced my mother, tears in her eyes, and then left the room.

My mother and I gathered up a few bits of luggage, not talking very much, checked out of the hotel, and headed back to Vermont. For the trip back the highway had again become a simple road. We talked some. Mostly we just sat in silence. Somewhere along the way I asked about the woman I had met in the hotel room, and my mother told me this story: When my father had collapsed in the hotel's hallway — even after all these years it is still hard to imagine, this towering figure, suddenly crumpled on the floor — my mother asked someone who was waiting for the elevator to get an ambulance. While my mother waited for help to arrive, huddled over the crumpled figure of my father, this woman came and stood by very quietly. My mother couldn't remember her saying anything.

When the paramedics came to take my father to the hospital the woman offered to go with my mother. As they drove to the hospital, my mother said, "You know, I don't even know your name." When they exchanged names, the woman asked, "Are you any relation to Charles Copenhaver?"

"Why, yes," my mother replied. "He's my husband. He's the one in the ambulance."

"Well," the woman said, "your husband and mine are good friends. I have heard your name many times."

These two women had never met, and my mother had to confess that she had not heard the name before, but the two men had belonged to the same club in New York and so they had often dined together as a part of their meetings. In fact, the woman told my mother that she was on her way to meet her husband in New York and that she had taken this little detour to Hanover, something she had never done before, because she was not used to traveling alone.

Beyond this bit of conversation, they did not talk much. The woman just sat with my mother while she awaited news from the doctors, and while she received word that my father could not be revived. My mother reported that she did not know what she would have done if that woman had not been there. Her very presence was a comforting shelter. There was a stillness and peace in her manner that came as a gracious gift to one who was in such profound need, as my mother was at that moment. She stayed with my mother until I arrived. And although one of the first notes my mother wrote after my father's death was to thank her for her presence, and although she received a gracious reply, they did not see each other again after that night. In some sense, they did not need to.

My mother and I arrived at my home in the early morning hours. I had so looked forward to taking her and my father for a tour of our new home, but a tour was now the furthest thing from my mind. We had to get some sleep. Or, at least, we needed to try. The next morning — with Karen, my brother, and my sister all on their way — my mother and I started working the phones, calling those with whom we thought we should share the news and making arrangements for my father's memorial service. Death may be simple for those who die, but it is quite complicated for those who remain. In the midst of all the cascading emotions, there is just a lot to do.

Among the things I had to figure out right away was what to do about worship the next day. My father died on Friday night. It was now Saturday. Until I got that phone call, I had planned to finish preparing my sermon before my parents were scheduled to arrive on Saturday afternoon. Now the sermon lay unfinished on my desk. I kept thinking, "I have to get back to that sermon." That thought pestered me all day, even as my mother and I chatted or made phone calls, even as Karen arrived, and later when my brother and sister joined us: "I have to get back to that sermon."

Grief has many faces and one of them looks confused. In retrospect I can see that, in my grief, I had lost my grasp on common sense. It never occurred to me that I wouldn't preach the next day. My thinking — if one can call it that — went something like this: The church had not yet called a new associate minister. What guest preacher could we get on such short notice? Besides, I had just started. This would be only my fourth Sunday in the pulpit as the new senior minister. The first three Sundays had gone well, but we needed to keep up the momentum. I was also quite young to be senior minister of this church so, at some level, I probably hoped that showing up to lead worship would help demonstrate that I was up to the job. Beyond all that, this was a particularly important Sunday. It was the last Sunday for the departing associate minister. It was a complicated parting. There was still some residue of conflict in the congregation over whether he should have been encouraged to stay after the new senior minister arrived. I wanted to be particularly gracious to him on this Sunday, both because it was the right thing to do and, to be truthful, so that I could be seen doing it. I thought it was a good opportunity to contribute to some healing and to exercise leadership in doing so. So I had to be there. Or, at least, that's what I thought at the time.

Now all of that thinking seems a bit off-kilter, at best. But no one in my family tried to dissuade me from preaching the next day. Perhaps they saw how determined I was to do so. Or perhaps they, too, were caught in the disorienting swirl of grief and so could not think any more clearly than I was capable of doing in that moment. By Saturday evening, however, I did conclude that I didn't need to finish that sermon. I could pull another sermon from my files and use that.

After a fitful night I said good-bye to my family, drove to the church and preached at both services. At least, I think it was me. I made a point of speaking with an extra measure of conviction, hoping that no one would notice that I wasn't really there at all, that it felt to me as if someone else were speaking. I held onto the pulpit as if I were holding on for dear life to the gunwale of a boat that was pitching in a stormy sea.

For most of the morning I told no one about my father's death. I said nothing during either worship service — not even at the point in the service when I shared prayer concerns from the congregation — and not after worship during the reception for the departing associate minister. At the time I told myself that was because I did not want to become the focus of attention on a day when it was important to say a proper good-bye to the one who was leaving. My time would come. To everything there is a season, a time to share and a time to keep silent, a time to weep and a time to go on autopilot. Or so it seemed at the time. And it is partly true. But it is also true that I was so overwhelmed that I did not know how to talk about my father's death. To speak the reality would be to make it all the more real to me. And I was not ready to face the depths of my own reactions, no less prepared to respond to the reactions of those around me. I was particularly unprepared to interact with my parishioners. I was in only the very beginning stages of trying to figure out how to be their minister. That was challenge enough. To be their minister while grieving myself added a degree of complexity that seemed beyond me.

As the reception was winding down, I sought out the president of the congregation. He followed me to my study, where I told him that my father had just died and that I would like to take the week off. He was clearly stunned by the news. It was an awkward conversation, neither of us really knowing what to say, but I remember thinking that, if I have to start dealing with parishioners' reactions, this is a good and kind man with whom to begin. Now that I had uttered the words, I was more eager to get out of the church than I had been all morning. I wanted nothing more than to seek refuge in the company of my family.

Later that afternoon, the president and the chair of the search committee that had called me to the church came by my house to pay a call. They brought flowers (I don't think I had ever received flowers before). I introduced them to my family. They didn't want to sit. As true New Englanders, they were men of few words. But whatever words were exchanged seemed entirely sufficient. It helped that they both already knew the news, that I didn't have to say the words. And just having them show up made a difference. Here were two men, one about my father's age and the other not much younger, who were willing to wade into unfamiliar territory themselves in order to express care for their new minister.

They also said that they were impressed by how composed and "brave" I had been that morning, which is something I would hear from others in the weeks that followed. This is not what I wanted to hear. I had not been brave. I had been numb. And, if given a choice, bravery is not something I would want to convey at such a time. I did not want my new parishioners to conclude that they are supposed to be "brave" in the face of grief. But, most of all, I think I resisted their characterization because it made clear that people were watching me and noting how I responded. My grief would not be private. There were no curtains to close. I was a rank beginner in the ways of grief — no one close to me had ever died before — but in some way people in the congregation were looking to me to show them how it's done. And that was a scary prospect. No, I did not feel brave.

The challenges of ministry are magnified for pastors who are going through personal difficulties themselves. It is hard to be attentive to the needs of others in a time when you are in great need yourself. And yet I have known pastors who are seriously ill, or depressed, or going through a divorce, or recovering from addiction, or grieving the loss of a spouse, and somehow — through a combination of grace and will — still they are able to function well as pastors. One pastor I know, who battled cancer for many years before he eventually succumbed to the disease, regularly called on parishioners in the hospital, listening with compassion, in many instances to those whose illnesses were far less serious than his own. Pastors who are going through a painful divorce (is there any other kind?) continue to meet with couples to plan their weddings and to help prepare them for their marriage. A number of pastors I know are regularly pursued by the black dog of depression, and yet they stand in the pulpit each week to preach good news to their congregations. Under such circumstances, the ability to perform even routine pastoral duties can seem almost heroic. Or so it can seem from the outside. If you were to ask one of these pastors, however, they would probably insist that they are just putting one foot in front of the other.

After the two church leaders left, my family and I again turned our thoughts to planning the memorial service. It was good to have some concrete tasks to focus on. A number of times through the years, I had told Karen, "When my father dies, I cannot imagine letting anyone else conduct his memorial service." Now that he had died, the surge of grief swept that thought so completely from my mind that it was hard to imagine that I had ever entertained such a notion. After my father's death, I knew in a moment that, during this time, I was not to be the minister. I was the son. My job was not to preach the good news, but to receive it.

Among the phone calls that were starting to come in, one was from a pastor who had known my family for many years. I heard my mother tell him the story about the woman who had stayed with her in Hanover and about the connections through their husbands they discovered. She concluded by saying, "Isn't that strange?" Afterward she told me what he said in reply: "That isn't strange, Marian. That woman was one of God's angels sent to minister to you."

"Do not be afraid." That is what the angel Gabriel said to Mary when he approached her to tell her of the promised birth of the beloved one. That is also what an angel somehow communicated to my mother at the death of another beloved one, my father: "Do not be afraid."

The memorial service for my father was held in the church from which he had retired from ministry just eight months earlier. This was the first time any member of my family had been back.

Before the service in the sanctuary, our family gathered outside at the columbarium that was built into the very foundation of the church. The only one outside our family in that little circle was Scotty, the gray-haired Scottish sexton of the church. He was there in an official capacity, because it was his job to open the niche where the urn with my father's ashes would be placed. But it was also entirely fitting that he was there, because he and my father had been devoted to one another. In a gesture she had not planned, my mother asked Scotty if he would place the urn in the niche, which he did. When he turned back to us, he let out a partially suppressed wail of grief and reached for his handkerchief. In the moment when he brought the handkerchief to his face, it was as if the levees broke. He sobbed great swelling sobs that made his shoulders heave. My mother put her arm around his shoulder, to comfort him. But, in a way that he certainly did not intend,

Scotty was showing us how this is done, giving more audible and visible expression to his grief than we had yet allowed ourselves. His tears invited ours.

When our family walked into the sanctuary before the service was to begin, I was overwhelmed by the sight of all the people, hundreds of them, some of them standing along the perimeter of the large sanctuary, like a great sea of faces that was washing over me.

The service was conducted by the new senior minister of the church, who had succeeded my father, and the eulogy was delivered by my father's best and oldest friend. It was the kind of service my father might have conducted were he still alive, comforting and stirring at the same time. When the last hymn concluded and the congregation sat down, I stood up from my place with the family and walked up the chancel steps to give the Benediction. We had decided that it would be good for the congregation to hear something from a member of the family. A Benediction — which literally means "good words" — is an ancient form of blessing. So it seemed fitting that, representing the family, I bless the congregation that my father had felt so blessed to serve for eighteen years.

Looking out at the sea of faces, I said, "Now, as we leave this place, let us leave with these words of our Lord Jesus cleaving to our hearts . . ." And then I read from my father's Bible the blessing, recorded in John's Gospel, that Jesus offered to his followers. It was not difficult to find the passage. In anticipation of this moment, I had highlighted it in bright pink — the only marking in the entire Bible that my father never would have marked — just so I could find the words on the page. I knew I would need all the help I could get. I read, "Peace I leave with you. My peace I give to you. Not as the world gives do I give to you. Let not your hearts be troubled and neither let them be afraid." Then I said, "And now may this peace of which our Lord speaks, the peace which indeed passes our understanding, be with you and remain with you this day and always. Amen."

I was grateful for the chance to fill the sanctuary with those words of triumph — not my own words, because at that point I had no words of my own, but Jesus' words, said in my own voice and expressing my own belief that death does not get the last word. It felt as if I were hurling powerful and defiant words into the face of death and, at the same time, offering words of comfort to this congregation that my father had served and that had nurtured me.

With the words "peace" and "always" still hovering in the air, I walked down the chancel steps and joined my family to walk out of the sanctuary.

As members of the congregation departed, or gathered with one another after the service, our family stayed in the minister's study. We had planned it that way. The members of my family had all agreed that we would not greet members of the congregation after the service. The prospect of responding to hundreds of people in a receiving line just seemed too overwhelming to us. We remembered how draining it had been to stand in a receiving line after my father's last worship service as senior minister just a few months before. And this would be even more challenging. So we decided not to greet people. I have since concluded that this was a mistake. To be sure, it would have been hard. But grief is hard. People want, and somehow need, to connect with one another at such a time, to touch, to say a word, or even just to share an awkward moment in which neither of you knows what to say. Many of those who came to the service wanted that and needed that — and I think I did, too, but in ways I was not able to recognize at the time.

When my mother arrived back at her home in Connecticut after my father's memorial service, she found on his typewriter a letter, the last one he was ever to write, which happened to be to the husband of the woman who had stayed with her the night my father died. In the letter, my father was sending regrets that he could not attend the next meeting of their club because of a "previous engagement" — a statement that proved ironically true.

That letter helped point us back to the mystery that, indeed, in the midst of the fire and fog of grief, we had been visited by angels — not the kind of winged angels who are depicted on Christmas cards or in Renaissance paintings, but rather another kind of angel who is described in the Bible. They embody the literal meaning of the word *angel,* a word that means "messenger." These angels are messengers from

God bearing good news. One of their roles is to comfort and to protect the faithful. The psalmist had this sort of angel in mind when he wrote, "God will command his angels concerning you to guard you in all your ways" (91:11).

One such angel came gently to my mother's side in the hallway of the hotel and stayed with her. Others came to the door of my new home with a bouquet of flowers and a few words. Another angel could only weep as he placed my father's ashes in the columbarium. And, indeed, there were other angels whom we were not ready to see, no less receive, on the day of the memorial service. At the time they looked like a sea of faces. In recollection, we could affirm that the members of the congregation gathered that day were something like a multitude of the heavenly host, praising God, and in their own way witnessing to the good news that death does not get the last word. On that day the church gathered to proclaim the good news that I could not yet utter myself, but so needed to hear. We had been ministered to by angels all along.

CHAPTER 25

Palm Sunday

LILLIAN DANIEL

About nine years ago, a few days before Palm Sunday, I was doing what ministers do. I was preparing for my big week and, to be honest, for my favorite Sunday.

I have always looked forward to Palm Sunday, from my childhood memories of waving the palms in processions at any number of churches; to the adults who could miraculously transform those long palms, with just a few folds, into a small cross that I kept all year long; to the pageantry and the choruses of "All Glory, Laud, and Honor"; and to the giggles that erupted among the children whenever the minister said the word "ass." (I still think that's funny.)

But now as a minister, Palm Sunday had become the gateway to the busiest week of my year. There would be an attendance surge at church, multiple worship bulletins to put together, so many services to plan, with Easter, the biggest of all, around the corner.

I still loved Palm Sunday, but I had now come to love it the way an accountant loves April 15. It signaled the most intense week in my working life, the week I was made for, the week I saved up for, the week that reminds me why it is that I do what I do, even as I see certain exhaustion around the corner.

Our eight-year-old son was under the weather, so, given the time of year, it was my husband Lou who volunteered to cover the doctor's appointment and the inevitable trip to the drug store for whatever prescription would clear up this little infection. "You go to the gym," he said. "You need to relieve some stress." And I took my hall pass freely.

I was drinking a cup of coffee in the gym's café, with the post-workout glow of relaxed self-righteousness, and picked up a call from Lou reporting on Calvin's appointment. "We're being admitted to the hospital," he told me. "They say that Calvin has diabetes."

My first reaction, I must confess, was one of judgment. "I should never have let Lou take Cal to this appointment," I thought to myself, as mothers, who believe they can do everything just a little bit better than their husbands, often do. I thought, "Lou has gone and messed everything up. And now they are admitting our son to the hospital for no reason." I was calm as we made the plans to meet there in a few minutes.

I was calm because I knew that there was absolutely no possibility that this could be true. Calvin was healthy in every way. Juvenile diabetes was something that ran in families, and we didn't have any in ours. I drove calmly to the hospital, ready to clear this up for everyone. And instead, they were waiting to clear things up for me.

A chronic condition is impossible to understand to those of us who don't have one. But as a parent, I needed to understand as much as I possibly could. At the hospital we were bombarded with information about this strange disease.

Unlike the more common type-two diabetes, which is growing to epic proportions in this country, the much rarer juvenile or type-one diabetes cannot be reversed by diet or lifestyle. With type-one diabetes, the body's immune system attacks its own pancreas, for no apparent reason. The pancreas then shuts down slowly over the next few months and there is absolutely nothing you can do about it. Suddenly, out of nowhere, our son was to be dependent upon insulin for the rest of his life.

All this happened just days before Holy Week; ironic, because Holy Week begins with that cheerful procession of people waving their palms before Jesus, shouting, "Hosanna!" His followers are ecstatic. They are having a party in the street. But in a matter of days, the disciples will be eating their last meal with Jesus. He'll be betrayed. They'll be afraid. The cheering and partying will seem like a distant memory from a time when they thought life was easy.

Those days spent in the hospital, I later realized, were more about us as parents than they were about our son. His health stabilized quickly once he received the insulin his body had stopped making. (It's a lot better to have something like this happen in 2001 than in 1901.) But we, his parents, needed a lot more treatment. The doctors would not release Calvin from the hospital and into our care until they were convinced that we could manage his treatment, that we had adjusted to this change.

We learned about what he could eat and should eat to avoid high blood sugars. He would have to monitor his carbohydrates, and cover them with the right dosage of insulin. This would keep his blood sugar at the right level and allow him to live a "perfectly normal life."

But just when we got that straight, we learned that when his blood sugar was too low he should eat the very things he shouldn't eat at other times. This disease was frustratingly counterintuitive. "I thought diabetics couldn't eat sweets," I said. "Not really," the doctor said, "and in a case of low blood sugar, when he's had too much insulin, he has to have sweets, in order to avoid a diabetic coma." This was not sounding to me like a "perfectly normal life."

What is a "perfectly normal life"? Have you ever noticed that the only time that phrase gets invoked is at times when life is neither "perfect" nor "normal"?

But is life ever perfect or normal?

We had been tag-team parenting for days, alternating between the hospital and home, where our five-year-old daughter was. We had friends but no family nearby. My mother had died a year before, and I don't think I ever grieved for her as much as I did in those days.

Calvin was a trooper, positive, interested in the treatments, but mostly interested in the hospital's Nintendo, since video games were something he did not have at home. But as flexible as my eight-year-old was being, my heart became consumed with one desire: Calvin must come home. I think I thought that if we left the hospital we could leave all this news there as well.

"I just want to get him home, and deal with all this there," I said to the doctor. "Everything will be fine if we can just get out of here."

"He can't be released until you are able to manage this," was the doctor's response.

"Well, what else do we need to do?" I asked.

"You and your husband need to learn how to give your son his shots," he said. "I'm going to have you practice with saline solution so that you can get the hang of it." Calvin grimaced, brave but doubtful as to our abilities.

My husband gave his first shot with confidence. Calvin took it with similar confidence. Between the two of them I saw a strength that I knew I did not have.

I held the syringe in a hand that was not steady, but shaking. I winced away myself, a person with a lifelong fear of needles, twitching uncomfortably in my own skin, sorrowfully squeamish, utterly convinced I could not do this one simple thing. But this was our only way to get home.

Finally, I jabbed the needle into him, the most counterintuitive action a needle-phobic mother could perform on a child she loves. When it made contact, he screamed in pain — I had hit a muscle, and then I did the worst thing you could do: I jerked the needle out again, causing more pain. "You have to put it in," the doctor said, and so I jabbed again, this time doing an even worse job. I watched my sweet boy lunge away from me, grabbing his arm protectively, glaring at his mother who had in one clumsy moment hurt him, failed him, and frightened him. We were not going home from the hospital yet.

Meanwhile, by now, it was the Saturday before Holy Week. Our thoughts turned from getting Calvin home to the more reachable goal of getting him to church the next day, for Palm Sunday. Finally, the doctor agreed that Calvin could leave the hospital for a few hours to attend the service. Lou stayed at the hospital and I spent that Saturday night at home, sleepless and unprepared for the most important week in my year, which suddenly seemed, I confess, a lot less important.

Because I love Palm Sunday, I had planned a lot for that day. There was to be the usual grand procession with the palms, the special music, the triumphant entry into Jerusalem. But because I had assumed this would be a celebratory day, I had decided that this would also be the day that new members would join the church.

Now, early that Sunday morning, I sat at the desk in the front office with no celebratory feelings whatsoever.

I wondered if it would be easier to simply lead the congregation through the service and then tell them the news, or tell them first. It seemed like a different person who had planned this festive Palm Sunday worship.

One of the new members who was to join that day, a young man who worked in the medical field, had arrived bright and early. "How are you this morning?" he asked innocuously, not realizing he would be the first person I had seen at church that morning, and that he was about to really find out.

"You know what?" I said, "I'm not doing too great. My son is in the hospital, diagnosed with diabetes, out of nowhere, and he may or may not get to come to church today. No, it doesn't run in my family, unless you count my great-uncle, who I am just now remembering, who lost his leg to it in his thirties and his life to it in his forties, leaving behind a widow and a little daughter, but then again they say he never took care of himself, but how do you make someone take care of himself? So how am I doing? To be honest, I'm a little shaky."

I realized that after I said it, I had said more than I had wanted to say, and more than he, a new member, had asked. I think I remember that I said, "Sorry," as we careful people do when we are accidentally honest with one another.

"Juvenile diabetes or type-two?" he asked, appearing to know a distinction that most people do not. "Type-one?" I nodded.

"Well, I have type-one diabetes," he said. "In fact, it's what drove me to go into medicine. I'm passionate about helping people to live healthy lives with this condition."

I looked at this young man who seemed to have it all together, the picture of health, a person who had talked about climbing mountains, kayaking, who traveled the world. Suddenly my image of this disease had a new face, and I liked it a lot better than my late great-uncle's.

"I think that's why I am joining the church today," he said, and we both stopped to take that in. "I'm going to be a friend to your son, and help you all to deal with this."

And that is exactly what happened. His friendship changed our lives in the years that followed, and none of that would have happened had we not been joined together in the body of Christ, not just in our good news but also in our bad.

On Palm Sunday, things change so quickly. The followers of Jesus move from triumph to tragedy in a matter of days. And that's how quickly life moves too. But as surely as the arc goes down, into the solemn services of Holy Week, we know it will go up again, too, on Easter Sunday.

Some resurrections are enormous and get recorded in scripture to be read year after year. Other resurrections are smaller. They happen in the midst of ordinary lives. And we witness one another's resurrections in church all the time. For me that Palm Sunday morning, what was resurrected was hope. And when my son ran into church that morning, finally out of the hospital, his energetic self, I knew that as quickly as things change, they can change in all directions, as much as they do in Holy Week.

It turns out my son was released later that Palm Sunday. But he was not released because we his parents had finally mastered it all. No, in fact, I never learned how to give that shot. I had failed and I would never succeed.

But in my failure, something remarkable happened. An eight-year-old boy, whose life must have seemed terribly out of control, decided to take control. After what I did to him, he said, "Nobody else is ever going to give me a shot. I'm doing it myself." And he did it, and because of what he was able to do, he was released that day.

I thought back to my devastation at failing to give the shot. I remember thinking that I had hit an all time low, not just unable to help, but contributing to the hurt.

But the lesson of Holy Week is that pain and sorrow do not have the last word. My failure had opened up the way for my son to succeed.

While I would have given anything to have gotten it right, in the midst of getting it wrong, God was working on the bigger picture, and my Holy Week story had yet another hero, an eight-year-old boy, now a sixteen-year-old young man, whose courage I admire every Palm Sunday, when I think about how quickly things can change.

But I also think of that new member. He probably thought that he was joining the church that day because he needed it. But sometimes the reason you are joining the church is because somebody there needs you.

CHAPTER 26

Hospital Visitation

MARTIN B. COPENHAVER

When I began in ministry, I would enter a hospital room with a bit of trepidation, as if entering a strange and alien land, because I was not sure what I would encounter there and how I might respond. I wasn't yet used to the sights and sounds and smells of this land — the sight of someone hooked up to every manner of tube, the occasional snoring or groaning of a roommate, the antiseptic smell that sometimes barely covers the various human smells that infuse the air. I didn't know the customs of this land, either — for instance, whether I should stop praying when a doctor entered the room, or whether I should introduce myself to the doctor, or whether I should leave the room when the doctor began her consultation (as to the answers, they are no, yes, no . . .and sometimes yes, no, yes).

But after twenty-five years as a pastor, I have been in hundreds of hospital rooms and by now they all look familiar. Even if I have not been in a particular room before, it still feels as if I have. After all, every hospital room seems to have the same linoleum floors in muted colors, the same adjustable beds, the same tables that can reach over the beds for patients to eat their meals, the same television sets bolted to the walls, the same chairs, upholstered in washable plastic, where visitors can perch at the bedside. Outside the window, there is usually a view of another part of the hospital or the parking lot. There is always the constant parade of nurses and doctors in and out of the room, carrying clipboards, checking charts, asking questions, giving a pill or taking a temperature. These rooms for me have become a neutral backdrop, where I am able to focus not on the place, but on the person I am visiting.

I have learned to love hospital visitation, one of the true privileges of pastoral ministry. In visiting someone in the hospital, I am representing the community of people who are bound together in the church. By the nature of my role, I get privileged access to someone's life at a time of need, and I am able to offer a reminder of the presence of God through prayer and perhaps other words of comfort. In such a setting we tend not to wade in the shallows of life, but are more likely to venture forth into something closer to the depths. So a hospital room is one of the places where I am reminded why I went into the ministry in the first place.

But one day, after twenty-five years of ministry, I found myself in a hospital room that once again seemed like a strange and alien land. Everything around me was familiar, and yet it looked different and unsettling. Suddenly, once again, I didn't know what to expect or how to behave. Almost everything I had learned and experienced about being in a hospital room had to be thrown out the window because it seemed not to apply anymore. This hospital room was different for one simple reason: it was the first one I had ever been wheeled into. I was a patient and, for the first time in my life, I was seeing a hospital room from the vantage point of lying in bed.

It happened quickly. I woke up in the middle of the night with the oddest sensation. It felt like my heart was trying to jump out of my chest. I sat up in bed and felt my pulse. My heart was beating very rapidly and irregularly. If a regular heartbeat resembles the strong and steady beat of a Sousa march in 4/4 time, this was a reggae beat. Mind you, I have always liked the syncopated rhythms of reggae, but when your heart is the only part of you that is dancing, it can be a bit disconcerting. I woke up my wife, Karen, and asked her to check my pulse. I said, "Well, I'm so glad I already have a check-up scheduled with my doctor for later this afternoon." She replied, "Are you kidding? We're going to the emergency room right now." We got in the car and, for once, I let her drive.

Within minutes of entering the emergency room, I was an intersection of monitors and intravenous tubes. The immediate and focused attention from so many doctors and nurses was both comforting and disconcerting at the same time. I was grateful that they took my condition seriously, but the way they responded brought home the realization that what I was experiencing was, indeed, serious.

They kept me there in the emergency room much of the day, doing a variety of tests. Karen sat at my bedside, listening intently to the doctors, taking notes on what they said. Most people would say that she was the picture of calm. But I knew better. I have learned that the more she is churning inside, the more placid her demeanor becomes. The telltale sign is the nail on her right index finger. It is always the first to go.

One doctor after another parted the curtains around my bed and stood over me, asking questions. I felt suddenly small. This was an unusual position for me to be in. Usually, I am the one who stands over people, either high in a pulpit, or standing as I teach a class to people who are seated, or as I enter a hospital room. Even when I sit down beside someone's hospital bed, I am perched a bit higher. And at committee meetings, if I sit up straight, I am at least as tall as anyone in the room. But not here. Not as a patient. Feeling small was a new experience.

My condition was "atrial fibrillation," which I learned is quite common and eminently treatable. The doctors expected that the drugs would bring my heart back into rhythm, but they would monitor me closely until then. Karen went home to get me a few things — my iPod, the book I was reading, some comfortable clothes.

It was then that Kathy, my pastoral colleague of over a decade, appeared at my bedside. I had always heard members of our congregation say that Kathy's very presence is calming, and now I knew what they meant. We chatted easily. Then Kathy said, "I have pretty much decided to postpone my trip to France." I knew how much she was looking forward to that trip, so I said, "Well, let's see. We can talk about that, but I don't think that is going to be necessary." She was looking out for me, and for the congregation, because she knew they would be anxious. It was best not to have both of us gone at such a time. But I wasn't ready to hear it. "It's up to you, of course," I said, stating the obvious, "but I feel quite sure I'll be back in the pulpit on Sunday and that you will be going to France." This was Thursday afternoon. "They say that they are planning to release me tomorrow, if my ticker kicks in." "Well," replied Kathy, "you don't need to decide that now. In either case, I'm quite sure that I will be staying." I prepared to object, but Kathy came back with words that were as firm as they were gently delivered: "I don't know quite how to say this, Martin, but this is not your decision to make."

We talked about what to say to the congregation. "Tell them I have had an unfortunate little episode with an irregular heartbeat, but that the condition is common, and treatable, and nothing that will prevent me from taking up my duties soon." As I had seen in so many of my parishioners over the years, I was trying not to make a big deal out of my illness. As a pastor, in such instances, I would try to help them move beyond their attempts to shrug off what had happened to them. But now, I wanted nothing more than to be able to try a little shrugging off of my own.

Torrential memories came surging back of my father's fierce determination to get back into the pulpit as soon as he could after his leg was amputated. I was a teenager at the time. Those of us in his family knew that he was still in great pain, but you wouldn't have known that from the way he hobbled into the church on crutches with his game face on. And he didn't want to come in any side door, either. He insisted on being part of the procession down the center aisle. When it came time for the sermon, with considerable effort that he tried to hide, he lifted himself into the high pulpit and sat on a barstool. After looking out over the congregation, he began his sermon by saying, "Surely this is not the first sermon ever to be preached from a barstool, but, to my knowledge, it is the first time in this place." The congregation laughed. Their relief was palpable.

But why do pastors, who spend so much of their time ministering to people in their vulnerability, have such a hard time letting themselves appear vulnerable to others?

I told Kathy that I would like her to communicate to the members of the congregation that I would welcome prayers and cards, but would prefer that they not stop by or call. I wasn't ready for a sudden reversal of roles in which I was not the minister, but the one ministered unto. I also suspected that, in some instances, the roles would not be reversed enough and that I would end up ministering to the one who came to visit me. I wasn't prepared for that, either, especially since, in this setting, my clerical garb would consist of one of those hospital johnnies with an open seam in the back.

Kathy assured me that she understood why I would make such a request, but still I felt a bit guilty in making it. Why can't I let myself be on the receiving end of the kind of care I have offered to others? Is it pride? In part, I am sure. But I was also sure that visits and calls from parishioners were not what I needed at that time.

Kathy offered a prayer and left. It occurred to me that, in the ten years we had worked together, I had observed virtually every aspect of Kathy's ministry, except for hospital visitation. Now I was not only given a chance to observe her gifts, I was able to receive them as well.

Sometime in that afternoon, my heart resumed its normal rhythm, as suddenly as it had been thrown out of whack. Soon after that they wheeled me out of the emergency room and into one of the regular hospital rooms where they could keep an eye on me and do a few more tests. The attending nurse explained that my roommate was a man with developmental disabilities who could neither see nor hear. "Perfect," I thought. "The last thing I want right now is a chatty roommate." The nurse went on to explain that my roommate, not understanding his situation, would occasionally try to slap the nurse or attendant when they tried to give him some form of treatment. Okay, not so perfect.

Karen stayed with me until I fell asleep and then went home to get some rest herself. In the middle of the night, I was awakened by the sound of commotion on the other side of the curtain that divided the two beds. The curtain was bulging with the press of bodies. It was as if a rugby game had broken out in the hospital and the push and shove of the scrum was taking place on the other side of the curtain. Then I heard the sound of a slap. "Ouch!" I heard one voice exclaim. "Don't do that!" Another voice said to the man who could not hear, "You've got to stop doing that! We are trying to help you."

Finally, a nurse came to my side of the curtain. She said, a bit out of breath, "I'm so sorry. He is terribly bloated and we are trying to give him a barium enema. He will be much more comfortable, but it is going to smell pretty bad in here for a while. I mean, really bad, actually. We could move you . . ."

"No, no," I said, "I'll be fine." I will spare you the details, gentle reader, but suffice it to say, I should not have been so quick to turn down the offer. Some time during the procedure that I could not see, but experienced acutely in other ways, I began to laugh. Not wanting anyone to hear me laughing, I laughed all the more. I don't think I was laughing at my roommate, poor fellow. In a way I was laughing at myself, that I could start the day as a healthy pastor who was used to striding into hospital rooms and shortly after walking out, and that by the end of the day I could end up in this position, draped in a hospital johnny, trapped in a hospital bed, all chained to tubes and monitors.

Early the next morning my friend Greg Groover, the pastor of Charles Street AME Church, stood at the foot of my bed. Greg, like my colleague Kathy, was someone I wanted to see. Greg did not sit down, but he did not seem to be standing over me, either. In his presence I did not feel small. We chatted a bit, and then he offered a prayer. He listened as I explained what atrial fibrillation is, and when I finished he said, "Yeah, I've had the same thing."

"Really?" He had never told me. I was beginning to wonder if silence around health issues is a characteristic of pastors.

Studies have revealed that the ministry used to be among the healthiest professions, but now it is one of the unhealthiest. Is that because we don't know how to talk about health issues? Or is it because the ministry today has unique stresses? Or because our full schedules don't allow much time for exercise? Or because focusing attention on our health seems contrary to our image of ministry as self-sacrificial?

Or because, of all the seven deadly sins, the one that is not only overlooked in clergy, but actually encouraged, is gluttony? (Let's have my doctor's patients each try to ply him with coffee cake at every consultation, and then let's see how long he remains thin.) Or do many of us pastors eat too much because it is a socially acceptable way of self-medicating? ("No, two beers is my limit, but could you pass the chips?") Or do we get ill because we have figured out that it is one of the circumstances in which we will allow ourselves to receive care? (One pastor's wife told me that for her overworked husband, "Illness has become his Sabbath.") Those may be some of the reasons why pastors are unhealthy, but there are probably others.

Later that day I was released from the hospital, but I did not preach the Sunday after my unfortunate little episode after all. I was exhausted, as everyone seemed to know I would be (everyone but me, that is). During my days away from the church, my mailbox at home was full of cards from parishioners. Many of them wrote notes saying that they were praying for me; some even wrote out their prayers for me, which I found almost unspeakably touching. For a number of years our congregation had placed increased focus on prayer in an attempt to deepen both our understanding and our practice of prayer. In doing so, it had never occurred to me that I would benefit personally from the congregation's increased fluency in the language of prayer.

The next week, I went for a follow-up appointment with my doctor of ten years. He's competent, thorough, and, as a charming bonus, he has a delightful Irish brogue.

After checking my blood pressure, he sat down and began to look through the thick stack of records that had been taken in the hospital, chronicling my unfortunate little episode. Without looking up from those records, he asked me questions about my eating, drinking, and exercise habits, which I rather awkwardly answered, knowing that my answers were not in every instance what he would want to hear.

He explained to me that the cause of atrial fibrillation is a malfunction in the part of the heart that sends the "electrical" signal to the heart muscle to beat at regular intervals, but there are also some common triggers. Speaking deliberately, he enumerated them: "There's fatigue . . . stress . . . alcohol . . . caffeine . . . cocaine . . ."

"No!" I said, with a little too much vehemence, to the last one. I was just relieved that at least there was one trigger I could take off the list. Then, just for emphasis, I added, "Decidedly not. No cocaine."

So he asked, "Do you experience stress in your life?" and I responded, "Well, sure." (I wanted to add, "Doesn't everybody?") He followed up, "At home or in your work?" "Not so much at home. Home is my haven. But in my work, sure." Then he asked, "How can caring for souls be stressful?"

What a lovely description of ministry. If I could only spend my day "caring for souls," as he put it, that would be wonderful.

If I could devote myself to visiting people in their homes or in the hospital, praying with them, leading Bible studies, preaching, conducting funerals, and those other pastoral duties that I imagine he had in mind, then I could understand what might prompt his question. If only that were the complete list of my responsibilities. But what sometimes keeps me up at night, wrestling with the angel (or with demons) are all of those things that don't fit so neatly under the category of caring for souls: the board meeting that didn't go well, the budget shortfall, the parishioner who is angry with me, the church leaders who are in conflict, the upcoming review of a staff member at which I need to bring up some difficult issues. Of course, I know how to interpret all of those things — and, indeed, everything I do as a pastor — as caring for souls, at least indirectly. But sometimes it doesn't feel that way, and I was quite sure this is not what my doctor had in mind when he asked the question. I didn't think this was the time to educate him about pastoral ministry, however, so I just said, "Well, there's a lot involved in my work that doesn't always seem like caring for souls."

After a few more questions, he finally closed my thick file. With his elbows on the file in his lap, he leaned forward and, for the first time that visit, he looked me straight in the eye. He said, "Here's the most important question. Are you praying?" At last, here is a question I could answer without feeling self-conscious or inadequate. "Why, yes,

I pray every day." But he was not finished with this line of questioning: "Half an hour every day, uninterrupted, no distractions?"

I felt like I was looking for a place to hide. "Uh . . . well, uh . . . hmm . . . not exactly. Not every day, at least." Without shifting his gaze — he wasn't about to give me any wiggle room — he went on to say, "It's the most important thing. For some people I might suggest meditation, but for you it's prayer."

This was not the prescription I'm used to getting from a doctor. But then I thought, "Half an hour a day, uninterrupted, no distractions? Does he have any idea what my life is like?"

I used to love to quote the spiritual advisor who said that we should each spend a half hour a day in prayer, with this exception: if the day is really jam-packed with too many things to do, then half an hour is unrealistic. On such days it should be a full hour devoted to prayer. I used to love to quote that. But now my doctor was saying something like that to me. "Hey, that's my line!" is what I thought. What I said was, "I'll try."

The following Sunday, feeling strengthened by rest and buoyed by prayers, I led worship. At the beginning of the service, during the time of welcome, I stood at the top of the chancel steps and took a moment to look out at the congregation, trying to meet as many eyes as I could. "Good morning," I said. Then I put my hand on my chest, patted it, and said, "Truly, it does my heart good to see you."

In that moment, looking out at the congregation, I think I finally saw the reason why my father was so eager to get back into the pulpit after his surgery. He wanted to see the faces. All those beloved faces. And to get back to caring for souls.

CHAPTER 27

The Preacher

LILLIAN DANIEL

My preaching colleague once preached a sermon that had an important refrain. Over and over again in the sermon, he would say, "We are all God's." He was reminding us that we all belong to God, first and foremost. In this individualistic culture, he was giving the countercultural message that we are not our own. It's not all about us. We are all God's. The repetition drove the point home.

I loved the sermon, and standing next to him in the receiving line, I noted the responses, one after the other: "Morning." "Why was Mary in the prayer concerns? I couldn't hear." "Can you tell me where the youth group medical waiver forms should be dropped off?" And occasionally, there was a reference to the preaching: "Nice sermon."

But finally one man came through the line and held the preacher's hand with intensity. "That sermon was what I have been waiting to hear preached in this church for years. Incredible. Life changing. Thank you."

Now, this man was actually an occasional critic of the preaching at the church, both mine and my colleague's. He was a devotee of an obscure New Age Indian guru whose pamphlets he passed along to us as examples of what we might say instead of "spouting doctrine." He came to church to appease his wife and children, but he was also clearly a seeker with a deep passion for matters of the spirit. So his praise was unexpected and notable in a sea of "Nice sermon's."

"What moved you?" the preacher asked.

"You finally got it right. I mean that one line said it all: we are all gods. Every one of us is a god. There is no one big god who is better than the rest of us. We are all gods ourselves. It's what I have been trying to say around here for years, and finally, you get it."

The preacher blanched. Others were pushing through the line, and there was no time for him to respond that this was not what he had meant at all. But after the receiving line, and by the time he preached that sermon at the second service, the refrain in that sermon was no longer, "We are all God's." It had become, "We all belong to God."

It was not the first time a preacher has been understood to be saying exactly the opposite of what he thought he was saying. Every preacher has a story in which someone has interpreted a sermon to mean the opposite of what we thought it meant. However clear our notes, however clear our delivery, sometimes something is lost in translation.

This isn't always a bad thing. Most preachers have experienced the flipside of my colleague's situation. We have delivered a sermon that was not our best. Perhaps we even thought it was our worst. And then later we hear that it touched someone in a particular way. They brought their lives to church that day — a recent diagnosis, a heartbreak, the thrilling news of a first grandchild on the way — and somehow our meager offering spoke to them, delivering more than our own efforts. The Holy Spirit was at work.

But was the Holy Spirit at work when my parishioner heard, "We are all gods," instead of, "We are all God's?" That is a question I am waiting to ask Jesus when I meet him in heaven and all questions are answered. But I hope he tells me this: not everything that happens in the preaching moment is of the Holy Spirit. Some interpretations are in error, just as some sermons are in error, and there needs to be a place for the discernment of the spirits. For now, I live in this awkward liminality, where somehow the Holy Spirit chooses to work through the broken vessel in me and the broken vessel in the listener to proclaim God's word.

Never was this clearer than when I decided to explain from the pulpit the social and historical context of the image of Jesus as the shepherd. "Most of us have no idea what life is like for shepherds," I explained, projecting my own urban prejudices upon the entire congregation. But I had at least taken the time to read something about sheep and their shepherds. "The shepherd really knew the sheep," I explained. "I mean, he really *knew* them." I noticed a few people in the congregation grimace, as if uncomfortable. I had no idea why, so I sought to be clearer.

"No, what I mean to say, is that the shepherd, he wasn't just in charge of the sheep; he cared about them. I mean, he was out there, all alone, with them. So he loved them. Really loved them." More expressions of people who looked somewhat disgusted.

"So my point here is that this wasn't a distant or disconnected relationship. Perhaps lonely himself, longing for companionship with those for whom he was responsible." I could tell by their expressions they were not following, so I had to explain. "The shepherd, God, was *intimate* with those sheep."

At that point giggling broke out and I moved on to my next point, baffled. It wasn't until after the sermon, when people with farm experience told me about the kinds of images that my words were bringing to mind, that I understood. I realized I had given the worst sermon about Jesus the shepherd that they had ever heard, and, sadly, that they would never forget. I had taken animal husbandry to a whole new level.

"How do you come up with what you say on Sunday mornings?" is a question that every pastor gets asked. There are few jobs in the world that require anything like a sermon once a week. Some people are impressed that we can do such an enormous thing. Others think we are making it up on the spot. Sometimes they are both right.

Preachers can make it look hard and impressive, or casual and easy. Either way, it is the most important thing most ministers do in a given week, and for me, it is the reason I do what I do. I am a preacher.

More than any other aspect of the job, this is the one thing that defines my particular call.

Yet I know there are ministers for whom preaching is not the central point around which their ministry revolves. They may be in a specialized ministry, where their focus is on youth, children, counseling, chaplaincy, or pastoral care. Increasingly the church is finding ways to use clergy's different gifts and acknowledging that not everyone's is preaching. But most clergy find themselves preaching at some point, whether they like it or not.

Few would admit it, but clergy know that there are pastors who preach every week, but do so grudgingly. It is the payment for getting to do all the other things they love to do. There are churches that faithfully exist without good preaching, in which the members are cared for at the hospital bedside, babies are baptized, and God's word is proclaimed at funerals. At some churches, the preacher may enjoy preaching but the congregation gets little out of it. And still the church goes on. It makes one suspect that the Holy Spirit may actually be at work.

But preaching, when done well, can change lives, build congregations, rebuke the haughty, inspire the discouraged, challenge the proud, and lift up the lowly. When we stand up to preach, we follow a man who started preaching as a youth at the Temple and never stopped, even on the Cross. There is much that the Son of God did that we could never hope to do. But in standing up to preach, in reflecting on the sacred texts, we really do follow Jesus.

I work more on my sermons than on any other aspect of my work. In ministry, much of our time management is triage. Most of the work that is demanded of us is worthy, good, and of God, but we cannot possibly do it all. So we make decisions. I am not ashamed to make the decision to put my sermon preparation at the top of my list each week. I have learned that of everything I do, the sermon is the thing that touches the largest number of people. It deserves the greatest amount of attention.

There are clergy who disagree with me on this point. They will drop everything to rush to the hospital, to respond to the latest need, to deal with an administrative matter because a lay leader is clamoring for something to be fixed right now. By Saturday night, the sermon is left undone. So they work into the wee hours, writing with the last scrap of energy from the week. These clergy are faithful. Some of them are excellent preachers. They claim to care deeply about preaching, but they believe that outside forces, such as the demands of the pastorate, are keeping them from giving the sermon the attention it deserves.

But my colleagues who are writing these sermons in the middle of the night or the early morning hours on weekends are exhausted. If they do care deeply about preaching, they feel somewhat guilty, too. They know in their hearts that they are not giving the task their best, but rather giving it their leftovers, drinking from a glass that is more than half empty. Their families and friends, who have waited until the weekend to get their attention, are also left shortchanged.

Laypeople might be shocked to discover how many clergy live on this hamster wheel, in which preaching has been stripped of both its joy and its privilege. If church members' demands and expectations have created this situation, they would do well to consider the consequences to the church as whole. But if this situation is caused less by the laity and more by the unrealistic expectations the pastor imposes upon herself, then lay leaders can help. They can tell the pastor how much they value the preached word. It is what every preacher longs to hear from a church member: that this particular work matters. The Sunday when the church says goodbye to the pastor is not the right Sunday to have this conversation. By then, it is too late.

But when preaching is given its due, started early and entered into as a gift of study, creativity, and generosity, it is the most life-giving thing I can do as a pastor. And the one receiving the gift is me. What a mind-boggling privilege to get to sit with the scriptures, to ponder the text, to wrack my brain in search of the right story, to read and take in the culture around me, to search myself with the passion of an artist, all in service to Christ. No other career offers such an opportunity. There are people all over the world stuck in jobs that offer nothing but monotony, yet we clergy are given the opportunity to create, teach, and preach. Why would a pastor leave such a thing hanging undone? When finally we approach this unique task, it should be with reverence.

Still, despite privileging this task so highly, I cannot imagine being a minister whose sole duty is to preach. I know there are a few ministers out there who have jobs that allow them to focus almost exclusively on the study and proclamation of the Word; and there are celebrity preachers who travel and speak in one place after another. But for me, preaching is rooted in the rest of my pastoral life.

When I visit a family in their home to prepare for a baptism, I am taking in their lives, learning in our conversation what matters to them. I want to see what state their living room is in, as well as hear about the state of their souls. The questions they ask about the church are often not the ones I would have assumed they had. I remember these points and they will find their way into a sermon down the road.

In meeting with couples in crisis, I realize that my own reflections on marriage are being shaped and enriched in ways that undoubtedly will make their way into my preaching. In the administration meeting where we agonize between two important budget items, my thoughts on stewardship are being shaped. Later when I read a text for the week, all these experiences will be part of what ends up on the page.

For this reason I am baffled to hear about preachers who use sermons that other people have preached. All ethical concerns aside (and I do find it entirely unethical), I cannot imagine it working. A congregation needs to see themselves in the sermon, and a sermon written for an entirely different congregation would have to ring false. Perhaps this is why pastors who steal sermons are often caught. The church can tell when a word is for them and when it is not. And congregations would rather have the preacher speak from her heart than use the polished and impressive words of another. They will forgive a poor word choice or clumsy structure when it is clear to them that the pastor knows them, cares for them, and is speaking to them.

Therefore, when I speak to groups other than my congregation, I know I am not doing my best preaching. While the gospel is constant, what I bring to it is in danger of being irrelevant, because I am winging it and working on hunches. On those occasions, I do my best, but I miss the intimacy that a parish minister has with a body of people. The best sermons are not written in a vacuum. They are crafted in community, each sermon part of a long conversation that continues week after week. The congregation shapes the preacher as much as the other way around.

Yet when the time comes to actually write the sermon, the congregation is with me in spirit only. I am alone with the task of putting all this into words. For this reason, for many preachers, the time of sermon preparation is a lonely set of hours. Here we are, with a job that no one else can do for us. With nothing but some texts from the Bible, we are stripped down. The blank computer screen, the unmarked legal pad, the pen that taps nervously on the desk — these are the reminders that we are on our own here.

But of course we are not. It is in the deep loneliness of sermon preparation that I find myself closest to God. At that moment when I feel like I have nothing to say, prayer comes easily. It is a prayer of lament, or petition, or a confession of my unworthiness for the task at hand. I feel Jesus with me at these times, encouraging me to try anyway. The moment before the writing begins is the loneliest time of the week, and Jesus uses it to get the attention of otherwise busy pastors. I have to listen to him at that moment. There is nothing left to distract me.

By this I mean that I have already fully milked every possible distraction. I have made myself a bagel. I have surfed the Web. I have tried coffee and soda and I am about to consider liquor. I have appointed myself the church janitor, taking care of some stains on the rug, and I have finally cleaned out the youth group's lost-and-found box. Now, I wander into the offices of other staff members, looking pathetic, asking them if they would like to hear my suggestions for a program for next year. They know how to respond. "So, you've got writer's block again, Lillian? Don't worry, something will come to you."

And, sent back to my lonely office, something does. I am convinced that the "something" is Jesus, who knows how hard this job is and picked me anyway. I am convinced that the "something" is God, who took seven days to create the universe, and so would probably prefer that I start my sermon on day one. I am convinced that the "something" is the Holy Spirit, who intercedes in the loneliness with sighs too deep for words.

I know the loneliness is a valley through which I walk to get to the rich pasture of Sunday morning. There, the day finally breaks and the loneliness ends. In preaching, the silence is broken. It is the moment I wait for all week. It's not always perfect. Sometimes it's not even good. But when the sermon is working, when the cóngregation is meeting me in this liminal moment with the gift of their attention, there is an electrifying presence of the Holy Spirit that leaves me feeling like I have run a race and won, not through my own legs but because there are wings on my shoes.

In every generation, somebody predicts the death of preaching. In our generation, technology has been lifted up as the big distraction. Churches make creative use of video screens and sound systems to keep up with the changes. But still, that preaching moment is decidedly low-tech. A person stands alone, telling a community what she knows of the Word of Life, and they listen. I am always struck by that and humbled. They actually listen.

After the Sunday services are over, I go home and experience a peace that is absolutely unique to that moment in the week. I really do relax. I can barely make conversation, I am so tired — but blessedly so. I would like to tell you I pray, but at that time, what I really do is eat pasta, watch mindless television, and sleep for hours on end.

Sunday afternoon, after preaching, is the Sabbath. Creation has been taken care of. Like the God who made us, we get to rest.

And in that rest, I reflect on what I have done — or, to be more accurate, what God has done through me. Sometimes I say that it is good.

Other times, I find myself reliving the quirky moments in the sermon, the ones that leave me wondering about questions like this: Why were they laughing at my explanation of the different streams within early Judaism?

After all, all I said was, "In the ancient world, they had sects just like we have sects."

CHAPTER 28

Staying in Church

MARTIN B. COPENHAVER

So many of my close friends have left pastoral ministry of late that I am beginning to feel like a character in an Agatha Christie mystery. As the other characters all start disappearing I cannot help but wonder, “Who will be next?” It has prompted me to consider again why I remain in pastoral ministry and why I still cherish this vocation.

I have been in pastoral ministry too long now to dismiss the challenges. It is not hard to identify with some of the frustrations that some of these departing pastors express: the sense of confinement, the relentlessness of the role, and especially the press of needy and quarrelsome people. I also recognize that some of the reasons given for leaving are, with the slightest turn of the kaleidoscope, some of the same reasons I stay in pastoral ministry.

Some pastors experience pastoral ministry as a kind of confinement. They feel hemmed in by the demands of the role and the needs of those around them. One friend, writing about her decision to leave pastoral ministry, likens wearing clerical garb to wearing the black-and-white striped outfits worn by prisoners.

To be sure, there are ways in which a pastor’s life is developed in confinement. It is anchored in text, font, and table — and also in a particular community of faith. One can feel hemmed in on all sides by the range of expectations people have regarding what a pastor should be and do. And there can be something exhausting about always having to be "on."

Nevertheless, I have found that there are ways in which the pastoral vocation confers an extraordinary amount of freedom, if I am willing to claim it. Perhaps no other vocation allows for the kind of flexibility in the use of one's time as does pastoral ministry. My wife is an attorney, so her vocational life is measured out in fifteen-minute segments of "billable hours." She is confined to an office, limited to a comparatively narrow set of responsibilities, with very little discretion over how her time is used — it is used in any way the paying client wants to use it.

By contrast, pastors do not need to think in terms of billable hours, quotas, the number of patients seen, or the amount of goods produced. To be sure, we must meet certain expectations and perform routine tasks, but there is nothing approaching the constraints on the use of time found in other professions. Pastors who fulfill basic expectations are given remarkable freedom to interpret their own sense of call.

That is why the schedules of no two pastors are alike. How each pastor spends time can reflect, in part at least, that person's unique gifts. So I have known pastors who have integrated their own interests into their ministries by writing hymns, producing plays, traveling internationally, building houses, reading theology, or even making pottery. People in other professions can only imagine having that kind of freedom when they retire.

It is true that, in order to exercise that freedom, a pastor has to master the diplomat's art of having a thousand different ways of saying no. It also requires the kind of clarity that does not confuse people's diverse expectations with a job description, which means that it requires being willing to disappoint people.

I have been helped by the reminder that Jesus was a pastor who was always running away from his congregation. That is, Jesus' life and ministry were marked by times of intense engagement with others in rhythm with times away, either alone or with his most trusted friends. Henri Nouwen often talked about the importance of a "ministry of presence." But certainly there is a "ministry of absence" as well, not only for the sake of the pastor's own health, but also for the bracing reminder that God can be at work even when the pastor is not present. For reasons I don't fully understand, more pastors are reluctant to exercise that freedom than there are congregations unwilling to allow it.

In whatever ways that freedom is exercised, however, there still is no escaping the pastoral role. Even though this characteristic of the pastoral life can be a source of stress, it also can contribute to an integrated life. The church I serve is in a suburban town where many people live remarkably fragmented lives: they have work lives, social lives, family lives, church lives. Those various lives may overlap somewhat, but more often they are each lived out in a separate location among different people, with little integration among them. Parents in my congregation participate in "Take Your Child to Work Day" so their children will have some notion of what they do with most of their waking hours. They long to have their lives gathered up into a more coherent whole. Most pastors' children see what their parent does for a living, not just on Sundays, but also in the integrated life of the week.

Pastors are given privileged access to the lives of people, but not in a merely therapeutic sense. Our interactions with parishioners are not confined to 50-minute appointments in a well-ordered office, on a fee-for-service basis. Our parishioners cannot be described in clinical, two-dimensional terms; they are not "clients" or "patients" because we see them in too rich a variety of contexts and relate to them in too many different ways. The pastor who listens to a parishioner's account of his life also shares in that life in important ways. The person who is counseled by the pastor may be the same person who, later in the week, takes part in a prayer group and presides at a church meeting — or encounters the pastor at the supermarket or soccer game or dinner party.

It is because God cannot be confined to any one area of life, even the one commonly deemed the "spiritual life," that the pastor cannot be anything but a generalist. The pastor brings unifying questions to every encounter and setting, as diverse as they may be. Those questions are: Where is God in this? What might God say to us here?

It is telling that *parson*, the old English term for "person," came to be used to describe a pastor, as though the person and the vocation were so completely integrated that they had become synonymous. Today we may not refer to "the legal life" or "the medical life," but we can still speak of "the pastoral life," because even in our time it is a way of life whose various parts can be more fully integrated.

Not being able to escape the pastoral role means particularly not being able to escape the people. William Willimon says that he worries when seminarians report that they are going into pastoral ministry because, "I just love people. I want to work with people." Willimon responds by asking, "Have you actually *met* any of these people?" St. Benedict, the same one who wrote about the blessings of community and gave instruction on how to live in community, also said, "Community is my penance."

Barbara Brown Taylor, who left pastoral ministry, reports in her book *Leaving Church* that when, in the baptismal service, she asked the congregation, "Will you seek and serve Christ in all persons, loving your neighbor as yourself," she had to stifle her protest: "How could I possibly seek and serve Christ in all persons? Did the author of that [liturgy] have any idea how many hungry, needy, angry, manipulative, deeply ill people I saw in the course of a week?"

Taylor testifies that her most frequent encounters with God are in the natural world. Given the demands of being in community with people, this should not be surprising. It is telling that the settings that we tend to describe as "peaceful" are invariably places with few, if any, people. So it's not hard to offer an "Amen" to elegiac testimonies to the immanence of God in nature. In fact, it's downright easy, perhaps too easy.

On a number of occasions I have hiked in the interior reaches of the Grand Canyon. To me it is a holy place, the most vaulted of natural Gothic cathedrals. It's not hard to feel close to God there, not only because of what is present, but also due to what is largely absent — the demands of living in community. The buttes don't quarrel with each other. The California condors make no demands of the living. The rollicking streams offer only comforting words. There is no need to raise money for a sanctuary roof because the blue sky has already supplied it.

But to me, the affirmation that God can be found outside the church has never seemed like much of a claim. The true wonder is that God can be found *inside* the church, among quirky, flawed, and broken people who may have little in common and yet are bound to one another. What an unlikely setting in which to encounter God! But the Christian God seems to like to surprise us by showing up in the most unpromising places, like a man from Nazareth and in a motley gathering of people known as church.

God throws us together in the church and says, in essence, "Here is where you get a chance to learn how to live with other people, to forgive, and even come to see God in one another. After all, if you can find God here, you can find God anywhere."

It is not coincidence that Jesus said both, "Love your neighbor," and, "Love your enemy," because often they are the same person. Living in community is an essential Christian practice because it gives us such ample opportunity to learn how to receive the stranger and practice forgiveness. If we can practice the art of reconciliation long enough with one another in church, then we have a chance to let reconciliation mark our relationships with others outside of church as well. The church, like the family, is the place where we learn to live with people we are stuck with. And when we stick together, it is a living reminder of the God who is stuck with us all.

As a pastor, I am expected to care about people I may not particularly care for. It is assumed that I will act with compassion even when I may not feel at all compassionate. I am expected to forgive when on my own I would be inclined to hold a grudge. Obviously, Jesus enjoined all of his followers to act in these ways, but in most congregations the expectations of a pastor in this regard are particularly high. And I am grateful for that. It is not easy to "seek and serve Christ in all persons," of course, but even attempting to do so has enlarged my capacity for compassion.

One does not have to be from a tradition in which the priest is called "Father" to find some resonances of the parental role in pastoral ministry. A pastor nurtures, feeds, guides, and teaches. There is a special bond between pastor and people. The pastor is charged with caring for the people in every circumstance, in and out of season.

Barbara Brown Taylor is particularly drawn to images of motherhood to describe her own ministry in the parish. She is the brooding hen, the single mother of a large and demanding family. At one point she says that her "breasts fairly leaked" when she would encounter people in need.

Nevertheless, parenthood is not the most apt, nor certainly the most healthy, image for the role of the pastor. We could take issue with the image on theological grounds, of course, but in addition, it is simply too exhausting to think of oneself as a parent to a congregation. The challenges of parenting my own two children is demanding enough without adopting the hundreds of parishioners who are a part of my congregation.

Instead, I have come to view my role as more like that of a midwife, someone who is trained to assist in the birthing process. A midwife performs her role in a whole range of ways, sometimes by coaching the parents and other times by providing direct assistance, and often, when little needs to be done, simply standing by in wonder and awe.

We pastors assist people in "giving birth" to a new or deepened relationship with God. We are not the center of the action, or even key players in the drama. Like midwives, our role can be quite important, but it is limited nonetheless. We perform our role in a variety of ways — for instance, by teaching, leading worship, and visiting the sick. We tell the Christian story, coach and encourage, listen and pray. What unites all these roles and activities is that each provides an opportunity to encounter God.

It is a joy simply to be present at a birth. It is something even more — a real privilege — to play a role, however small or incidental, in that birth. Actually, in my work as a pastor, often I am not aware that anything so momentous is taking place. But then someone will report, fresh from a kind of birth, that a particular worship service helped her experience Jesus Christ as a living presence, as if for the first time. Or a young person returning from a church service project will tell the congregation what it was like to encounter Jesus Christ disguised as one of the poor. Or someone will tell me that my prayers at his hospital bed provided ongoing comfort because, when I departed, it was as if I left God with him. Or I will conduct a funeral and the congregation will be so obviously hungry for whatever word might sustain them that they resemble a flock of baby birds with beaks open wide. To be able to offer the words of promise that their souls are aching to hear at such a time feels like a privilege beyond deserving.

In each of these instances I am very aware that I did not make anything happen. My role, like that of a midwife, was limited. Nevertheless, something I did not provide, something clearly beyond me, that "something" called the presence of God, was at work. On such occasions I feel like a wick that is in awe that it can be used by a flame.

So, much of the time, I feel like an invited guest to special places where wondrous things happen. I am not invited because I am a special person, or because I have a particular set of skills, or because I have greater faith than anyone else does. Nevertheless, I am invited to those places in people's lives because I have accepted God's call to do this holy work.

A few years back I wrote an article that argued that the pastoral life is a form of the good life. I commended pastoral ministry as a uniquely rewarding way of life, which, indeed, I have found it to be. I showed the article to a friend who is a pastor, who had only one comment: "Well, it is a good life, *if* you are called to it." And of course he is right. Pastoral ministry is a job laden with challenges and in certain ways it seems to get more difficult every year. So it is not the kind of job anyone would likely pick out from the classified ads or at a jobs fair. Then again, if it were a job rather than a calling, I probably would have quit long ago.

My friend's comment on my article captures an essential reason why people can have such different experiences of pastoral ministry. It still comes down to the matter of call. So I am able both to affirm my friends' decision to leave pastoral ministry and to reconfirm my own commitment to pastoral ministry.

On the occasion of his retirement, Harry Emerson Fosdick said, "If I had a thousand lives to live in this century, I would go into parish ministry with every one of them." That is perhaps the strongest affirmation of a call to pastoral ministry that I know. I'm not sure I could go quite as far. If I had a thousand lives to live in this century, I might use one or two to do something else, like become a jazz pianist or an NBA point guard. But, with just one life to live on this earth, I am grateful that God called me to be a pastor. And I am staying.